Isaiah Shembe's Prophetic Uhlanga

PETER LANG
New York · Washington, D.C./Baltimore · Bern
Frankfurt · Berlin · Brussels · Vienna · Oxford

JOEL E. TISHKEN

Isaiah Shembe's
Prophetic Uhlanga

THE WORLDVIEW
OF THE NAZARETH BAPTIST CHURCH
IN COLONIAL SOUTH AFRICA

PETER LANG
New York · Washington, D.C./Baltimore · Bern
Frankfurt · Berlin · Brussels · Vienna · Oxford

Library of Congress Cataloging-in-Publication Data

Tishken, Joel E.
Isaiah Shembe's prophetic uhlanga: the worldview of the Nazareth Baptist Church
in colonial South Africa / Joel E. Tishken.
p. cm.
Includes bibliographical references and index.
1. Shembe, Isaiah, d. 1935. 2. Church of the Nazarites—History.
3. Zulu (African people)—Religion—20th century. 4. Independent
churches—South Africa—History—20th century. 5. Zionist churches
(Africa)—South Africa—History—20th century. I. Title.
BX7068.7.A4T57 2013   289.93—dc23   2013003549
ISBN 978-1-4331-2285-9 (hardcover)
ISBN 978-1-4539-1107-5 (e-book)

Bibliographic information published by **Die Deutsche Nationalbibliothek**.
Die Deutsche Nationalbibliothek lists this publication in the "Deutsche
Nationalbibliografie"; detailed bibliographic data is available
on the Internet at http://dnb.d-nb.de/.

Front cover photograph courtesy of Campbell Collections
of the University of KwaZulu Natal

The paper in this book meets the guidelines for permanence and durability
of the Committee on Production Guidelines for Book Longevity
of the Council of Library Resources.

© 2013 Peter Lang Publishing, Inc., New York
29 Broadway, 18th floor, New York, NY 10006
www.peterlang.com

Printed in Germany

To my partner, Lee Ann Powell;
to my parents, James and Judith Tishken;
and to Diana, Apollo, Ceres, Iris, Mercury,
Mars, Neptune, Pluto, Victoria, and Venus.

Contents

Acknowledgments

Like all significant projects, this book has come to fruition only with the assistance of a great many people. Many individuals in South Africa helped me fulfill my research goals. My sincerest appreciation goes to Robert Papini, formerly of the Local History Museums, Durban, who was of great assistance to my research. He provided me with access to the museum's holdings on the Nazareth Baptist Church (the overwhelming majority of which he compiled) and arranged my visits to Ebuhleni. My thanks to the staffs of the Durban Local History Museums; Killie Campbell Africana Library, in Durban; the Pietermaritzburg (Natal) Archives Repository (NAB), in Pietermaritzburg; and the National Archives Repository (SAB), in Pretoria, for their research assistance. The images in this book are from the Campbell Collections of the University of KwaZulu-Natal. I thank Mwelela Cele for arranging permission for their usage in this book. I wish to express my gratitude to Irving Hexham for collegially permitting me access to two volumes of manuscripts on Shembe and the Nazareth Baptist Church prior to their publication with Edwin Mellen Press. To my guide, Linda Cele, thank you for patiently answering my questions and expertly escorting me around the grounds of Ebuhleni. I must also gratefully thank all of the members of the Nazareth Baptist Church for their kindness and graciousness in answering my questions and permitting me observation of their worship.

I would be severely remiss if I did not thank all those individuals who provided comment on draft chapters of this book. My collegial gratitude to: Emily Anderson, Alfred Andrea, S. Davis Bowman, Todd Butler, Gregory Cushman, Toyin Falola, Tyler Fleming, Eugene V. Gallagher, Virginia Garrard-Burnett, Trevor Getz, Daniel Haworth, Matthew Heaton, Andreas Heuser, Brenda Ihssen, Lauren Jarvis, John-Marshall Klein, Matthew Kustenbauder, G. Howard Miller, David Northrup, J. Patrick Olivelle, Robert Papini, Allison Sellers, Jesse Spohnholz, and the members of the Washington State University/ University of Idaho Interdisciplinary Religious Studies Scholarly Group.

On a personal level I thank my parents, James and Judith Tishken, for their loving support over the years. To my partner, Lee Ann Powell, thank you for your patience, love, and support that helped make this book possible.

Headquarters and Major Temples of the Nazareth Baptist Church

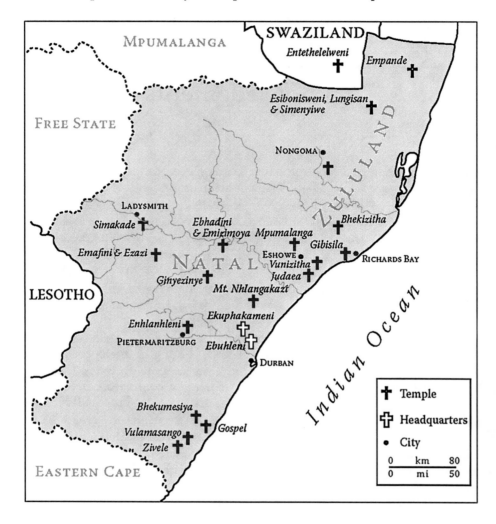

Introduction

In missionary as in all religious history, the impact of the saint, the truly charismatic individual, the prophet, is something of primary rather than marginal weight.
—Adrian Hastings, *The Church in Africa 1450–1950*, pp. 200–201

I n January 1915, Isaiah Mdliwamafa Shembe, a middle-aged Zulu man, climbed Mt. Nhlangakazi in the Ndwedwe district of the South African province of Natal. He was not a surveyor, geologist, or even an intrepid hiker, but a Christian preacher and the individual who had founded the Nazareth Baptist Church five years earlier. He was climbing the mountain with the firm belief that he had been prophetically instructed to do so by God. Shembe was fearful to make the climb, due to the mountain's wild reputation as a refuge for dangerous animals and poisonous snakes, yet felt he had no choice but to obey the prophetic command.[1]

Over the course of eleven days, Shembe was visited by a series of preternatural creatures including beautifully clad maidens, apparitions of black and white clergymen, phantoms of the deities of the ancestors, skeletal humans with rattling bones, a giant, and several talking animals including a leopard, a lion, and a snake.[2] Each, in turn, asked Shembe if he was waiting for them in an effort to lead him off of the mountain, and some even asked to take possession of him. Each time Shembe insistently responded, "No! I don't know you." On Shembe's twelfth day on the mountain he reported that he heard glorious singing, smelled the loveliest of scents, spotted a light in the east, and felt as though his entire body was being filled with energy. The entire landscape, from the mountains and rivers to the trees and the grass, even the dead in their graves, was thrumming with this energy and singing about Shembe, "He is Holy!" It was amid this overwhelming sensory experience that Shembe claimed to have received a vision of God himself. With a roar of thunder and a flash of lightning, God soared toward him upon a white cloud, accompanied by the saints of heaven. Shembe reported that God came and stood before him with a vessel in his hand. He gave Shembe a heavenly meal of communion from the vessel, and then anointed him with the oil of grace. God then told Shembe, "Today, I give you all the authority to go all over the earth and to preach the message of the Nazaretha Church to all the nations under the sun.... Go now and teach all nations the way of God that leads to heaven, and baptize them in the name of the Father and of the Son and of the Holy Spirit. Today, I make a covenant with my Brown people."[3]

Shembe understood this particular prophetic event to be the moment of his transfiguration, when God fully and personally anointed him as his special emissary charged with the divine mission to illuminate the path of salvation among his new chosen "brown" people, and eventually all of humanity.[4] Shembe recounted this prophetic tale to his parishioners. Some followers retold the story orally, while others wrote the story in the notebooks that Shembe encouraged the literate to compile. For Shembe and the members of the Nazareth Baptist Church, this story was no legend but a factual account of

Isaiah Shembe on horseback, early 1930s
Used by permission of the Campbell Collections of the University of KwaZulu-Natal

a real event that demonstrably proved the prophetic might and divinely appointed mission of Shembe. For many scholars, a narrative of skeletons, apparitions, talking animals, and God sailing upon a cloud would sound like a fanciful fairytale generated by a charismatic individual, and a figurative or metaphorical interpretation would be assigned.[5] However, to accurately understand a thoroughly prophetic institution like the Nazareth Baptist Church, for which prophecy underwrites and circumscribes its documentary record, history, memory, theology, and identity, one must seriously consider, by which I mean treat as literal statements, such prophetic source material.[6] These accounts have defined, shaped, and reified the religious worldview of the founder, the leaders, and the members of the Nazareth Baptist Church.

By prophecy I refer to the process by which an individual believes they have received supernatural communications and convinces others of their validity. It is my contention that prophecy should be considered the Nazareth Baptist Church's *uhlanga*,[7] if you will, "the source" that originated, defined, shaped, and reified their worldview.[8] In the Zulu creation story, the maturation of *uhlanga*, the original bed of reeds, produced all the features of the universe. The Nazareth Baptist Church's universe was likewise born from a common source: in this case that font was a prophetic one that stemmed from the prophetic experiences of Isaiah Shembe, the church he founded, the worldview he constructed and articulated and that members embraced and reified.

More than that, the prophetically defined worldview of Shembe and his congregation served them as a particular navigational mechanism through the course of colonial South Africa, and was maintained by their documentary record, history, memory, identity, and theology. Normative definitions of empire, resistance, salvation, theology, and the like, will fail to accurately understand the actions of Shembe and his congregants because their notion of these concepts was informed by Shembe's prophetic experiences and the worldview they produced. The response Shembe and his congregation had to colonialism was neither resistant nor acquiescent, neither strictly Western nor African, neither exclusively Christian nor indigenous Zulu, but was a unique composite and hybrid response formed largely by Shembe's prophecies and the faith members had in him and the worldview he articulated. According to the beliefs of church leaders and members, every feature of the universe had a role to play in God's cosmic plans for bringing about the salvation of Africans (and eventually all of humanity) through the theology taught by Shembe, as they believed God had instructed him to preach. Within this worldview even colonialism and white supremacy were but agents of God's divine plans in advancing the salvation of Africans. Within the church's own narrative, empire, politics, the ascendency of whites, the Zulu past, and in fact anything one could name, were all subsumed into the grander, and, from their point of view, much more significant, story of how God's new chosen people were bringing about the salvation of God's "brown" people through the prophetic messages of Isaiah Shembe.

The church's history of itself, from within a prophetic paradigm, reveals a fresh and compelling means of understanding the experience of the colonized within colonial Africa. Shembe, church leaders, and church members endorsed a prophetic account of contemporary Africa that placed their church at the epicenter of their own history, and subsumed the story of imperialism within it. Scholarly accounts of Africa's colonial period have traditionally seen the forces of empire and resistance to colonialism as the principle motivations of human actions during this era of Africa's history. Yet historians would be mistaken to suppose that "everything that happened under colonialism was in some way a result of it."[9] An emic account of the history of Shembe and his church, indeed, reveals a different view of Africa's colonial era, one in which colonialism was not the sole or even the chief determinant of the history of the era. Shembe and the Nazareth Baptist Church resolutely accepted colonialism as part of a divine plan, prophetically revealed, that would bring about redemption and salvation for God's new chosen people, Africans. God, Shembe, and prophecy were the heart of their colonial-era experience, not British colonialism or white supremacist South Africa.

Colonization and Missionization in Eastern South Africa, 1820s–1930s

The peoples of eastern South Africa, like all of Africa, experienced considerable change across the nineteenth and twentieth centuries. Among those changes was the emergence of a Zulu identity, from the 1810s–1830s, during the Mfecane—variously translated as "time of troubles," "crushing," "forced migration," and "total war."[10] During this period, the tiny Nguni-speaking chieftaincy of the Zulu, under the famous king Shaka (r. 1818–1828), violently consolidated a constellation of northern Nguni-speaking peoples and realigned the political, cultural, linguistic, and ethnic landscape of southeastern Africa. Like most every process of ethnogenesis and ethnic amalgamation, the creation of the broader identity of Zulu never erased subethnic ones. As a result, "Zuluness" has experienced numerous contestations since the era of Shaka.

Settlers and missionaries began to arrive in the region in the 1830s and 1840s, not long after the consolidation of the Zulu. Afrikaner settlers striking out from the Cape established the short-lived province of Natalia in 1838 on land taken from the Zulu. In 1842 the British claimed Port Natal, absorbed Natalia, and declared establishment of the colony of Natal one year later. Most Afrikaners in Natal left for Transvaal or Orange Free State, and white British settlers soon began to take their place. The first wave of British settlers in Natal was quickly followed by multiple missionary societies.

The first missionaries arrived in the 1840s from Anglican, Congregationalist, Catholic, and several Lutheran mission societies. While the Zulu state remained intact, the number of converts remained very low. Forbidden by missionaries to swear allegiance to the Zulu monarch or fulfill their military obligations to the state, Zulu converts became "dead" people or strangers to other Zulu. Most Zulu converts to Christianity prior to the British conquest of the Zulu were those individuals who had nothing to gain from continued membership in Zulu society—criminals, deserters, captives, those accused of witchcraft, and those fleeing disagreeable marriages.[11]

The Zulu kings after Shaka, Dingane (r. 1828–1840), Mpande (r. 1840–1872), and Cetshwayo (r. 1872–1879), employed appeasement tactics in dealing with the British. While such diplomatic tactics generally worked for Dingane and Mpande, British demands accelerated during the reign of Cetshwayo. After Cetshwayo refused to concede to a thirteen-point ultimatum, the British declared war in January 1879. While the Zulu enjoyed a great victory at the war's first major encounter, Isandlwana, with more efficient supply lines and superior military technology, the British defeated the Zulu by July 1879. The British divided the former empire into thirteen chiefdoms, annexed Zululand in 1887, and incorporated it into Natal in 1897. Over the next few years more and more land was opened for white settlement; by 1905, the land slated for Zulu occupation was one-third the size of the former Zululand.[12]

The rate of conversion to Christianity began to increase following destruction of the Zulu empire. As precolonial structures diminished in power and resources, the social, economic, and religious allure of the missions grew. As the rate of conversion increased, so too did the number of Africans serving as teachers, catechists, and itinerant preachers. Indeed, indigenous preachers gained many more converts than their European or North American counterparts, as was true globally. As the number of African Christian converts and preachers grew so too did discontent over the lack of leadership positions for Africans within white-led mission churches, resulting in formation of a number of independent churches. Taking inspiration from Psalm 68:31[13] many such churches began to use the term *Ethiopia*, as a metaphor for ancient Christian Africa, in their names. The term became prevalent enough that scholars picked it up as well, and even today these sorts of churches continue to be identified as Ethiopianist churches.[14] Such churches were almost indistinct theologically from Protestant or Catholic variants of Christianity, yet they possessed an entirely African membership and leadership, free from the control of Western missionaries and denominations.

Beginning in the first decade of the twentieth century, a number of African Christians began to challenge the theologies of their Protestant, Catholic, and Ethiopianist brethren. Based upon prophetic inspiration and/or biblical exegesis, these dissenting Christians arrived at different theological concepts and practices than those of other Christians. Some of these new churches split off from existing congregations, others formed when members were forced out for their supposed heretical beliefs, while still other churches were formed almost ex nihilo through prophetic inspiration. Because of the preponderance of the term *Zion* in the names of many such churches, these churches are collectively called *Zionist* by scholars. Most possess a common set of characteristics: members believe themselves to be God's new chosen people; they typically possess a holy city; they accommodate African cultural expressions; and many emphasize prophetic inspiration. Shembe's Nazareth Baptist Church, while not the first Zionist church in South Africa, was the first to form independently, rather than as a result of a schism from an existing church.[15] The growing theological and ecclesiastical autonomy of Africans, however, was not matched politically or economically. In these realms it was the machinations of the British and Afrikaners that largely determined the fates of black South Africans.

Following the conclusion of the South African war in 1902, the four provinces of South Africa (Cape, Natal, Transvaal, Orange Free State) operated as autonomous British possessions until 1910. As negotiations took place on the future of South Africa, the question of black rights was sacrificed for the sake of political unity and peace among whites. The Union of South Africa was declared in 1910, the same year Shembe founded the Nazareth Baptist Church. From the time the union was formed in 1910 through 1931, South Africa was a self-governing dominion within the British Empire.

After the Statute of Westminster in 1931, British dominions, including the Union of South Africa, gained legislative autonomy, ending South Africa's colonial status in a constitutional sense. In most other ways, however, South Africa remained colonial until the advent of majority rule in 1994. During this entire period, as Mahmood Mamdani has convincingly demonstrated, all forms of colonial rule, regardless of their name and the metropolitan rhetoric surrounding them (indirect rule, direct rule, assimilation, association), were grounded in segregation, the use of indigenous agents, and the exploitation of ethnic politics.[16] While the South African state was once seen as brutal beyond compare, and therefore an anomalous situation, Mamdani has illustrated that colonialism by any name employed the same institutions and practices of control. While South Africa's white minority rule outlasted colonial rule of most of the world's colonies, its chronology is the only aspect that makes it anomalous to the rest of colonial Africa. In the words of Mamdani, "neither institutional segregation nor apartheid was a South African invention."[17] The bulk of this book's analysis concerns the 1910s–1930s, when South Africa was both practically and literally colonial. Yet even where the narrative and analysis continues past the 1931 Statute of Westminster, I will continue to employ the term "colonial Africa" in recognition of the fact that: (1) next to nothing had changed for South Africa's non-white populations after 1931; and (2) whatever South Africa's constitutional status, the experience of South Africa's non-white peoples was much more like that of other colonized peoples than it was not.[18]

A Brief History of the Nazareth Baptist Church

The Nazareth Baptist Church recently passed its centennial anniversary. Space does not allow an examination of the entire century of the church's history, nor does my narrative and argument concern the entirety of the church's history. The bulk of this book focuses upon the formative decades (1910s– 1930s) during the central leadership of Isaiah Shembe. This was the time when Shembe developed the church's overall prophetic worldview, which was embraced by the church's membership and then routinized and institutionalized as the church became one of Africa's most significant Zionist churches.

The Nazareth Baptist Church emerged within a colonial context due to the determined efforts of its founder, Isaiah Shembe. Both Shembe and church members recount Shembe's early life as an uncanny one that revealed his distinctiveness even prior to formation of the church.[19] This special nature was supported through his recounting of how he had received prophecies by a variety of media including visions, dreams, and hearing a voice throughout his childhood. In an effort to find the source of these prophecies, the teenage Isaiah engaged in a period of religious exploration into both Zulu indigenous religion and Christianity. This period of exploration in the early 1900s included attendance at Methodist services and the African Native Baptist Church, an Ethiopianist church led by the Rev. W. M. Leshega. Through this exploration he eventually came to the conclusion that the high god of the Zulus, Unkulunkulu, was the same god as the Christian's Jehovah, and was the source of the supernatural communications. He also became convinced that other Christians were in serious error concerning their sacramental and soteriological theologies.

Shembe married and began to produce a family, in spite of prophetic admonitions to be celibate. He continued to receive repeated prophetic warnings not to defile himself through sex that eventually culminated in a series of profound prophetic experiences that convinced him to leave his family and preach full time, as he believed God was commanding. Nazareth Baptist Church lore is full of stories of the healing miracles Shembe performed in his subsequent travels.[20] Shembe worked as an itinerant preacher for four more years before creating his own church.

The moment of the church's formation was rather unspectacular considering the founder had such an astounding prophetic record. As he had done throughout his years as an itinerant preacher, Shembe brought a number of converts to an American Board of Commissioners for Foreign Missions station for further instruction in 1910.[21] The converts were refused admittance because they were in Zulu attire. Unwilling to depart without giving these converts an opportunity to learn more of God, Shembe felt it was his responsibility to care for them. From this point onward he ceased directing converts to existing congregations and instead encouraged them to join his own, and the Nazareth Baptist Church was born. Shembe subsequently had a number of prophetic experiences that affirmed how pleased God was with him and the church, whose congregants were God's new chosen people, following the path of salvation being illuminated by Shembe through God's prophetic instructions.

Shembe instituted a new theology based on his prophetic experiences and biblical exegesis. According to Shembe, salvation could only be achieved through strict seventh-day Sabbatarian observance, as this more than any other action of the worshiper demonstrated proper adoration of God. Shembe also instituted a strict code of conduct based upon his understanding of God's laws, and four sacraments: baptism, communion, *ukusina* (dance worship), and *umnazaretha* (uniform). Beyond development of the church's theology, among Shembe's initial goals was the purchase of land to build a holy city that would maintain the purity and economic viability of his followers. Shembe purchased thirty-eight acres of land at Inanda (on the outskirts of Durban), and there constructed Ekuphakameni (the exalted place)—a name he said just came to him—and permitted followers to settle there.[22] The church grew modestly, gaining most of its converts from other Christian denominations, and homes (temples) began to appear in many parts of eastern South Africa, principally among Zulu-speakers.

Shembe continued as the central leader of the church until his death on 2 May 1935. He was succeeded by his son Johannes Galilee Shembe. During the era of Galilee the church grew considerably, from around 20,000–40,000 at the time of Isaiah's death to hundreds of thousands. This growth included many converts from indigenous religions, unlike during Isaiah's era, and also included expansion into neighboring countries, principally Swaziland and Mozambique. Galilee had a considerable tenure as the head of the Nazareth Baptist Church, remaining in the position until his death at the end of 1976.

The central leadership position was hotly contested between two male descendants of Shembe following Galilee's death: Amos Shembe (Isaiah's son) and Londa Shembe (Isaiah's grandson, and Galilee's son). Despite intervention by the Zulu King Goodwill, the South African Council of Churches, the Supreme Court of Natal, and the prophetic intercession, via dreams, of Isaiah and Galilee, no compromise was forthcoming and the church split in 1980. The Supreme Court awarded Londa Ekuphakameni and most of the church's properties, but only 10–15% of the membership followed him.

Amos lost the battle for the holy city and most of the church's holdings, but won the contest for popular support with 85–90% of the membership supporting him.[23] On land ceded by the Qadi-Zulu Authority, Amos established a new Ekuphakameni—or a new New Jerusalem—about ten kilometers away from Ekuphakameni and named it Ebuhleni (the place of splendor). The church has maintained two New Jerusalems ever since.

Amos continued as head of the Ebuhleni branch from 1980 until his death in October 1995. Roughly six factions formed around rival claimants in the mid-1990s, though none was successful at displacing Vimbeni, the son of Amos, who Amos had named as successor.[24] Vimbeni served as head of the Ebuhleni faction from 1995 until March 2011, when he died at age 74. At the moment of this writing, court cases over central leadership are pending and the future of the Ebuhleni church is uncertain.

Londa served as central leader of the Ekuphakameni section of the church until his murder in April 1989. The Ekuphakameni section was ruled by a church council from 1989–1998. In 1998, the ruling committee selected Londa's second-born son, Vukile Shembe, as central leader and he remains the head of the Ekuphakameni branch. While the Londa-Vukile branch continues to be far smaller demographically, it does possess greater symbolic currency than the Ebuhleni section, given that they control the mausoleums of Isaiah and Galilee and the original holy city. With the Ebuhleni section currently embroiled in a succession dispute, the Ekuphakameni branch may begin to capitalize on this currency.

African Responses to Imperialism: Historiography and Theory of Colonial Africa

Our understandings of empire and the experiences of the colonized, in short what it means to be colonial, have undergone multiple historiographic shifts over the past five decades, moving from nationalist, to materialist, to postcolonial interpretations. Scholars writing about the colonial period from a nationalist perspective in the 1960s–1980s emphasized the agency of Africans, highlighting those who resisted, whether militarily, politically, culturally, and so on. Studies written from a materialist approach, in the 1970s–1990s, critiqued nationalist works for presenting resisting Africans as an imagined whole who always resisted. Through class and gender analysis, such works demonstrated how economic and social groups reacted to colonialism differently, meaning that some resisted while others collaborated. In the last two decades many scholars have applied postcolonial theories to the study of colonial Africa and illustrated how the binary categories of resistance or collaboration are far too simplistic; most historical actors operated somewhere between those two archetypes, even moving between degrees of resistance and collaboration.[25] Despite such intellectual shifts, all these schools of thought agreed that the forces of empire and resistance to them were the principle determinants of history during Africa's colonial era.

Scholarly attention to African responses to colonialism blossomed in the 1960s–1980s with the advent of the nationalist school of thought. The timing was not coincidental, and many of these studies were closely tied to nation-building, hero construction, and the establishment of new national narratives and curriculums for recently independent countries.[26] These nationalist histories challenged earlier imperialist narratives of Africa that had focused upon European endeavors in Africa, and thereby painted a seemingly passive and static picture of Africans. Nationalist works, rather, demonstrated the continually active nature of Africans even under the oppressive conditions of colonialism.[27] These scholars brought a much-needed historiographic correc-tive to the Eurocentric scholarship before them, and provided new narratives for recently independent African nations. Yet the nationalist perspective had two shortcomings. First, many nationalist works focused on armed resistance and political organizations, and generally ignored other, less spectacular sorts of responses.[28] Second, those who did not resist in some manner were neglect-ed entirely. Africans who took collaborationist or accommodationist positions did not fit within the nationalist scholars' agenda, either their research agenda or their political one, and were simply not written about in this era.[29]

The same nationalist sentiments can be detected among many studies of Zionist churches. Zionist churches were depicted as communities of resistors who defied missionary efforts and Westernization, and exemplified a stage in the "evolution of anti-colonial protest, lying between early armed resistance and the rise of modern nationalist parties."[30] Such studies portrayed Zionist churches as strongholds of indigenous culture built upon cultural and political resistance.[31] Some works endeavored to illustrate the strength of indigenous religions and the weakness of Westernization, rejected the "Christianness" of Zionist movements, and attributed the majority of such theologies to continui-ties from indigenous religions.[32] Nationalist sentiments within the study of Zionist churches is even revealed in the preferred term for the era, *African Independent Churches* (AIC), suggesting a previous state of religious dependence that had now been liberated to a state of independence.[33]

From the late 1960s and into the 1990s, materialist narratives fuelled another major historical approach to studies of African responses to colonial-ism. These narratives critiqued the nationalist ones of the 1960s–1980s for characterizing resisting Africans as a monolithic whole. These materialist historians, many with Marxist political leanings, brought class and gender analysis to bear on the study of resistance, and illustrated how different eco-nomic and social groups reacted to colonialism differently. Resistance, they suggested, was not simply the purview of the elite, who tended to be the focal points of nationalist studies. Materialists demonstrated how resistance could be found across the socio-economic spectrum. In an effort to show how even the humblest individuals were capable of resistance, materialist scholars wrote about a variety of "subaltern" voices that were found infrequently in nationalist studies, including peasants, women, and even outcasts.[34] Some materialists additionally challenged nationalist studies further by noting that collaboration with the efforts of the colonial state, and not just resistance to it, was also part of colonial history.[35]

The shift toward materialist analyses is likewise reflected in understandings of Zionist Christianity from the 1960s through 1990s.[36] Whereas nationalists had depicted members of Zionist churches as heroic resistors and preservers of tradition, materialists transformed Zionist organizations in two manners. One trend was to portray Zionists as humble resistors who, because their class kept them from positions of power, instead used religion as a vehicle to resist. While the churches began as genuine religious movements, according to these scholars, they all eventually drifted toward black nationalism and political resistance as a means of actualizing the resentments of non-elites.[37] A second, later trend was to depict Zionists as politically acquiescent groups who "studiously avoided political action" and who did not possess the "proper" political consciousness.[38] This was particularly the case in studies of South African Zionists who were criticized by portions of the Africanist intelligentsia and some Protestant and Catholic theologians for their dual lack of a liberation theology and an overt, anti-Apartheid stance.[39] To such critics, the emphasis on traditional culture within Zionist churches, and their self-segregating nature, further suggested an acquiescent posture to such critics.[40]

Whether nationalist or materialist in orientation, studies of resistance from the 1960s to 1990s shared a common goal. Both scholarly approaches were intent upon showing the uniformly transformative and inescapable nature of colonialism, while at the same time highlighting the unbreakable vitality of African cultures and peoples. Both sorts of studies unquestionably served an important historiographic function and challenged earlier Eurocentric imperialist narratives of African passivity. The emphasis upon resistance was warranted, though overstated.[41] Surely there were plenty of peoples for whom resistance was their central concern. It is not difficult to imagine that many Western-educated elites, those Africans working in colonial bureaucracies and mission bodies, industrial workers, or youth, for instance, might indeed have had considerable interest in choosing courses of resistance.[42] However, the focus on resistance in the 1960s–1990s says a great deal about who was doing the writing. Within African academies the quest to locate resistance and resistors served the purposes of nation-building and identity construction. Within North American and European academies, our own concurrent histories of counterculturalism, the civil and indigenous rights movements, feminism, and secularism, made us seek resistors and agitators in order to glorify those Africans in colonial Africa who had behaved in the manner we most admired in ourselves.[43]

From the 1990s onward, resistance to colonialism has continued to be a popular subject of study, yet scholars have complicated their perspectives still further. With the application of various postcolonial theories, resistance, a singular unilateral response, and its antithesis, collaboration, were transformed to plural responses, to represent the array of possible positions for the colonized. Many scholars of the last two decades have argued that a binary notion of resistor or collaborator is a much too simplistic way to view colonized peoples of the past. While some peoples resisted and some collaborated, most individuals were somewhere between those binary archetypes, and even moved between degrees of resistance and collaboration, taking different positions as colonial circumstances and self-interests shifted over time.[44]

Postcolonialism also brought changes to scholarly understandings of Zionist Christianity. These newer approaches contended that Zionist churches should be understood as complex engagements with both tradition and modernity, and were simultaneously something old and something new, a trend reflected in approaches to colonial Africa as a whole from the 1990s onward.[45] The earlier term of *African Independent Churches* was replaced by *African Initiated Churches* or *African Instituted Churches* (though the acronym remained the same) in recognition that Zionist churches were unique hybrids, some of which were not schismatic reactions to missions, never had a connection to Protestantism or Catholicism, and whose creations were therefore not necessarily purposeful acts of cultural resistance. Postcolonial sensibilities also redeemed the political image of Zionist churches. While some materialist scholars a generation before had implied Zionists were not political enough, postcolonial approaches countered by arguing that this critique only holds if one insisted upon European notions of politics and resistance. If, however, one looked outside of Western norms, other forms of resistance could be found among the memberships of these churches. Because the Zionist faithful were generally politically and economically marginalized, recent scholarship has argued that they manifested their resistance in symbolic and internal ways.[46]

Studies of African responses to colonialism over the past five decades have revised scholarly understandings of Africa's colonial period and developed greater nuance regarding the experiences of the colonized. Scholars have recently added that same sort of complexity to our understanding of empires as well.[47] During the nationalist era of scholarship, empires were viewed as monolithic and uniformly oppressive. In the past two decades, historical understandings of empires have grown more refined, with recognition that empires were complicated affairs that varied in their agenda, strength, impact, pervasiveness, and tenacity. Time period, responses from the colonized, metropolitan affairs, imperial strategies, the presence of white settlers, changing administrative policies, and even the personalities of the colonizers all altered the texture of empires over time and space.[48] Empires were not, then, totalizing hegemonic forces that forced all the colonized into a constant posture of resistance. Rather, spaces existed where the full impact of imperialism was not experienced by some populations, at least at some moments in time, allowing the colonial subject to view that impact as secondary to other interests, as an obstacle that could be worked around, or even as an opportunity to embrace.[49] By this understanding of empire, it is not difficult to imagine communities of people whose first concern was not imperial oppression and the need for resistance. People in such communities may have narratives of their place in the colonial world that defies the traditional scholarly trope of constant imperial oppression in need of regular resistance. Given the array of possibilities from empires, and the range of possible experiences of colonized communities, historians can no longer assume that the central concern of all imperial subjects was resistance, nationalist agitation, or political consciousness as though these were evolutionary inevitabilities of being colonized.[50] These remarks should not be mistaken as minimizing the consequences of empire. Empires quite clearly had costly and transformative effects and destructive, even genocidal, consequences and potentials. But that does not mean that every colonial population had constant oppressive experiences in need of resistance, or more importantly, interpreted such experiences as imperial oppression.

Such is the case with Shembe and the membership of the Nazareth Baptist Church. Even living within a white supremacist state, the church's founder still developed and advanced, and his membership embraced, an internally inspired worldview grounded upon prophecy, and not an externally inspired one defined by the politics of empire. Shembe and his congregation engaged in neither resistance nor acquiescence. Rather, they developed their own unique response to colonialism, a prophetic response that explained empire as but a necessary facet of God's plans, of which they and their church were at the epicenter. This prophetic worldview was an involutionist one that could weave any event of the external world into the tapestry of God's prophetically revealed cosmic vision for Shembe and his new chosen people.

Shembe's Prophetic Response to Colonialism

In post-Apartheid South Africa, Shembe and the membership of the Nazareth Baptist Church have been cast as heroic figures of cultural resistance in two manners, one public and one scholarly. First, the image of the Nazareth Baptist Church has experienced a nationalist public revitalization. Within the narrative of the new South Africa, the Nazareth Baptist Church is remembered as serving as a refuge for the preservation of Africanness and the racial uplifting of Africans.[51] This new attitude is best reflected in an award given to the late central leader of the Ebuhleni branch, Vimbeni Shembe. In March 2001, a number of "heroes of the South African struggle" received awards amid the Third African Renaissance Festival in Durban. Vimbeni Shembe received the King Cetshwayo African Image Award on behalf of his grandfather, Isaiah, in recognition of Isaiah's role in subverting the barriers of a segregated society.[52] Such an award is emblematic of the new image of the Nazareth Baptist Church, and Zionist churches generally, in post-Apartheid South Africa. Scholars too have contributed to the image of Shembe as resistor by applying a postcolonial notion of cultural resistance to Shembe and the Nazareth Baptist Church. By this reckoning, Shembe is seen as a resistance figure who used an alternative rendering of Christianity as a form of passive and symbolic resistance.[53] Such contemporary reckonings of Shembe are much like earlier nationalist readings from the 1960s–1980s that cast Zionist leaders as cultural resistors, and shares the fact that it emerged in what could be called South Africa's post-independence period.

This post-1994 postcolonial image of Shembe, however, suffers from the same shortcomings as nationalist renderings from decades ago. The inspiration and historiographic moment is the same—new narratives, heroes, and symbols for a new nation. It is the chronological gap between most of Africa's moment of independence in 1960 and South Africa's transition to majority rule in 1994 that accounts for the temporal distance between otherwise parallel arguments. Yet whether informed by earlier nationalist sentiments or more contemporary postcolonial sensibilities, we must be careful in casting the colonized in the role of resistors, whether the resistance is deemed active or passive, external or internal, lest a focus on resistance blind us to zones of creativity.[54] Does every cultural expression of the colonized constitute an instance of resistance?[55] Some cultural activities, either individually or collectively, were assuredly purposeful expressions of resistance; it is not difficult to imagine indigenous cultures being used to resist imposition of imperial ones. However, Shembe practiced Christianity, something South Africans had initially learned from whites. While Shembe's Christianity was original, he would not have known about Christianity if not for whites. So ultimately, was Shembe a cultural resistor, a Zulu man who resisted Western notions of Christianity while preserving Zulu culture, or a politically acquiescent accommodationist who allowed Zulu culture to be overwhelmed by its imperial counterpart?[56]

There is no need to force Shembe to conform to the nationalist quest to locate resistors, or mine for hidden clues of symbolic resistance in a post-colonial manner to demonstrate that Shembe was not acquiescent. Moreover, being resistant or acquiescent does not exhaust a colonized population's range of potential responses. Shembe was quite clear about what motivated him—prophecy. State and church records both reveal that Shembe's worldview was prophetically defined from start to finish. We would, therefore, be doing Shembe and the members of the Nazareth Baptist Church a disservice in calling their actions resistance, although they do unquestionably constitute a response to colonialism. That response is a prophetic one that subsumed colonialism within their own narrative. Though living within a white suprem-acist South Africa under British and white minority rule inevitably influenced the leaders and members of the church in their daily lives, archival documents and church records both reveal that the church tells its own story within a prophetic narrative where God, prophecy, and their church, not imperialism, constitute the center, the *uhlanga*, of their history.

Within the historical narrative church members tell of their institution, colonialism was not the chief determinant of their history, God was. Their destiny, and ultimately all of Africa's, they believed, was being generated by God and prophetically revealed to Shembe. Shembe taught that God had revealed the correct path of salvation to him that required observation of a Saturday Sabbath, bolstered by proper adoration from worshipers through the maintenance of God's laws. Shembe believed it his mission to spread this message of salvation, an indication that Africans were now God's new chosen people in need of spiritual redemption. When God felt the appropriate period of atonement for Africa's past sins of improper worship and ancestral violence had passed, only then would the political landscape of South Africa change. In the meantime, white overrule of South Africa was part of God's cosmic plan of African salvation.[57] Therefore, one who fought against whites would be fighting God and running against the current of God's salvific plan for Africa. Colonialism, then, was by God's design, and was but a fragment within the larger mosaic of human history being constructed by God, a portion of which he was sharing with Shembe via prophecy. Prophecy thereby created, defined, and reified the church's worldview, a worldview that subsumed politics within their own salvific narrative.[58]

Consider, for example, an excerpt from the *Catechism of the Nazarites*, a volume of church lore compiled by church secretary Petros Dhlomo, who was appointed to the position in 1949 by Galilee Shembe. One of the documents within the *Catechism* is "Shembe's Prayer in Remembrance of His Nation," that records the following prayer of Isaiah Shembe,

4: Let the curse of Shaka to his descendants be forgotten.
Let us forget the curses of Kings Dingane, Mpande, and Cetshwayo,
Over the Zulu nation.

5: They were bad ancestors of our nation.
Let us now turn to the new Thixo, who has appeared in our midst...

7: I come now to the new Thixo
Who is today inside the gates of Ekuphakameni...

12: One day, while the Servant of the Lord, Shembe, was mourning for our scattered
nation, and not knowing how it could be gathered together again, he heard the sky
thundering. Shembe awoke and sat up, trembling with fear. There came a Voice
which said to him: "Do you hear the thunderstorm?" He said: "Yes." The Voice said:
"The noise you hear is not a thunderstorm, but the footsteps of the kings entering
Ekuphakameni."[59]

It would be easy to read this prayer as evidence of indigenous retentions living
on in the guise of Christianity and therefore as a form of cultural resistance to
the dominant colonial white culture. After all, as the early stanzas illustrate,
the prayer is concerned with one's ancestors, and not just any ancestors, but
the royal ones. But this prayer was no evocation of cultural resistance or neo-
monarchic dreams. When one reads on to the twelfth, and penultimate,
stanza, one can see that a concern with ancestors or Zulu kings is not the
central focus of this prayer. In the twelfth stanza Shembe describes a prophetic
experience. It is through this prophetic experience that he knows, with the
sort of confidence brought about by faith bolstered through prophecy, that the
sins of the royal ancestors have been forgiven by God, and the kings have
entered into Ekuphakameni, a Christian space and the Nazareth Baptist
Church's holy city. In this fashion, Shembe and Ekuphakameni were bringing
about a new Christian era for Africans, made real through Shembe's
prophecies. As this source preliminarily indicates and later chapters will
reinforce, time after time, and no matter to whom he was speaking, Shembe
insisted upon a prophetic and Christian explanation of his activities. His
progeny likewise continued this practice in the maintenance of Shembe's
prophetic charter for the church. In short, the interpretation of history and
historical memory of the founder, the subsequent central leaders, and the
membership, is told through a prophetic paradigm. This is what gave their
world meaning and subsumed colonialism within their prophetic worldview; it
was not colonialism and resistance to it that defined the parameters of their
universe.[60]

In this manner, Shembe and the Nazareth Baptist Church reveal a new
way of thinking about colonial Africa, the range of responses produced by
colonized populations, and the ways in which the colonized explained imperialism within their own epistemologies. Additionally, the worldview of Shembe
and the Nazareth Baptist Church faithful is predicated upon their own under-

standings and prioritizing of concepts such as empire, politics, Christian theology, God, and tradition. Scholars must be wary of employing normative definitions of these concepts in an examination of the Nazareth Baptist Church. Normative uses of these concepts will marginalize Shembe and his followers as the scholar aligns himself or herself with modes of authority other than Shembe. The leaders and members of the Nazareth Baptist Church possessed unique understandings of these important concepts, understandings that derived from the authority and prophecies of Shembe and the worldview he advanced.

This study is based upon research conducted at the Killie Campbell Africana Library and the Durban Local History Museum, both in Durban; the National Archives and Records Service of South Africa in Pretoria; and the Pietermaritzburg (Natal) Archives Repository in Pietermaritzburg, KwaZulu-Natal. These collections offered a variety of sources: police reports, court documents, news articles, recorded interviews, church constitutions, hymns, prayers, and memoirs. Especially central to this study were the records of visions, dreams, and other prophetic experiences that have been compiled and archived by government agents, church members, and academic researchers over the course of the history of the Nazareth Baptist Church.[61]

The next chapter explores the history of the Nazareth Baptist Church through the history of the evolution of its documentary record. Isaiah Shembe, his son Galilee, archivist Petros Dhlomo, and an array of members produced and preserved several major sources including: the church's hymnal (*Izihlabelelo zaManazaretha*); a collection of Isaiah's primary accounts dubbed the "Grave Book;" a compilation of church members' and leaders' oralture and literature assembled during the era of Galilee, the *Catechism of the Nazarites*; and an additional compilation begun in the era of Galilee and continued during the administrations of Londa Shembe and Amos Shembe, the *Acts of the Nazarites*. I argue that the church's documentary record served as a legitimating device in two ways. First, the traditions that were preserved and compiled into the church's documentary record were intensely prophetic. These narratives amplified the very teachings and beliefs Shembe had composed into a systematic worldview of the church's place within colonial Africa. It became much easier to sustain one's faithful commitment to the church's worldview when there were ample traditions in circulation that supported it. Second, as the documentary record took shape, it grew increasingly Christian in form, assuming normative expressions such as a printed hymnbook, rule code, and catechism. This was quite purposeful and an attempt to enhance the church's Christian legitimacy. I conclude this chapter by evaluating the usefulness and trustworthiness of these records for the historian. The sources are not without their complicating factors for scholarly usage, including such issues as uncertain provenance and unclear "voice." Yet despite such concerns, I conclude that the documents possess a considerable degree of authenticity and can reveal both the memory and history of the church.

Having established the legitimating purposes of the church's overall documentary records, in chapter 3 I utilize the texts of particular sources to analyze the history and historical memory of the biography of Shembe up to 1910, the date of the church's founding. The biography of Shembe, both as he told it and as his church has preserved and recounted it, reveals a thoroughly Christian and prophetic narrative replete with visions, voices, and miraculous events. Shembe's prophetic abilities and uncanny life generated a prophetic aura around him that not only reinforced but amplified his teachings, explanations, and even the record itself. From these prophetic experiences, Shembe believed God had revealed to him the path of salvation, his desires for his new chosen people, and portions of his cosmic vision for humanity. Thoroughly convinced of the veracity of these prophecies and of his prophetically bestowed mission, Shembe developed a prophetic worldview, and it directly informed how he understood his own life, the conditions of colonial Africa, and the future of Africans. Shembe's development as a theologian and preacher, and later as a church founder and leader, was entirely colored by this worldview and his prophetic experiences. This worldview was so powerful it became part of the church's theology and was embraced by the church's membership. Shembe's biography, therefore, from the perspective of the church's membership, was not merely a historical account but a sacred record of God's revelations to Shembe that explained and divinely justified their faith and prophetic worldview.

Chapter 4 analyzes the history of the church from its founding in 1910 until Shembe's death in 1935. The first portion of the chapter examines the interactions between the fledgling church and officials of the colonial province of Natal. Like many autonomous black churches of the time period, Shembe and the members of the Nazareth Baptist Church came under near immediate suspicion from white administrators, missionaries, and citizens. However, over the course of the 1920s and 1930s, Shembe and the Nazareth Baptist Church were gradually cleared of the accusations leveled against them and permitted to operate with a surprising degree of freedom. From the perspective of the state's officials, Shembe's congregation grew to become an acceptable picture of assimilation; not too much, that they became interested in integrating into the white world, and not too little, so that they remained "uncivilized." I contend that this was largely by coincidence on Shembe's part, and not by design, and will explore the question of whether or not he was "playing politics." Regardless, the relative *laissez faire* attitude of colonial officials provided a space that allowed this group of imperial subjects to view their world as determined by God and prophecy, and not by oppression in need of resistance. Even when the state intervened in the church's affairs, by insisting that members be vaccinated or in mandating permits for the annual pilgrimage to the holy mountain, Shembe assigned a religious and prophetic interpretation that he shared with the congregation. At no point did the actions of colonial officials dissuade Shembe or his congregants of their prophetic worldview and the place it assigned them within early twentieth century colonial Africa.

In chapters 5 and 6 I explore the ways in which theology reinforced the identity and worldview of Shembe and his congregation. Chapter 5 analyzes the church's theophanic sites and their soteriology. Both of these theological elements contributed to the identity Shembe and his congregation ascribed to themselves as a unique community of God's chosen people. The belief in their chosenness was a true cornerstone of how Shembe and his congregation defined themselves, and also informed how they related to the world beyond the church. The church's two theophanic sites of Ekuphakameni, the New Jerusalem, and Nhlangakazi, the church's holy mountain, coupled with the church's soteriological theology, generated a religiously based identity for Shembe and his congregants, an identity that trumped other possible identity options available to them, including political and ethnic ones.

The sixth chapter continues an investigation of the impact of Shembe's theology upon the identity of the Nazareth Baptist Church's congregation. While the previous chapter looked at the role of the church's theophanic sites and soteriology, this chapter analyzes the church's four sacraments (baptism, communion, *ukusina* (dance worship), and *umnazaretha* (uniform)) and the role that the church's sacramental theology played in both reinforcing Shembe's distinctiveness and prophetic might and in reifying the identity of the membership as God's new chosen people. Shembe's status as a prophet imbued all the decisions he made on these sacraments with a sense of legitimacy and truth for worshipers, regardless of the number of direct prophecies he received on the matter, or even whether he received any at all.[62] The aura of Shembe's prophetic might legitimated his theological conclusions for himself and his congregation, whether direct prophetic inspiration was absent, as it was with communion, or voluminous, as it was with the *umnazaretha*. Regardless of the degree to which a sacrament was legitimated by direct prophetic inspiration, Shembe's prophetic aura, or most commonly a combination of the two, all the sacraments were ritualistic celebrations for worshipers of their chosenness in the eyes of God. Such communal events bolstered the faith of members, affirmed the teachings and worldview of the church, and enhanced the membership's sense of community and identity.

The seventh and last chapter returns to the issues of empire and the responses of the colonized. Shembe and the members of the Nazareth Baptist

Church engaged in neither resistance nor acquiescence but rather produced their own unique prophetic worldview that explained empire as a necessary element of God's divine plans. While Shembe generated a unique prophetic worldview and response to colonialism, the Nazareth Baptist Church is not beyond compare. This chapter additionally offers some comparative insights from other colonized communities, suggesting that the leaders and members of the Nazareth Baptist Church were not alone in responding to colonialism in a manner that was based on neither resistance nor acquiescence.

Prophecy, Oralture, and Literature: The Documentary History of the Nazareth Baptist Church, 1910s–1990s

[W]e want all the personal testimonies just as they were told. Then we shall get real history, you see.

— J. Galilee Shembe to Bengt Sundkler, 1958[1]

I n a letter dated 22 August 1931, Shembe wrote to his lawyer, Mr. Dickson, seeking legal counsel. The month before, the Native Affairs Department had ordered Shembe to shut down some provincial temples within three months. Shembe was intending to comply with the order but desired to write the names of the temples upon whitewashed stones because he believed that in the future a "white Lord will come from Europe" to seek and restore them. Shembe sought Dickson's advice about whether or not he should ask permission from Native Affairs to leave the names of the temples inscribed upon the rocks. Shembe wrote that, "My conscience tells me to do it: but I wish to obtain permission from the government."[2]

This incident illustrates Shembe's respect for the written word, though illiterate himself. This respect was deep enough that it inspired and shaped the documentary record of the church. Shembe encouraged his followers to preserve his prophecies, sermons, hymns, and parables to memory and to paper. A documentary record was begun from the church's earliest days, but it was one in both oral and written forms that was neither strictly oralture nor literature, but complexly both. Following Shembe's death in 1935, his successor J. Galilee Shembe was intensely interested in preserving the history of his father and the early decades of the church's history, as revealed by the epigraphic quote. Through the efforts of the indefatigable church secretary Petros Dhlomo, the support of Galilee and the church's ministers, and the cooperation of the church's membership, several major compilations [hymnbook,

"Grave Book," *Catechism*, and *Acts of the Nazarites*] of material were amassed at the church's headquarters, Ekuphakameni.

Beyond telling the story of how these records were produced, this chapter has several other, more analytical concerns that are interwoven into the narrative of the church's documentary history. First, I examine how the documentary record served as a legitimating device. Like any archive or compilation of source material, the church's documentary record is selective. Archives, whether produced by government agencies, individuals, or churches are generally not random in their selection process of what information is preserved.[3] In the case of the Nazareth Baptist Church, those tales which were prophetic or miraculous had far greater odds of being transmitted and recorded than pieces of ordinary history recounting mundane events. There is a clear reason for this, and that is because such pieces of church lore strengthened the faith of members in multiple ways. From reinforcing their beliefs about Shembe, his distinctive prophetic status, his prophecies, and his theology, to bolstering their confidence that they were a new community composed of God's new chosen people, the telling, preservation, and retelling of these supernatural communications aided in reifying the church's worldview. The nature of the documentary record, itself intensely prophetic, amplified the very teachings and beliefs Shembe had composed into a systematic worldview of the church's place within colonial Africa. It became much easier to sustain one's faithful commitment to the church's worldview when there were ample traditions in circulation that supported it.

The content and form of the church's documentary record also served as a legitimating device in a second manner, and this was through the generation of Christian legitimacy. Isaiah had instructed members to preserve his prophecies, sermons, hymns, and parables by whatever means was within their literacy skills. But during his time as leader, the written records were decentralized and took the form of individual copybooks. His son and immediate successor, Galilee, was interested in producing a centralized version of the history of Isaiah and the early church. As that centralized version was compiled, preserved, and published it took an increasingly Christian form. The church's hymnbook and catechism have clear analogues throughout Christendom, while the church's *Acts of the Nazarites* purposefully echoed Acts of early Christianity, thereby Christianizing the story of Shembe.

Lastly, I conclude by assessing the overall reliability and credibility of the church's documentary record, and highlight methodological windfalls and pitfalls in its scholarly usage. Despite the challenges posed by provenance and "voice," I ultimately conclude that though careful usage is required, the main sources of information on the church's history do contain a general veracity. The church's own documentary record does allow the historian access to the words and actions of the founder and early members of the Nazareth Baptist Church.

Oralture and Literature: The Genesis of a Prophetic Church Record, 1910–1935

The Nazareth Baptist Church's own historical record was generated through a complex intersection of orality and literacy. As with so many features of the church, the reason for this can be traced back to Isaiah Shembe. Shembe had a powerful respect, a respect that one might say bordered on awe, for written texts and literacy. For some African converts to Christianity, literacy was an avenue for advancement within the colonial world. Shembe too was susceptible to this impulse, and insisted that his sons receive a formal education at a mission school. One of them, Galilee, even became an educator himself.[4] Yet literacy as a key that unlocked the door of opportunity within the white world had little meaning for Isaiah personally; he never pursued formal Western education nor became fully literate in any language. Like many first generation African Christians of the era, for Isaiah the power and mystery of literacy came from its ability to unlock the Christian Bible and allow one access to the Word of God.[5] In a conversation with journalist and neighbor Nellie Wells in the early 1930s, Shembe shared the wonder the Bible had for him. While he had learned of the Bible as a youth, while working on a Boer family's farm, it took "a long time before he dared touch that sacred book.... The Great-Great-One for whom he yearned, and who had manifested himself to him, had sent a message in that book."[6]

To access that message within the sacred words, Shembe believed God had bestowed a supernatural form of literacy upon him in response to his prayers. In an April 1931 interview, in Natal's provincial capital of Pietermaritzburg, agents of the Native Economic Commission asked Shembe, "Have you not learned to read & write?" The particular wording of the state official who asked the question suggests the commission members assumed a Christian church leader must have been formally educated. This had been generally true of African ministers to that point, but was becoming less so with the growing emergence of Zionist churches in the early twentieth century. Shembe responded to the query by saying, "No, I have not been taught to read & write, but I am able to read the Bible a little bit, and that came to me by revelation and not by learning."[7] Shembe believed his limited literacy to be a miraculous power bestowed by God that gave him access to the Word of the Bible.

Shembe's ability to "read" the Bible, in addition to being a God-granted ability in his mind, provided the bridge that connected orality and textuality for him. As was true of many individuals within predominantly oral cultures who possessed limited literacy, Shembe was reputed to have had a powerful memory and acute mnemonic skills that had allowed him to memorize the Bible. A reporter for the *Illustrated London News*, for instance, noted that Shembe was able to spontaneously quote Bible verses in response to any inquiry.[8] Shembe's mnemonic mastery of the Bible quite likely enabled him to begin recognizing words and verses as he engaged the written form. Shembe's considerable mastery of the Bible as oralture, therefore, began granting him entrée into the Bible as literature. Yet oral mastery of a text will never bestow full literacy upon an individual, which is why Shembe admitted his literacy was partial. Moreover, Shembe admitted that his literacy was not just fractional but conditional and his skills in literacy were entirely limited to the Bible. The fact that Shembe's partial literacy was circumstantial, and only applied to a single text, demonstrates that it was Shembe's skills in orality that began the development of his singular aptitude in literacy. The more time he dedicated to the Bible, in both oral and written forms, the greater his abilities became with both versions.[9] But such a rational explanation of how an otherwise illiterate individual might develop a limited literacy with a particular text was not how Shembe understood or explained the talent. For Shembe there was only one explanation for how a man with no formal education could come to read the Bible, and that was because God granted him the ability to do so.

Shembe also viewed the Bible as the Word of God one had to engage, recite, and perform. This approach to the Bible as simultaneously oral and written—a text for memorizing and recitation as well as for reading and preservation—informed Shembe's thinking about, and instructions for, the creation and preservation of the church's history and records. Liz Gunner has convincingly demonstrated how orality/oralture and literacy/literature interacted and overlapped within all the records produced by members of the Nazareth Baptist Church, a cultural development with equivalents in many parts of colonial Africa.[10] The line, then, between oral lore and written documents within the records of the Nazareth Baptist Church is not crisp or dichotomous, as many records contain dimensions of both oralture and literature and were recorded in writing while they simultaneously continued to circulate as oral traditions. The relationship of orality and textuality within the Nazareth Baptist Church, then, is not an evolutionary model, with the traditional oral Zulu form "graduating" into the modern written Western one. The church's historical record was a symbiotic combination of old and new, traditional and modern, and in this case, oral and written.[11]

Among the first church records to emerge were Shembe's hymns, which assumed oral and written forms virtually simultaneously. Shembe claimed that he began receiving hymns around the time of the church's formation in 1910.[12] Many of the hymns in the church's hymnbook are undated, but this is particularly so with the earliest hymns. It is therefore not possible to date

Shembe's first hymns with precision, only that the earliest hymn production was contemporaneous with the earliest years of the church. Shembe described how the words and melody of a hymn would simply "come to" him in a dream or waking vision, as he heard a voice singing the hymn. Lacking the ability to write but with the desire to record the hymn in writing, Shembe would seek out school children among his converts, wherever he was at the time, to do the transcribing. The young scribe would handwrite the hymn as Shembe recited what he had already committed to memory. Shembe urged all of his followers to memorize the hymns and disseminate them throughout the church's membership. He further urged those who were literate to record them in writing in their own handwritten notebooks. The hymns thus circulated in both oral and written forms from the moment of their composition, or as Shembe and his followers believed, their revelation. Shembe produced no new hymns from 1914–ca.1920, a fact Hans-Jürgen Becken attributed to the chaos of World War I.[13] From around 1920 until just months before his death, Shembe continued to receive hymns prophetically, memorize them, and recite them to an *ababhani* (literally, the writers) who would record them in writing. From there the hymns would be distributed among the membership, who in turn memorized them and transcribed them if they were able.[14]

A nearly identical process to the hymns occurred with Shembe's liturgies: the Morning Prayer, the Evening Prayer, and the Prayer for the Sabbath. The three liturgies contain Shembe's spoken moral lessons, biblical reminders, and admonishments for proper worship directed to members, with pleas to God for blessings and mercy upon his chosen people. Each liturgy also contains performative portions for the congregation including verses to recite and hymns to sing. When Shembe generated these three liturgies in the 1920s, they too were memorized, recorded, and disseminated in oral and written forms, much as the hymns were.

As Shembe's ministry advanced in the 1920s and 1930s, his prophecies, sermons, counsels, parables, and epistles were added to the church's emerging corpus of oralture-literature. As each prophecy, sermon, counsel, or parable was performed or spoken by Shembe, or in the case of the epistles transcribed according to Shembe's oral instructions, church members both memorized and recorded them too, with one appreciable difference from the hymns and liturgies. The hymns were numbered and their order was therefore obvious, and there were just three liturgies. The memorizing and recording of the other elements had no standard order, nor was an order necessary. As Shembe traveled around Natal, gaining converts and visiting existing congregations, the various supernatural experiences, moral lessons, and instructions he shared with worshipers were memorized and recorded, and then disseminated. These prophecies, counsels, and the like radiated outward from multiple epicenters as Shembe moved about Natal, meaning that each congregation had a particular timeline of when particular sermons or parables reached them, depending on their spatial relationship to the sermon's or counsel's origin. Therefore, the order and number of this portion of church lore, whether oral or handwritten, varied by congregation and individual, unlike the standard order of the hymns.

Shembe's admiration for the power of the written word is further demonstrated by the fact that he had his own notebook of hymns and church traditions. John Dube, African nationalist, founder of Zulu Christian Industrial School, and neighbor of Shembe, noted in his biography of Shembe that, "in this book he used to write his prayers and his hymns."[15] Since we know Shembe did not write it himself, the text was clearly compiled by his amanuenses. The scribes were multiple and drawn from the congregation he was with at the time he wanted something recorded. This notebook was dubbed the "Grave Book" as it was placed atop Shembe's grave upon his passing in 1935.[16] Yet in what manner was it "atop" the grave? Was it merely atop the gravesite as a votive offering, later retrieved by a minister or family member, and thereby preserved? Or was it atop Shembe's body, entombed with him, and ultimately destroyed by decay? Both scenarios for the fate of the "Grave Book" are possible, but the latter seems more likely. To begin, this was the fate of the notebook described by John Dube, an eyewitness to the funeral and burial.[17] Second, contemporary church oral tradition holds that the "Grave Book" was interred with Shembe.[18] So it seems likely that Shembe's original notebook was ruined by its interment.

The loss of the original "Grave Book," though, had no impact on how church members have approached the authority of their historical record. For many of the world's religions, the admitted loss of a textual original would be devastating to their legitimacy.[19] Given that Shembe had encouraged widespread reproduction of the material, authenticity and authority could be maintained even in the absence of a textual original due to the manifold versions that existed in many memories and notebooks of church members. For instance, a praise singer of Galilee Shembe, Azariah Mthiyane, told Liz Gunner in 1976 that the praise poems (izibongo) he was reciting for her were identical to the ones "Written in our great book at Ekuphakameni."[20] Whether one could still put one's hands on Shembe's original "great book" was not of consequence within the mind of Mthiyane, because he believed his oral form was an exact replication. Mthiyane's belief in the authenticity of his oral accounts of the teachings and actions of Isaiah Shembe, decades after Isaiah's passing, appears to be more than an idle boast bred from faith too. Gunner discovered in her extensive fieldwork on the church's oralture that there was indeed a remarkable stability within the church's oral traditions. Narrators of the church's oralture did not make the small substitutions and shifts in sequence that typified performance within Zulu oral traditions. The oral traditions of the Nazareth Baptist Church, then, do not conform to the cultural expectations of Zulu oralture, but to their own priorities in preserving their historical record. Gunner attributes the remarkable degree of stability and conformity in the church's oral traditions to the intersection of orality and textuality that brought the permanency of printed texts to members' perceptions of how oral traditions were to be preserved and transmitted.[21] Moreover, the very identity of the church requires faith in the fact that Shembe's prophetic record, hymns, biography, and teachings have survived from the time of Isaiah to the present. This confidence in the preservation of Isaiah's prophecies, teachings, and instructions is more than faith or rhetoric, however, and can be factually corroborated with surviving records and testimonies.

Preserving a Prophetic Church History, 1935–1990s

Isaiah's successor, his son Galilee, likewise possessed a keen interest in preserving the history and teachings of the church. This interest of Galilee's may have come from the fact that he was a man of letters, an educator with a formal Western education. But the stronger motivation was likely his passionate determination to hold to the course of his father. On more than one occasion Galilee described his role as central leader as continuing his father's vision for the church.[22] This philosophy of his leadership likely determined Galilee's attitude about the church's historical record, and generated a passionate determination to preserve the records, both oral and written, produced during the life of Isaiah.

Even as early as late 1935/early 1936, Galilee had six notebooks at the church's headquarters at Ekuphakameni, a fact reported by Esther Roberts. While conducting research for her master's thesis, Galilee had allowed Roberts to view six large books containing Isaiah's "dictation, parables, addresses, and paraphrases of the Bible he thought were suitable for his services." Roberts recorded the name of just one, with the lengthy title, "The Book for conducting Religious Services and other Ceremonies of the Nazarites as Inaugurated, Arranged and Authorised by Isaiah Shembe, Servant of God, Prophet and Servant of Sorrows of Ekuphakameni, Phoenix, Natal, South Africa."[23] It is unlikely this was Shembe's original notebook. It was likely a facsimile of the contents of the "Grave Book," perhaps Galilee's own, or that of a member. Roberts dedicated just a few sentences to the matter before moving on to a general discussion of the teachings the books contained, so there is no way for us to know the exact origins of this book, or the other five. Given the wordy title, we can surely not blame Roberts for omitting the other five titles from her thesis, but it does leave us with an incomplete knowledge of the books in Galilee's possession at Ekuphakameni in late 1935/early 1936.

Yet regardless of the exact identity of these six books, their existence does indicate that Galilee had begun to build an archive at Ekuphakameni from the earliest moments of his tenure as central leader. Galilee had requested that church members "who had been writing about his father to bring their work to the office, and those who knew anything about him to start writing without delay."[24] Many members did just that from the late 1930s onward in handing over their copybooks, or in offering their oral testimonies for transcription, for the sake of contributing to the preservation of the church's history and Isaiah's memory.[25] One member, Lazarus Maphumulo, even wrote a reminder to himself in the margins of his copybook, "It is important that you write these things down and then give them to the king [referring to Galilee] at Ekuphakameni."[26] The original "Grave Book" had been lost, but its contents had been reproduced, memorized, and disseminated prior to Isaiah's death. For members of the Nazareth Baptist Church, Shembe's notebook was not an immutable master copy, but one version among many, albeit a symbolic version, given that it was the personal possession of the church's founder. Yet the loss of Shembe's notebook did not represent the ruin of the church's history and traditions. They continued, rather, in the oralture and literature of the members that Isaiah Shembe had encouraged them to produce.

Our knowledge of what the archive looked like in the early years of Galilee's administration is limited, and we do not know how much material was compiled or all the individuals who contributed. But we can gain a partial sense of this from contemporary memory and documents. Contemporary oral tradition recalls those members who contributed a great amount of written material to the church's archive, among them Philip Ngubane, Muntuwezizwe Buthelezi, John Mabuyakhulu, and Malingakwenzeke Mhlongo (Mpungose).[27] A number of other written notebooks recorded by members in the 1920s and 1930s, containing "Grave Book" material, have survived to the present and are housed in public archives. Photocopies of the copybooks of members Imilando Nemithetho, Meshack Hadebe, and Lazarus Maphumulo are housed at SOAS (School of Oriental and African Studies) at the University of London. They were translated and edited by Liz Gunner, and published in Zulu and English in 2002 as the volume *The Man of Heaven and the Beautiful Ones of God*. Two other collections are housed at the Durban Local History Museums: (1) the "Memela," written by Mailethi Memela, Jabulani Memela, and Ntombikayise Memela, and (2) a duplicate of the "Mpongose/Khuba" file compiled by Bhekinhlanhla Mpungose (nicknamed Goodluck Khuba).

Each of these surviving copybooks is unique, not only because there was no standard order or number for the recording of sermons, prayers, and the like, but also because each included first-hand experiences the author had in the church, a sort of log book or diary. The copybook of Meshack Hadebe, for example, describes his journey from the interior, "the land of Mshoeshoe," to

Durban, in search of the holy people to the east who produced the heavenly music and drums he heard in a dream.[28] This conversion testimony is quite clearly personal, and therefore is not found in the notebooks of other members. Likewise, the Memela notebook contains a five-sentence counsel from 22 October 1933, spoken by Isaiah at Judiah (Judea) temple. In the counsel Isaiah tells the assembled congregation that a priest who leaves the church may rejoin but can never again be restored to the priesthood.[29] It is not the content that is unique, as this church rule was one Isaiah said elsewhere, but the record of this particular utterance at Judea in October 1933.[30] Despite such instances, however, the essence of each member's notebook is the same. Each notebook is principally devoted to the recording of Isaiah's biography; liturgies; hymns, identified by number; teachings, as revealed through his various prophecies, sermons, counsels, parables, and prayers; and the church's early history. The survival of these personal copybooks allows for crosschecking across sources, enhancing the trustworthiness of such records and accounts.

Galilee's initiative to amass the literature and oralture of the church's members was driven by a genuine desire to preserve his father's teachings and the church's history. Yet as the 1930s progressed Galilee developed an interest in not merely compiling material, but also in producing a standard version of these church records. Through the 1930s and 1940s, the membership grew: demographically into the tens of thousands; spatially with temples founded beyond Natal and neighboring locations; and culturally with increased growth among non-Zulus. With these forms of growth the number of transcriptions, and therefore the potential for errors, had likewise been growing. Given the considerable expansion in church membership, it is clear Galilee developed an interest in more effectively ensuring that the flows of information accurately conveyed the words of his father, and ultimately himself too. As such centralization and standardization proceeded, the church's documentary record took on an increasingly Christian appearance, and this was quite purposeful.

Galilee's first venture in standardizing church tradition was the printing of the church's hymnbook. The *Izihlabelelo zaManazaretha*, printed in Durban in May 1940, in Zulu, was a compilation of Isaiah's 219 hymns, the three liturgies, and a few of Galilee's hymn compositions. With the exception of hymn 133, which is the Lord's Prayer, all are original compositions of Isaiah or Galilee that both individuals attributed to prophetic inspiration.[31] There were subsequently four more editions to account for the fact that Galilee continued to compose, or as he saw it prophetically receive, hymns until 1948, giving the final version of the hymnal a total of 242 hymns. (The hymnal has remained the same since, and Galilee's fifth edition remains in use.)

Standardizing and publishing the hymnbook had multiple consequences. Printing the hymnal eliminated the need for hand-written copies, and reduced the chances that transcription errors could enter into the hymns and be distributed. Given the tremendous growth of the church in the 1930s and 1940s, reducing the potential for copying errors among the increasingly diffuse (demographically, spatially, and culturally) membership was assuredly among Galilee's concerns. Yet production of an official hymnbook was also an exercise of prophetic authority. A standard official version made clear that in the Nazareth Baptist Church there were only two composers of hymns and no others. Church members were not allowed to draft hymns for the church as this was the prophetic prerogative of Isaiah and Galilee alone, a belief about leadership and prophetic control that a printed official hymnbook made theologically and physically evident.

A printed hymnal additionally lent Christian legitimacy to the church. Hymnals are certainly a fixture of Christian congregations around the world, and individuals living in South Africa would have been familiar with this, either personally or anecdotally. Possessing one of the features of the historical Protestant churches in South Africa, like the Anglicans, Lutherans, or Methodists, lent the Nazareth Baptist Church some of the same Christian credibility associated with those denominations. A printed hymnbook was also much lovelier in appearance, lending a sacral element to the hymns and hymnbook. There is a reason that religious works are generally printed on high quality paper with a comely and durable cover, and this is to set the book apart from other texts, a physical indication of the special nature of what lies within. Though the handwritten copies produced prior to Galilee's publishing of the *Izihlabelelo zaManazaretha* were individual labors of love and expressions of faith, they collectively had an almost amateurish appearance, physically symbolizing that the church was new, immature, and humble. A printed version, conversely, symbolized a church that was mature and Christian in its accoutrements. In short, a printed hymnal standardized and centralized the hymns and hymn production, while simultaneously elevating the church's Christian profile.

Galilee's second regulating initiative began with the appointment of a permanent secretary and archivist to organize the material that had been submitted in the 1930s and 1940s, and continue to amass additional material, with a long-term goal of producing collections of church history and teachings for reproduction and distribution. Galilee selected Petros Musawenkosi Dhlomo for the position in 1949, a post Dhlomo maintained until his death in 1994. Originally from Swaziland, Dhlomo and his family had converted to the Nazareth Baptist Church in 1929. Dhlomo hints that he had an instinctual, almost supernatural predisposition toward the church in remarking that prior to that point he "did not yet know anything about faith," yet he still refused medicines because he would "recover by the love of God." Upon his first visit to a Sabbath service, he felt the Nazareth Baptist Church was the right place for him because "their mode of worship appealed strongly to my heart...I enjoyed their talks and their singing of hymns, which were written on papers...the message of these hymns sounded clearly."[32]

Dhlomo described his appointment by Galilee as an uncanny experience. In August 1949, Galilee summoned Dhlomo to join the crowd of people next to the main building at Ekuphakameni, where Galilee would "hold court" and attend to members. Upon Dhlomo's arrival, Galilee showed the crowd a typewritten paper that contained "a report on the deeds of our great father, Isaiah Shembe." Galilee lamented that he had been wanting someone to "work on them" but nobody wanted to, saying they needed to work for whites. A non-member, Mngadi, had expressed willingness, but Galilee did not like "that the work of God should be done by unbelievers." Dhlomo later reported that he felt like he was "being called by these words" and all the people there looked at him as though he had been selected by a "silent ballot." Galilee then asked Dhlomo where his typewriter was, to which Dhlomo replied it was in Johannesburg. Galilee asked why he had left it behind when Dhlomo knew he was coming to Ekuphakameni. After giving him money for train fare, Galilee instructed Dhlomo to retrieve the typewriter and return to his new home at Ekuphakameni. Upon Dhlomo's return, Galilee gave him a house, two barrels for water storage, and then told him all the rules, with a pastor serving as witness, that he must obey now that he was living within the holy city. During the following night, a messenger roused Dhlomo at 4 a.m. summoning him to Galilee again. Galilee again repeated all the rules, even including some additional ones he had not stated the first time. Dhlomo expressed feeling depressed at all the rules he had to follow, yet awed by the sanctity and hallowedness of living in the place the rules were designed to protect.[33]

So began Dhlomo's four-and-a-half decade tenure as the Nazareth Baptist Church's official archivist and secretary. For Dhlomo, compiling, recording, and preserving the church's historical record wasn't a job but a sacred duty, and he embarked on the projects with the industrious work ethic that had been advocated by Isaiah Shembe and emulated by many church members. His first decade, or more, as archivist was dedicated solely to the amassing of material, a project we might rightly call "Words of the Founder."[34] In an interview with Bengt Sundkler in 1958, Galilee expressed regret that the corpus of materials had not yet been sorted out.[35] Galilee's expression of regret suggests that any serious arranging and cataloguing of material by Dhlomo, something many observers later noted he was meticulous about, did not begin until the late 1950s or early 1960s. From the late 1950s/early 1960s, through the remainder of his life, Dhlomo continued to amass traditions, whether sorting and cataloguing material that had been written by church members, or typing and filing oral traditions he transcribed through interviews (and later began to record on cassette tapes). Dhlomo's research and editing efforts were dedicated to two projects: (1) the *Catechism of the Nazarites* and

(2) the *Acts of the Nazarites*, both of which reached print, but along different textual trajectories.

Catechism of the Nazarites

Dhlomo's first project, the *Catechism of the Nazarites* (hereafter *Catechism*), or *Umngcwabo*, was the church's second major work of literature, after the hymnal, to be printed for mass distribution. Like the hymnal, the compilation and reproduction of the *Catechism* was an effort to preserve and distribute a centralized official version of the church's documentary history. A catechism, like the hymnal, also fit within normative expectations of what sort of literature a Christian congregation generally possessed. The creation of the *Catechism*, a compiled and printed text, was an effort by Galilee and Dhlomo to enhance the church's Christian legitimacy by expanding its literature. Unlike the hymnal, however, the several editions of the *Catechism* contained greater differences. Whereas newer versions of the hymnal simply had a few additional hymns from Galilee, the later versions of the *Catechism* contained wholly new material. The revisions to the later editions were purposeful attempts to make the *Catechism* appear more Christian.

The earliest version of the *Catechism* was printed in the early 1960s, likely 1963, and untitled. Scholars have colloquially dubbed it the "white book," so named because of the color of the cover. In the 1990s, Goodluck Khuba, secretary for Londa Shembe, and several ministers at Ebuhleni verified that this earliest version of the *Catechism* contained historical materials only, without the liturgical material of later editions. The historical materials, however, were not strictly chronicles, but a blend of the teachings of Shembe, purportedly in his own words, within various counsels, prayers, parables, and epistles, some of which were identified by date.[36] The church's archive certainly contained more material than what was included in the short book and some sort of selection process took place. Yet who engaged in that selection of material is not entirely clear.[37] It is possible Galilee trusted Dhlomo to make these decisions alone, perhaps believing that Dhlomo's choices would be preternaturally guided by God or the spirit of Isaiah. It is also feasible that a committee of ministers played some role in the selection process.[38] Did Galilee have a role? Galilee's very appointment of Dhlomo suggests that sorting the archive was not a task he saw as his own. The growth of the church also placed great demands on Galilee's time, in visiting congregations and attending to the needs of members, and it doesn't seem likely he would have dedicated the time to personally sorting documents and weighing their significance, after entrusting the task to Dhlomo. It does seem safe to surmise, though, that Galilee granted his blessing to the final compilation prior to its production and distribution. So while it is unlikely Galilee personally organized the material, he surely must have contributed some level of secondary, post-sorting approval to the process.

There are several reasons we can be certain the documents in the *Catechism* are based upon content from the "Grave Book," even though it was compiled in Galilee's era. First, church leaders and members were sincerely motivated to preserve the heritage of their church's formative era. This factor alone does not guarantee a record's authenticity, but it does solidly point to the purpose behind the compilation of the records, which was to preserve the words of Isaiah. No evidence has yet been unearthed to suggest that the original source of the *Catechism*'s records is someone other than Isaiah Shembe. Unless and until such evidence is discovered, a basic level of trust by the scholar that church members preserved the words of Isaiah is not unwarranted when combined with the factors below.

Second, the content of the "Grave Book" is consistent with what we know of Shembe and his teachings from extra-church sources. To take one example, in two documents from the *Catechism* Shembe praised the value of hard work and industriousness.[39] Both Esther Roberts and John Dube recorded that Shembe advocated such morality.[40] Though neither of them quoted Shembe's exact words, their texts confirm that the essence of these two traditions in the *Catechism* are consistent with what these two non-members observed. With much less frequency, a few of the pieces of lore preserved in the *Catechism* can also be found verbatim elsewhere. For instance, John Dube preserved two full-text traditions in his biography of Shembe, *Ushembe*, that were also preserved in the *Catechism*.[41] The pieces of lore recorded by Dube in 1936 are identical in content and style to those in Dhlomo's *Catechism* of decades later, suggesting considerable consistency and stability within these traditions over time. Unfortunately few of the traditions within the *Catechism* can be cross-checked in this manner with extra-church material. Yet even this small sample alludes that church members have preserved their church's lore in a conscientious and reliable manner.

Finally, numerous scholars over the course of several decades have not uncovered evidence of manufactured or falsified texts, with a few exceptions, in the church's historical record. The record is full of the prophetic, fantastic, miraculous, and generally unbelievable to the non-member, to be certain. But scant evidence exists of post-dated apocryphal inventions that make claims inconsistent with other accounts of the church's formative era. To the contrary, scholars have vouched for the general authenticity of the church's preserved lore.[42] It seems difficult to imagine that scholars the caliber of G. C. Oosthuizen, Hans-Jürgen Becken, Robert Papini, and Irving Hexham, with decades of experience with the church and its records, would not have discovered distorted or manufactured traditions if they existed. This means that either a wide conspiracy of knowledge has been successfully manufactured, uniformly maintained, and kept secret to all outsiders by the church's leaders and members for decades, or, we can trust that the records allow us access to the words and deeds of Shembe with as much credibility as is scholarly allow-able for records with uncertain provenance. Those few records that can be cross-checked with extra-church versions allow a considerable degree of assur-ance that we have the words of Shembe before us. In cases where the luxury of such crosschecking is not afforded us, which is most of them, the intent behind their preservation, the style and content of the texts, and the learned opinion of a previous generation of scholars suggests we can have confidence that these records provide an accurate window into the early decades of the church's history and Shembe's role within it.

The ca. 1963 "white" version of the *Catechism* was composed entirely of historical-theological documents from the "Grave Book." Two later versions of the *Catechism* were more than reprints of the "white" one, and contained three augmentations. In addition to the "Grave Book" material from the "white" edition, the ca. 1970 and 1993 versions added: (1) doctrinal material, in the form of a catechism, (2) funerary and marriage rites, and (3) a written compila-tion of the church's rules. The second edition of the *Catechism*, or "red book," was printed around 1970 with a red cover and the title *Umthetho Nezimiso eBandleni lamaNazaretha* (Laws and Foundations of the Nazareth Baptist Church). The 1993 reissue of the "red book" carried the title *Nazareth Baptist Church Umngcwabo: 1993 Edition*, and a yellow cover, hence the appellation "yellow book." Papini has verified that the "red" and "yellow" versions of the *Catechism*, with the exceptions of the title and the color of the covers, are identical.[43] The "red" and "yellow" catechisms, with the three supplements, served multiple purposes spurred by the interests of two constituencies: Dhlomo and the ministers.

For the man at the center of the *Catechism*'s production, archivist Petros Dhlomo, the goal of the "red" and "yellow" *Catechism* was to revise the "white" *Catechism* in a manner that made it more Christian. To do so, he added doctrinal material in the form of a catechism, the "Catechism of the Naza-rites" (hereafter "Catechism") to the "red" and "yellow" versions.[44] Dhlomo had reached the conclusion that the format of the first "white" *Catechism* did not represent a "true" catechism. While the 1963 version revealed a great deal of the church's theology through the teachings of Shembe, the teachings were not concisely presented, but distributed throughout the historical and bio-graphic material. Nor were the teachings presented in the traditional question and answer format that typifies Christian catechisms. Dhlomo clearly viewed a genuine catechism as a critical element and legitimating device for any church, and included a catechism in the ca. 1970 and 1993 versions of the *Catechism* for this reason. The "Catechism" was composed and recorded by Dhlomo sometime between 1963 and 1970, perhaps with assistance from some ministers or Galilee. Like other Christian catechisms, the "Catechism of the Nazarites" provides a comprehensive distillation of the church's basic theology in an easily readable question and response format (132 total). The nature and format of the "Catechism" reveals Dhlomo's interest in enhancing the Christianness of the church's literature by adding a common feature of the literature of Christian congregations, a printed catechism.

Dhlomo's second augmentation to the "red" and "yellow" *Catechism*, scripts for funerary and marriage rites, was similarly prompted by his interest in making the church's literature more Christian in appearance and form. The text of both rites could be considered practical, containing instructions for ministers on how to prepare and perform the rites, and liturgical, with scripts to be performed at the ceremonies. The order of burial is the first document in the red and yellow versions of the *Catechism* and is what gave the 1993 edition its Zulu name, *Umngcwabo* (The Funeral Service). The name bespeaks Dhlomo's interest that the book be considered part of the genre of catechismal literature akin to *Luther's Large Catechism* within Lutheranism or Anglicanism's *Book of Common Prayer*; these Christian catechisms likewise contain educational material and ministerial instructions.[45]

The third addition to the "red" and "yellow" *Catechism*, a written compilation of the church's rules, was the results of a grassroots ministerial campaign of the 1960s known as the "Revived Law." Three decades had transpired since Isaiah's passing, and the church was experiencing tremendous growth. Amid these changes, the ministers were interested in ensuring that the church maintained the theological vision of Isaiah under the changing conditions of the Galilee era. Galilee's interest in recording and preserving the material of Isaiah's era was combined with the revivalist spirit of the "Revived Law" in producing a written code of behavior for application in the present. This document, the "Reminder of the Statute" (hereafter "Statute") was issued in 1970, and included in both the "red" and "yellow" *Catechism*. The "Statute" concerned everything from the ordination of guards to protect Ekuphakameni, to acts prohibited on church grounds, to proper hygiene. The text of the "Statute" blended older rules, attributed to the instructions of Isaiah, with discussion of conditions in the present and the need for renewed enforcement of Isaiah's rules. More rarely, the "Statute" outlined Galilee's modification of a previous law. The compilers of this document, then, do not present the text solely as a preservation of Isaiah's teachings, but as a revival of the founder's teachings within the Galilee era with occasional additions from Galilee.

Yet the reprising venture of the "Statute" (and the "Revived Law" more broadly) could easily have been conducted orally. Ministers could have hounded their congregations with revivalist sermons and admonitions, and most certainly did so. The additional step of writing it down derived from the same impetus in the codification of most any law or rule code. Once written the rules become permanent and applicable to the entire community, one cannot as easily claim ignorance of a centralized and permanent code of conduct. Interpretations of a law that is "on the books" can be disputed, but cannot be readily denied. Members of a congregation are expected to obey a church's rule code, and can be punished for not doing so, even if they have never read it in its entirety or are unable to read altogether. An oral rule code surely allows for the maintenance of order as well, as many pre-colonial organizations aptly demonstrated. But a written "Statute" fulfilled the revivalist desires of the ministers while also increasing their power to punish transgressors. In addition to making the rules more easily enforceable, a written rule code is a common feature of many Christian organizations.[46] Like the question and response "Catechism" and the ritual material, the written "Reminder of the Statute" recreated a common feature of Christian congregations for the Nazareth Baptist Church.

The fact that all three of these additions to the "red" and "yellow" *Catechism* are from the 1960s explains the noticeably different narrative style compared to the "Grave Book" material in the previous "white" version. Unlike the fused historical-theological material of the "Grave Book," which had the avowed intent of recording the exact words of Isaiah Shembe, these "Revived Law" efforts were principally motivated in reviving the teachings of Isaiah and enhancing the church's Christian profile. The authors, Dhlomo and a council of ministers, with perhaps even the occasional input of Galilee, were not attempting to disguise that they were drafting original documents. The numerous discussions of the authors' present (i.e. the 1960s) in the "Statute" clearly indicates this. For the leaders and members of the Nazareth Baptist Church, however, that does not make these additions to the "red" and "yellow" *Catechism* wholesale inventions divorced from their past. The documents, despite a post-Isaiah production, possess authority because they are considered to convey the essence of the past (Isaiah's teachings) through their compilation by learned individuals. Though I have never unearthed such a statement, it would not be surprising to discover that the authors of these documents believed they were guided by God and/or the spirit of Isaiah in their endeavors.

For worshipers of the Nazareth Baptist Church, the fact that these additions to the *Catechism* are redactional products of the 1960s was not troubling. They believed that the "Statute," ritual scripts, and "Catechism" were new in form, but not in content, and were consistent with the overall teachings of Isaiah. The authority of them is, however, secondary to the "Grave Book" material. The relationship between the new additions to the *Catechism* and the older portions that derived from the "Grave Book" is not unlike the *Mishnah*'s relationship to the *Tanakh* in Judaism. Within most sects of Judaism, the *Mishnah* is an acknowledged secondary text compiled later than the *Tanakh* by learned individuals that was new in its form but not in its content. Likewise within the Nazareth Baptist Church, the additions to the *Catechism*, though derivative and not constituting a separate text, were for members a learned compilation of teachings, with some modern day reflections, that were consistent with those of Isaiah Shembe. More significantly, a more robust *Catechism*, one with a Christian-like question and response catechism, rule code, and ritual explanations and scripts, was Dhlomo's purposeful effort to bring greater Christian legitimacy to the church's emerging corpus of literature.[47]

Acts of the Nazarites

Dhlomo's second great labor, with the support of Galilee, over four decades, was the *Acts of the Nazarites* (hereafter *Acts*), a compilation of elders' testimonies of the words and deeds of Isaiah Shembe. Dhlomo gathered accounts written by members, tape-recorded and transcribed the oral testimonies of hundreds of individuals, and carefully catalogued them at Ekuphakameni.[48] Like the *Catechism*, the *Acts* assumed an increasingly Christian character and were used as a legitimating device of the church's Christianness by the church's leadership.

The name, content, and intent of the *Acts of the Nazarites* was purposefully parallel to the compilation of the various Acts from early Christianity, both canonical and apocryphal, including the Acts of the Apostles, the Acts of the Martyrs, the Acts of Thomas, and the Acts of Andrew, among others. In the ancient Mediterranean, acts referred to a recognized literary genre that described great deeds of people or cities.[49] The various Acts of early Christianity are dedicated to recounting the heroic and miraculous deeds of the apostles as evidence that they were vehicles of God's power. In the narratives this power is used to heal the sick, exorcise demons, raise the dead, destroy "pagan" temples, and shame practitioners of other religions or "false" forms of Christianity due to the overwhelming "truth" the individuals presented.[50] The Acts additionally served as a means of reinforcing the identity of early Christians, by showing what the religion meant to those who had already joined, and as a tool of conversion by portraying what it could mean to those considering it.[51]

Use of the word *Acts* by Dhlomo in the title of his literary compilation was quite purposeful and an attempt to generate the same sort of legitimacy for the Nazareth Baptist Church that early Christians had in the second through fourth centuries with their Acts. The choice of the title *Acts of the Nazarites*, rather than "Gospel of the Nazarites" or "The Gospel of Shembe" may have been calculatingly done by Dhlomo. A gospel recounted the life of Jesus and use of that term could have been viewed as a theological undermining of Jesus or the New Testament gospels by granting the literature on Shembe the same term. Shembe's prophecies and teachings, as revealed in the *Acts of the*

Nazarites, were considered a contemporary supplement to the Word within the theology of the Nazareth Baptist Church, but were not thought of as a challenge to or displacement of those of Jesus in the New Testament. An act, on the other hand, recounts the great deeds of a remarkable Christian individual, a servant of God filled with God's power. The name *Acts of the Nazarites*, then, could simultaneously apply the same sort of legitimacy to the emerging corpus of the Nazareth Baptist Church that was associated with other Christian texts with the name *Acts*, while also remaining within the bounds of orthodoxy by avoiding the term gospel and suggesting that the narratives of Shembe were equivalent to that of Jesus.

Not only was the same term, *acts*, shared by both sets of literature, but the overall content of the *Acts of the Nazarites* was also quite parallel. Like the Acts from the second to the fourth centuries, the *Acts* of the Nazareth Baptist Church also showcased the spectacular travels and miraculous deeds of an uncanny individual and agent of God. Within the *Acts* one can find details of Shembe's biography, his ministry, records of the prophecies he received, healing miracles, parables, sermons, and historical details about particular events or church services, just as one can find across the various Acts of early Christianity.[52] Consider two examples, the first concerning healing and the second the power to command animals.

Both sorts of acts, for instance, are brimming with testimonies of healing miracles. To take one corollary example, the apocryphal Act of Peter recounts how Peter healed a paralyzed woman by commanding her to rise and walk in the name of Jesus. She did so, according to the narrator, to the crowd's amazement and delight. In response, Peter said "Behold, your hearts have been persuaded that God is not powerless regarding anything we ask of him."[53] Similarly, in an account from the *Acts*, a crippled boy from Zululand came to Ekuphakameni to see Shembe. According to the narrator of this testimony, Shembe prayed for the boy "in an astounding way," moving his hand over the boy's body. As he did so, the boy's spine shifted to a normal position and the boy was healed.[54]

In another case of how both sorts of acts reveal the special powers of the central characters of the account, while also demonstrating God's might, several testimonies in the *Acts* discuss Shembe's special relationship with animals. One particular set of narratives in the *Acts* describes how Shembe asked aquatic creatures of various kinds to move to a different location so he might perform baptisms. In each of the tales, the narrators state that the animals obeyed, the baptisms were performed, and Shembe thanked them for their compliance upon conclusion.[55] Asking creatures to move so that they do not impede the work of the agent of God has direct parallel in the Acts of John, one of the most significant of the apocryphal texts. In verses 60 and 61, John and his travel companions took refuge at an inn. The companions granted John the honor of the sole bed while they slept on the floor. According to the narrator, John awoke in the middle of the night plagued by bugs and spoke to them saying, "I say to you, you bugs, be considerate; leave your home for this night and go to rest in a place which is far away from the servants of God!" The travel companions laughed at John's nocturnal speech. But when they all awoke, they were amazed to discover a mass of bugs huddled near the door. When they roused John and called it to his attention, he addressed the bugs again saying, "Since you have been wise to heed my warning, go back to your place!" The narrator continues by noting that the bugs then ran from the doorway to the bed, climbed up the bed's legs, and disappeared into the bed.[56]

In both cases (the testimonies of healing miracles and those about commanding animals) the moral lessons of the stories are clear. The explicit lesson is that the men at the center of the act are unlike the rest of humanity and possess uncanny power granted by God. That power provides them with the ability to heal and command creatures as these examples reveal, but also, as revealed in other stories, to exorcise evil spirits, resurrect the dead, convert unbelievers by the power of their words and deeds, and shame those who oppose them. The implicit lesson is that the listener or reader of the tale would be wise to take heed of this individual and their religion; their power is so mighty that one ignores their displays of power and speeches about the real "truth" at great risk.

In this manner, the Acts of the Nazarites fulfills the same sort of purposes as those of early Christianity. First, the Acts served as a means of preserving accounts of a great leader in the generations subsequent to the leader's death. That Galilee and Dhlomo were interested in putting it in writing suggests their interest in producing a literary corpus that approximated that of early Christianity. Echoing the form and content of books from early Christianity was a legitimating strategy, an attempt to connect the present to the formative era of the Christian past. Appealing to history in this manner is a common tactic among emergent religions in order to demonstrate that their religion is an extension of the past being recreated in the present and is no modern invention.[57] Even early Christians employed the same logic; second-century apologists appealed to the Jewish roots of Christianity to demonstrate how Christianity was the culmination of Judaism and not a new creation.[58] Second, the Acts, like the Catechism, amplified Shembe's reputation and reified the faith of those who followed his teachings. For those considering joining the church, such narratives displayed what the religion could mean.[59] Third, the Acts of the Nazarites also bolstered the prophetic worldview of Shembe and his church's members by presenting the world beyond the church as profane, hollow, and an easily explainable extension of God's divine plans that had the church at the center. So when Shembe encountered practitioners of other religions, he dismissed their teachings as misdirected and empty, much as the central characters of the early Christian Acts.[60] The "correctness" of Shembe's teachings and his explanation of the universe appeared even more truthful when placed next to the grave "errors" of other religions. Applying additional legitimacy to their church and the teachings of Shembe, through the above means, is what Galilee and Dhlomo had in mind when Dhlomo began to compile records for the *Acts* starting in the 1950s and continuing through the 1990s.

Galilee Shembe proudly discussed the emerging literary compilation with several scholars. Lutheran missionary and seminal author of Zionist churches Bengt Sundkler noted Galilee's interest in preserving all the testimonies "just as they were told." Sundkler was awed by the collection calling it, "one of the most amazing in the history of African religious movements...a record of the effort of the Nazarite faithful to interpret the nature of Isaiah Shembe's personality and to gather his revelations."[61] Shortly thereafter, across the 1960s, Hans-Jürgen Becken, a professor at Lutheran Theological College, Umpumulo, Natal, had numerous conversations with Galilee where Galilee expressed a keen interest that the material be used to write a comprehensive church history. He was concerned that such a history be written by an insider, or at least a friend of the church, so that the church's image was not misman-aged, and suggested Becken take on the enterprise.[62] Becken did not take on the task and returned to Germany in 1974, though he would be an indispen-sable part of the collection's preservation and dissemination later.

Following Galilee's death in 1976, a factional struggle emerged between Amos Shembe (Galilee's brother) and Londa Shembe (Galilee's son). The archive and the *Acts*, like everything else about the church at the time, became a site of contestation between the two claimants and their supporters. Amid rumors that Galilee had been poisoned, some members of Galilee's family drove all the ministers out of Ekuphakameni, extorted money from Dhlomo (who had been in charge of banking), and let him know his life was in danger. Dhlomo hurriedly fled, too quickly to take the archive with him. This thuggish group sacked the archive and scattered the records. In an effort to restore calm, a group of Londa's supporters occupied Ekuphakameni and the remain-ing records were rescued and turned over to Londa. Dhlomo returned to Ekuphakameni for a very brief time, but fled in January 1977 after shots were exchanged between the factions. He moved to Imbeka on the northern edge of Inanda, where church member and chief of the Qadi-Zulu Montane Ngcobo had offered Amos refuge.[63] The factions drifted further apart over the next two years until, in 1980, Amos founded a second New Jerusalem, Ebuhleni. From this point onward there would be two churches and two archives. The hymnbook and *Catechism* were already in print, widely distributed, and those records were in no danger of being lost. But the *Acts* only existed as archival records at the time of the split and would have a bifurcated history from that point onward.

At Ekuphakameni, Londa and his supporters felt they had saved the church's historical record at an uncertain and potentially violent moment. Yet they did not take control of the records until after they had been scattered by some individuals in the Shembe family, acting out of outrage at the possibility that Galilee had been poisoned. That the archive was ransacked is clear, but there is no way to know if records were destroyed, and if so, which ones. The one individual who might have surmised if anything had been lost, Dhlomo, never had the opportunity to reorganize the remnants of the collection. Not only was the period of his return to Ekuphakameni in December 1976–January 1977 very brief, but Londa had retained control of the surviving records, likely believing they were safer under his control.

Some supporters of Amos viewed Londa's seizure of the strewn archives not as an act of preservation but political usurpation. They claimed Londa wanted to see if there were any records in the *Acts* that supported his candidacy and then destroyed those that did not. Londa never put forward any of the recovered *Acts* as elements to advance his candidacy, so presumably none existed. Given the bitter and protracted struggle for control, it is difficult to imagine that Londa would not have used records from the *Acts* that put him in a favorable light had he located them. No evidence suggests that Londa destroyed any of the records he recovered either.

The original *Acts* survived the succession dispute, though perhaps pillaged, and were in the possession of Londa after 1976. Londa appointed his own secretary, Goodluck Khuba, who served as steward of the collection. Khuba later relayed how his close relationship with Londa aroused jealousy. In 1983 some individual set fire to his two rooms, next to Londa's quarters, where the records were kept. Many documents and photographs were lost or damaged by the fire.[64] Following the fire, Londa took several additional steps, besides continuance of a church archive, to disseminate the surviving collection for posterity. First, he gave copies of some of the documents to Arthur Konigkramer, publishing director for the Zulu-language newspaper *Ilanga*, asking that they be published there in Zulu. Second, he began translating a number of the documents into English, with the goal of publishing them through partnership with the scholar Irving Hexham.[65] By March 1989, just a month prior to his murder, Londa Shembe had finished his translations of the documents, and expressed approval of Hexham's editorial work.[66] Copies of Londa's translations are housed at the Killie Campbell Africana Collection in Durban, and were eventually published in 1994 as *The Scriptures of the amaNazaretha of EKuphaKameni*. Shortly after Londa's murder, theologian G. C. Oosthuizen found two boxes of unsorted material at Ekuphakameni, from Dhlomo's original archive. He received permission to photocopy them and deposited copies of this material with the Killie Campbell collection and the NERMIC (New Religious Movements and Independent/Indigenous Churches Research Unit) archive at the University of Zululand.[67] The *Acts* at Ekuphakameni had quite an odyssey: from their compilation in the 1950s and 1960s they endured a ransacking in the 1970s and a fire in the 1980s, and yet survived, reaching print in the 1990s, with further preservation in multiple locations.

At the second New Jerusalem, Ebuhleni, the *Acts* began a second independent trajectory from January 1977 onward. The original *Acts* survived at Ekuphakameni, at least in part. Yet from the perspective of Dhlomo and the members at Ebuhleni the records were lost as Londa did not relinquish them. Like some ninety percent of the membership, Dhlomo followed Amos in the succession dispute. The resulting chasm that emerged between the two branches eliminated any chance of Dhlomo, or the members at Ebuhleni, gaining access to the original *Acts*. Seeing it as his sacred mission and life's work to record the testimony of members, Dhlomo rebuilt the *Acts*, even working into the night by kerosene lamp.[68] No doubt some of the individuals whose testimony Dhlomo had transcribed the first time had since died. But even by the 1980s, there were still plenty of members yet alive from Isaiah's era to recite the oral traditions they had committed to memory. Becken observed, in 1989, that Dhlomo had built the *Acts* back up to 250 testimonies of some 550 narrow-typed folio pages.[69] The reconstituted 1980s *Acts* of Dhlomo were supplemented by scholars in two manners. G. C. Oosthuizen duplicated the salvaged Ekuphakameni material from the NERMIC archives and gave them to Becken for translation. In addition, Becken gathered oral traditions of his own from throughout greater Natal (or as he described it, from Transkei to the Mozambican border) from May to October 1989. He was accompanied by church members throughout the more than 7500 kilometers (4660 miles) of travel, and reported that the congregants he met received him with warm hospitality and freely shared their traditions with him.[70] From nothing in 1977, the Ebuhleni *Acts* had been substantively rebuilt by 1989 through the efforts of Dhlomo and Becken, and the many church members whose testimonies they recorded, supplemented with material from Ekuphakameni and the NERMIC archives. This compilation of traditions was translated by Hans-Jürgen Becken in the early 1990s, with funding from NERMIC, and the blessing of Amos Shembe.

Translation projects raise several legitimate concerns over the reliability of the translated material. The most obvious potential issue concerns the language skills of the translator. In this particular case, however, Becken's aptitude with Zulu is not in question. In fact, Becken's comprehension of Zulu was so sophisticated that some native Zulu-speaking church members considered him to be a Zulu in his ability to comprehend the language and its cultural nuances.[71] Numerous scholars have additionally not found fault with his translations and knowledge of Zulu. Reviewers of the translated volumes did, though, question Becken's skills with English, pointing to grammatical errors such as "We digged a pool..." and "When I waked...." Such renderings, however, were not shortcomings of Becken's English but his desire to capture the essence of the original texts, grammatical shortcomings and all. As even some church leaders have acknowledged, a good portion of the church's membership came from humble backgrounds with little education. For some of these individuals their grammatical skills, even in Zulu, often lacked the sophistication of the formally educated. This was something Becken chose to preserve, "warts and all."[72]

Every translator must wrestle with the tension between fidelity to the original text and the beauty and readability of the translated text in the target language. In the words of Friedrich Schleiermacher, from his famous lecture "On the Different Methods of Translation" (1813), the translator can choose to move the writer toward the reader, with an idiomatic, grammatically conforming, readable version that lends the appearance that the original was written in the target language to begin with. Or, the translator can choose to move the reader toward the author with a faithfully rendered version that preserves the foreignness of the original.[73] Becken, like Schleiermacher, favored the latter approach. Becken desired to capture the subject's way of thinking through the exact means they expressed it. In faithfully translating the originals, some of the testimonies may appear to be less than smooth, even poorly worded, in English. For instance, while a native English speaker would use the phrase "bit by a snake," Becken preserved the original meaning of "hit by a snake." Not only does use of "hit" over "bit" more faithfully represent the language of the original, it also captures the local understanding more accurately. In coastal parts of Zululand, snakes often hide in thick foliage and lunge at people, catching them very much by surprise, as though they had been hit.[74] So ultimately the grammar errors in the English rendering were not the result of Becken's weak grasp of either English or Zulu, but a purposeful and deliberate translation decision to favor the "spirit" (no pun intended for religious texts) of the original over their smooth expression in English.

Becken's translations were, in turn, lightly edited and organized by Irving Hexham.[75] Like Becken, Hexham strived to convey the essence of the originals with minimal alteration. The *Acts* were published by Edwin Mellen Press in three volumes organized by period of central leadership and geography.[76] The first volume, on the era of Isaiah, was absolutely vital for this book. To the handful of us studying the Nazareth Baptist Church in the twenty-first century, with the church's centenary now past, these volumes are absolutely indispensable. Compiling this quantity of material on one's own would be a huge task, given that the volumes represent the culmination of the work of several individuals over decades. More importantly, though, with added chronological distance from the era of Isaiah, those of us writing today would have greater difficulty in reliably securing such traditions, particularly in this quantity. The preservation and publication of these oral traditions was to the benefit of church members and scholars alike.

While these published volumes may be hugely valuable and propitious to scholars like myself, to what degree can they be considered authentic and trustworthy? It is sensible for any scholar to approach source material with some degree of care, even caution. A scholar should not approach any and all church traditions uncritically, as there is occasional evidence of church traditions being politically doctored to legitimate present conditions in the guise of remembering the past. For instance, supporters of Amos Shembe, during the leadership struggle with Londa, advanced a tradition that purportedly originated with Isaiah, yet there is no such evidence that it did. In this invented tradition, the supporters of Amos claimed that Isaiah supposedly said, "The sun will shine, then the moon will rise," referring to the nicknames of Galilee and Amos as *Ilanga* (sun) and *Inyanga* (moon) respectively. Yet no such prediction can be found in the early literature of the church.[77] As this piece of invented lore indicates, members of the Nazareth Baptist Church were, like any human community, not immune to playing with tradition to serve political ends, and some traditions must be approached prudently with this in mind.

Despite the warranted note of caution, in the main, the *Acts* display considerable authenticity, more than one might first be inclined to assume could be true for such a colorful textual trajectory. In a text- and print-oriented culture, like most contemporary Western ones, recreating oral testimonies some four decades after the events would raise concerns over the reliability of the information. Were similar documents produced within our own culture, one might indeed have to approach them with the attitude that there may be as many distortions, even outright errors, as facts. Yet there are three means by which the recreated *Acts* are more reliable than they may appear at first blush from a Western point of view. First, as noted earlier in this chapter, the members of the Nazareth Baptist Church, past and present, have a hybrid oralture-literature, with a complex interrelationship between orality and textuality. As a result, the mnemonic aptitude of the average member of the Nazareth Baptist Church was considerable. In addition, the dual and reinforcing oralture and literature granted elements of each form to the other. The church's traditions display a greater level of stasis and stability than would be true of a solely oral form, suggesting the permanency of printed texts had impacted the members' perceptions of how oral traditions were preserved and transmitted.[78] Second, members of the Nazareth Baptist Church have seen preservation of these traditions as a hallowed duty, a means of honoring their faith and telling the story of Shembe, the illuminator of the path of salvation. For this reason alone, memorization and oral recitation of the traditions was a task treated with care and gravity and practiced regularly. That the task was seen as hallowed and serious does not necessarily eliminate every possibility for distortion over time. But in addition to the two variables above, the integrity of the traditions was thirdly maintained by the fact that many traditions existed in a multiplicity of memories and notebooks and could be crosschecked with several versions. This was not true of all accounts, as personal experiences and conversion narratives were generally, though not always, singular or localized. For traditions of church-wide significance certainly, such as the historical and biographical traditions of Shembe, there were multiple holders of such traditions across congregations. The multiplicity of a tradition allowed for verification across accounts.

Crosschecking across such traditions demonstrates that while some details differ from one piece of lore to another, the basic story, the essence of the tale, if you will, is the same across them. This can be seen, for example, in the tale of Shembe's transfiguration, a tradition I recounted at the beginning of chapter one. Dhlomo and Becken recorded four versions of Shembe's transfigurative moment upon Mt. Nhlangakazi. Each version differed in reporting the sort and order of the supernatural tempters that tried to lure Shembe from the mountain. Yet the versions agree upon the essence of the story that Shembe told and church members retold. Each version reports that: Shembe was tempted by a series of supernatural creatures in a variety of forms, he was visited by God, nature celebrated the moment, and God commissioned Shembe to lead humanity to salvation.[79] Clearly some level of distortion entered into the memory of the transfiguration narrative as these four versions are not perfectly identical. I would aver, though, that distortions of this sort are not of much consequence.[80] They do not matter to church members, who can maintain faith in the fact that Shembe had a transfigurative experience and was visited by Jehovah upon the holy mountain, regardless of the precise nature of the tempters. Likewise, such differences are inconsequential to my analysis as well. The core of the story is consistent and accurately conveys the fact that Shembe believed he had a series of prophetic experiences upon the mountain, stood in the presence of God, and was appointed as God's envoy to humanity. Though slightly altered in detail, the distortions in these transfiguration tales are minor enough for me to use these traditions from the Acts with confidence that it reflects Shembe's first-hand account of this important matter in his prophetic ministry. Whether the prophetic experience was "real" or "imaginary" is not of relevance to my analysis. What is important is that Shembe believed it was real, he told the story to his followers, they believed it, retold and recorded it, and the story has reached us in the present. The story's existence in the present reifies the faith of members in the distinctiveness and might of Shembe, and the overall correctness of their church and its worldview. In this manner, the story has power and veracity for church members, a fact I can explicate and analyze, regardless of whether the prophecy is "genuine" or "false" by any rational or scientific measure.

The *Acts of the Nazarites* had a colorful trajectory over the decades. From the initiative of Galilee to preserve testimonies of his father "just as they were told," the records that composed the *Acts* were later pillaged, divided between claimants, and burnt. But through the combination of Galilee's vision, Londa's commitment to carry on the work of his father, Dhlomo's determination, and the involvement of several Western scholars, the *Acts* did eventually reach print as Galilee and Dhlomo had initially intended. There is little doubt that a good portion of this information would have otherwise been lost, and the *Acts* are indispensable to scholars like myself in the twenty-first century.

But beyond their scholarly significance, the *Acts* were of vital importance to the overall literature and legitimacy of the Nazareth Baptist Church. The name, content, and intent of the *Acts of the Nazarites* purposefully reproduced the same aspects of the various Acts from early Christianity, thereby serving as a Christian means of legitimation. By telling Shembe's story in the same form as that of John or Peter, Galilee and Dhlomo were extending the legitimacy of the apostolic past upon Isaiah Shembe in the present era. But more than that, the *Acts* also bolstered the faith members had in Shembe as an uncanny individual who served as a conduit for God's power, just as the central characters did in the other Christian Acts. This faithful confidence in Shembe, in turn, reified the faith members had in his prophecies, his teachings, and the worldview he provided the church and its membership of their place in colonial Africa. The *Acts* were not simply a composite of miraculous stories but a work of literature that endorsed the explanation Shembe provided of himself, his ministry, his theology, and the role he believed he and his congregation had in advancing the salvation of Africans within colonial Africa.

The Nazareth Baptist Church's Documentary Record and the Historian

In this last section, I offer some final assessments and summations regarding the church's overall documentary record and its potential for the historian. Even given the general reliability of the church's literature, there are nonetheless several issues that complicate their scholarly usage.

Provenance

The first thorny issue the documentary record of the Nazareth Baptist Church raises for the historian is the factual details surrounding the provenance of individual pieces of church lore. With all the major sources of church lore the time and place of an account's origin, whether that tradition is a prophecy, hymn, biography, chronicle, sermon, counsel, parable, or epistle, is identified with less frequency than the scholar would wish. The amount of chronological and geographic provenance identified by authors, scribes, or editors varies according to each major source. Of the church's major sources, the *Catechism* contains the most information of this sort. By way of illustration, I offer a segment of the *Catechism*, its counsels, as a statistical sample. Of the fifteen counsels in the "yellow" *Catechism*, four describe both the time and location for the counsel's origin, four the location alone, and the remainder have neither time nor location identified. This ratio is roughly proportionate throughout the *Catechism* with approximately half of the records containing some marker of provenance. With both the hymnbook and the *Acts*, roughly one-quarter of the records are identified by a place and/or time of origin, though such information is distributed differently in each. The first half of the hymnbook (to hymn 126, from Judea, 24 June 1926) contains no such information, while in the second half, approximately fifty percent of the hymns are tied to a place and/or time. The absence of dates and locations in the first half of the hymnal, compared to their frequency in the second, suggests that Isaiah began to see this as worthwhile information to transcribe as the volume of recorded material grew, a practice continued by Galilee with the hymns he authored. The *Acts*, on the other hand, have no pattern to such information, and the provenancial data is peppered throughout the traditions. Whether the date and location were not included with the original account, were lost in the retelling or copying, or were abandoned by Dhlomo, Galilee, and other redactors, cannot be known. Taken together, then, some two-thirds to three-quarters of recorded pieces of church lore lack overt provenancial data.[81]

These ratios obscure an additional fact, however, regarding provenancial and contextual markers. The proportion of chronological and geographic details is far higher among those traditions that connect to significant events beyond the church. For example, the bureaucratic show-down between the church and the Public Health Office of the Union of South Africa regarding compulsory vaccinations was preserved in the *Acts*. The lengthy testimony of John Mabuyakhulu, that describes this instance of church-state tension, identifies the event as taking place in July 1926.[82] Another instance of church-state tension regarding a government shutdown of several provincial temples emerged in 1931. Two accounts identify 22 August 1931 as the exact date of Shembe's remarks on the matter.[83] In short, for the most significant events, where chronology matters most for the scholar, provenance is quite often evident. In other cases inferences can be made within and across pieces of lore that can also establish, or at least often estimate, the provenance of a tradition. The burial liturgy, for instance, contains hymn 235. That hymn is identified as having been written by Galilee in May 1946, a clear indication that the burial liturgy text we have today was composed, at least in part, in the era of Galilee's administration and does not come from the time of Isaiah. The vast number of testimonies without overt or inferred provenancial information are, for the most part, matters such as healing accounts, conversion stories, and the like. While these are most certainly a significant part of church lore, chronology is, in the main, not terribly consequential to their analysis. The relative scarcity of chronological and geographic markers is not, therefore, a tragedy for the scholar, as such context is sometimes evident or can be established on the most significant historical matters.

When provenance cannot be established, whatever the nature of an account's content, we must remember that the traditions were memorized, recorded, and transcribed for the benefit of internal, and not scholarly, usages.[84] The volumes of church lore were not intended to be chronicles, or a linear recounting of events with carefully identified provenance. The goal of recording and preserving the traditions, from the point of view of the membership, was to recount their prophet's blessed biography and teachings, and the church's sacred history. In short, the goal was to explain and reinforce the church's overall worldview for the benefit of members, or prospective ones. Consider that when Shembe preached human kindness to animals because humans were God's stewards of the earth, and warned people not to abuse animals by placing ropes through the noses of cattle, overloading donkeys, or shirking responsibility for caring for their dogs, the fact that he preached it was far more significant to church members than the day it was preached or where it was spoken.[85] Kindness to animals, as part of the church's moral ethos as expounded by Shembe, was enough to give this counsel meaning and legitimacy for members, and knowledge of the place and time it was spoken was much less significant, even unnecessary. In short, the content of these church traditions, whether a counsel, biographic story, hymn..., outweighed the details of its delivery for church members. This quite likely impacted the degree of significance attached to an account's date and location, often leading to their omission, as church members recited and recorded their sacred history.

For members, an absence of provenancial information does not detract from the sacredness or accuracy of the preserved narrative, and it need not necessarily detract from the scholarly value either.[86] Clear provenance for every record would certainly make the scholar's task simpler and the resulting narrative richer, yet for my analysis here, it is often not necessary. My overall argument—that the unique worldview of Shembe and his congregation was prophetically defined and served them as a particular navigation through the course of colonial South Africa—does not require chronological or geographic data for every source I analyze in understanding how that worldview was built and maintained. The level of provenancial detail will generally be enough for my purposes as well. While the historian may lament the absence of such data for some records, its frequent omission is in itself evidence of the membership's inwardly focused interests that caused them to generate a historical record upon their own priorities that ignored outside conventions of documentation.

Narrative Voice and Shembe

There is another matter, trickier than the first, for scholars analyzing the documentary record of the Nazareth Baptist Church, and that is the matter of "voice." This issue does not apply to the hymnbook, for which the authors of the hymns are clear even if the identities of the transcribers of Isaiah's hymns are no longer known. We know, with certainty, that Isaiah and Galilee were the only authors of the church's hymns, and who authored which hymn is clearly labeled in the hymnbook. The words of the hymns, therefore, clearly allow us access to the "voice" of either Isaiah or Galilee Shembe. This issue is more complicated, though, for the *Catechism* and the *Acts*, where the identity of the speaker is not always clear. Are the traditions preserved in the *Catechism* and *Acts* direct transcriptions of Shembe's spoken remarks, as originally recorded in Shembe's "Grave Book" or an early member's copybook? Are they secondary copies of such original transcripts? Or are the preserved versions oral recitations from a church elder that later assumed written form?

There are rare instances in the *Catechism* and *Acts* where it is difficult to tell the original author at all. Consider one such item of lore in the *Catechism* titled "The Words of Shembe at Khethokuhle, 13 March 1916" that states, "I have words I received from the Lord."[87] Is this Shembe communicating to his audience that what he is about to say was a prophetic directive from God? Or, does this line come from the transcriber wishing to indicate to the audience that what they are about to read or hear are the direct words of Shembe, the Lord of Ekuphakameni? Our lack of a clear understanding of the trajectory of this piece of lore through the church's oralture-literature, from Shembe's spoken words in 1916 to print ca. 1963, makes it impossible to know whether the "voice" making this statement is Shembe repeating the words of God, or a scribal intervention by the narrator to alert his audience to the fact that what is to follow are the words of Shembe.

But unlike the example above, most pieces of lore, whether in the *Catechism* or *Acts*, make clear which words are those of Shembe and which are those of the narrator, other historical actors, or even those the narrator believes came from God and was communicated via Shembe. For instance, among the testimonies of Khaya S. Ndelu preserved in the *Acts* is one that recounts a sermon told by Shembe at Bekumesiah in 1931. Shembe told the congregation of a supernatural conversation he believed he had had the night before with a dog in the village. Shembe asked the dog why it was howling and it replied, "I want my food. In this village there is the smell of something which I ought to eat." Shembe understood the dog's remark to mean that his instincts were prompting him to consume an unclean item, and he chastised the congregation in the sermon by saying, "I also want to know what you have with you in this village which does not befit you; what is it? I see that you amaNazaretha here at Bekumesiah are weak; there are no others who are like you. I saw that the members of the Nazaretha Church in this village are not holy. You will perish, when Jehovah will shed light for me over this place of God."[88] Ndelu leaves no question that Shembe was the one who made this statement, and which words were attributed to the dog and which to Shembe is equally evident. Most of the material in the *Catechism* and *Acts*, like this one, makes clear distinctions in authorship, allowing the "voice" of Shembe to come through. The church's documentary record, then, allows the historian access to the thoughts, words, and actions of Shembe. His "voice" is attainable.

Yet even as these records allow access to Shembe's "voice," a question remains. Are they a word-for-word transcription of the remarks of Isaiah, and thereby a primary historical account, or the product of an elder's later recollection, and thereby historical memory? Dube's verbatim text of two traditions from the "Grave Book" verifies through an extra-church source that at least some of the pieces of church lore were recorded in Shembe's exact words. Yet as noted earlier, few traditions exist in extra-church sources to conclusively cross-check widely with sources beyond the *Catechism* and *Acts*. The overlapping literature and oralture of the church, moreover, make the distinction between history and memory less crisp than it might be in the documentary evidence of other historical contexts. It is perfectly possible that a written record within the *Catechism* or *Acts* based on an oral testimonial, even one provided decades after the fact, is a perfect replica of what was once a textual or oral first-hand version decades earlier. While this cannot be demonstrably proven in all cases, it is also perfectly plausible and cannot be summarily discounted. Therefore, some of the documents in the *Catechism* and *Acts* are certainly historical, first-hand accounts, even among oral recreations sometime after the fact, and others are quite likely secondary records of memory. Which is which, however, is quite often beyond scholarly discernment.

Ultimately creating such clear lines between history, or first-hand account, and memory, or secondary account, may not be terribly important anyway.

Even with an inability to conclusively distinguish between history and memory in some traditions, the material within the *Catechism* and *Acts* does unquestionably allow the scholar access to the historical data and events of the foundational era of the church and Isaiah Shembe's role within it, whether those remarks be first, second, or even third and fourth hand ones. Whether a narrator changed a verb, recalled the wrong date, or added punctuation does not detract from this fact. So while I do not always know whether each and every word may demonstrably be proven to be Shembe's exact remarks in his "voice," I do have a general confidence that they approximate the words of Shembe, and a full certainty that they convey the essence and spirit of Shembe's history and teachings, even allowing that there may have been some changes or distortions over time. Given the stability in the church's records generally, this is a reasonable conclusion and a sensible method to approaching the analysis of the material in the *Catechism* and *Acts*, even amid the challenges regarding provenance, voice, and memory.[89]

The Documentary Record and Church Membership

There has never been a single documentary record of the Nazareth Baptist Church. Even though Galilee Shembe, Petros Dhlomo, an unknown number of assistants and informants, and later some scholars too, did compile and publish the various centrally sanctioned sources this chapter has described, other versions could be found in a multiplicity of memories and copybooks. These alternative renderings ranged from the apocryphal (from the point of view of the church's leadership) to the small and essentially insignificant.

There are a few examples of alternative renderings of Nazareth Baptist Church history one might call apocryphal in the sense of providing a narrative of Shembe and church history that is at clear variance from the church's version. The most powerful example was produced by Unkulunkulu KaGcwensa, who during the leadership dispute between Londa and Amos generated her own alternative rendering of the church's history and future.[90] KaGcwensa made the claim that the spirit of Isaiah had entered into her, indicating that she should assume central leadership. Apparently getting nowhere with her own bid for central leadership, KaGcwensa left the Nazareth Baptist Church in 1977 and began her own church known as the iBandla lamaNazaretha Nkulunkulu kaGcwensa (Nazareth Baptist Church of God KaGcwensa). In her own church, she began to craft a new theology grounded upon that of the Nazareth Baptist Church, yet quite distinct. KaGcwensa claimed that Isaiah was not just a mighty prophet, as the Nazareth Baptist Church held, but God himself. Now that she was possessed by the spirit of Isaiah, she too was God; Jehovah was the invisible God while she was the visible form. To account for this theological variance that was at odds with the

Nazareth Baptist Church's narrative, oral histories were shifted to explain the divine nature of Isaiah and KaGcwensa and how the history of the church had been leading to her assumption of leadership. KaGcwensa additionally added twenty-four new hymn compositions of her own to the Nazareth Baptist Church hymnal known as "New hymns for the Nazareth Church."[91]

Clearly not all alternative renderings of Nazareth Baptist Church theology were as grand as KaGcwensa's total rewriting of Nazareth Baptist Church theology and history. For instance, in 1977, Mama Dainah Zama claimed to have received numerous prophetic communications from Zulu kings Shaka, Cetshwayo, and Solomon, and from Isaiah Shembe, all insisting that the Nazareth Baptist Church be transformed into a Zulu National Church. The concept of a Zulu National Church had roots in the emergent Zulu nationalism of the early twentieth century, yet it had few supporters in or out of the church after 1931–32, following the souring of relations between Isaiah Shembe and King Solomon.[92] Zama later made the claim that God was also telling her the same thing. Within the theology of the Nazareth Baptist Church, only Isaiah and his progeny could claim to know the will of God. While Zama's claims of prophetic inspiration fit within the bounds of church doctrine, the source, God, did not. Zama's incredulous claims were orally preserved and even reached print in the *Acts* because they served a political role in Amos' bid for central leadership. In a vision in 1978, Zama claimed that Shaka told her Amos should suspend everything, even church services, until the Londa faction was absorbed, because until that happened, everything about the church was spoiled. Shaka further instructed Zama to inform Londa that God was disgusted and angry with him and held him responsible for transforming the *umnazaretha* into a "gown of blood."[93] Normally Zama's unorthodox prophetic claims of knowing the will of Jehovah would not have entered into church lore, whether in an oral or written form. Zama's prophetic record was preserved so that the Amos faction might use the 1978 prophecy to legitimate Amos, provided one ignored Zama's earlier prophetic claims to speak for God. In the end, the obscuring of Zama from the historical record was imperfectly done and the church lore of the Ebuhleni faction preserved, rather contradictorily, both her heretical prophetic claim and the content of her 1978 prophecy. The case of Zama illustrates that there were indeed church members whose actions and beliefs were not always in accordance with those of the church's leaders and the church's central dogma. How many cases of this sort there were we will never know, but surely there were other individuals like Zama.

Nonetheless, despite the cases of KaGcwensa, Zama, and an unknown number of lost records of alternate renderings of church history, most memories and copybooks that differ from the *Catechism* or the *Acts* reflect differences of order and selection, and not the overall historical narrative they provide. In other words, they are generally not alternative in the sense of providing an image of Shembe, his teachings, or the church's history that might be viewed as apocryphal by the central leadership, in the manner of KaGcwensa, and to a lesser degree Zama. The image of Isaiah, the teachings attributed to him, accounts of his prophecies and miracles—in short the core history of the church—remain essentially the same across the various versions even amid the differences regarding the order of accounts, narrative details, and the inclusion or exclusion of some personal testimonies.

While there was some theological heterogeneity among the membership that differed from that outlined by Shembe, particularly over time and as the church grew demographically, highlighting such minority opinions and the impact that they did or did not have upon the church's documentary record would be a different project and research agenda. The existence of theological heterogeneity does not, however, negate the existence of a dominant position embraced by the large majority. The Nazareth Baptist Church, like most Christian institutions, still had an identifiable central dogma and historical narrative. Throughout this book I make statements such as "the membership believed that...." I am referring to the communally held opinion of the majority when making such statements. An individual who chose to join and remain with the Nazareth Baptist Church embraced a certain set of beliefs and narrative details about Shembe. It is difficult to imagine an individual remaining with the church if they largely rejected them, as the case of KaGcwensa illustrates. Therefore, while acknowledging that there were "subaltern" narratives, some of which may have escaped documentation, it remains accurate to refer to the membership as a collective as there was, and remains, a central dogma and church history endorsed by the large majority of the church's leadership and membership, as revealed in the church's documentary record.

Conclusion

Like many religions, the internal histories of the Nazareth Baptist Church began their existence in oral form. While the traditions of and about Isaiah Shembe (and his successors) have never stopped circulating in oral form they gradually assumed written form. That process began in a decentralized manner during the time of Isaiah, and reached a centralized and published form under the leadership of Galilee Shembe and the oversight of archivist Petros Dhlomo.

The church's literary corpus served as a legitimating strategy in two ways. First, the sorts of records that were selected for transmission and preservation helped to reinforce the beliefs of church members and reified the worldview articulated by Isaiah Shembe. The church's documentary record is replete with accounts containing supernatural, prophetic, and miraculous events, and this is not accidental. When church leaders and members memorized, recounted, and recorded their history, they most often transmitted and preserved those narratives that highlighted the supernatural history of Shembe and their church. Mundane affairs certainly had an impact upon their preservation efforts, but less so because the mundane failed to reify the church's worldview and beliefs the way the supramundane could. By underscoring those stories that describe Shembe's supposed performance of miracles and reception of divine prophecies, members reinforced their collective belief in Shembe as God's special messenger for the modern age. Reinforcing that status for Shembe thereby amplified the believability of Shembe's theology and worldview. This worldview included two important beliefs in particular: (1) that the imposition of colonial rule in South Africa was all part of God's plan to advance atonement and salvation among his chosen people, and (2) that the congregants of the Nazareth Baptist Church were God's new chosen people. The church's documentary record, then, provides the text that bolstered the beliefs of the members and affirmed this overall worldview.

The second manner in which the documentary record served as a legitimating mechanism was through the generation of Christian legitimacy. As the church's documentary record was gradually centralized and printed over the course of Galilee's era, it increasingly became more Christian in form. A printed hymnbook, a catechism, and a rule code all have analogues within many Christian denominations. This was certainly true of the Protestant churches in twentieth-century South Africa that the leaders and members of the Nazareth Baptist Church were most familiar with and likely emulating. Printed books of sacred literature physically symbolized a church that was mature and Christian in its accoutrements. The church's documentary record was also used to connect the present to the past and eliminate the sense that the church was a new invention that ruptured Christian history, but was rather the best manifestation of it. Compiling and distributing accounts of Shembe's prophecies, teachings, travels, and biography purposefully echoed the Acts of early Christianity. Doing so collapsed time by injecting Shembe and his sacred narrative into the apostolic past through parallel content regarding healing miracles, discredited challengers, and a sheer volume of supernatural displays of God-bestowed power to leave no doubt of Shembe's greatness.

Prophecy, History, Memory, and Legitimacy in the Biography of Isaiah Shembe, ca. 1870–1910

Without mentioning the name SHEMBE, Ibandla lamaNazaretha is non-existent.
—Mthembeni P. Mpanza, Submission to the Truth and
Reconciliation Commission, 18 Nov. 1997

Another day as I was praying, I felt the heaven rend asunder, as if it was thundering. I was alarmed. It was thus that for the first time I heard a voice—come as if from above, in heaven.
—Isaiah Shembe, testimony to Carl Faye, 5 Nov. 1929.

According to a tradition in the *Acts of the Nazarites*, during one of the annual pilgrimages, likely in the 1930s, to the church's holy mountain, Mt. Nhlangakazi, some church members were digging out a large stone. The workers lost control of the stone as they were digging, and it began to roll down the hill toward the encampment of the maidens who were doing laundry at the time. According to the narrator of the tradition, Khulumani Jinios Mzimela, when Isaiah Shembe noticed the rolling peril, he pointed his finger at the stone and broke it in two. He then pointed a second and third time at the two remaining pieces and broke each of those, and everyone, human and animal, escaped injury that day. Mzimela continues by adding that, "On this day, everybody could see the power of God. And this is not the first miracle Shembe did. He is not an earthly person, he is a man of heaven, who had this power to prevent a great accident from threatening the people."[1] Mzimela had learned of this miraculous tale second hand, and had first heard it from an eyewitness, an Indian church member named Aaron (surname unknown). In his telling of the story, Mzimela added no conditional language to allow for the fact that he was not a direct witness. Rather, he told the story quite straightforwardly as though the veracity of the tale was never in question, because for him the story was perfectly truthful.

For church members stories such as these were (and are) "facts," and thus it is important to analyze the words and deeds of these historical actors with this status solidly in mind.[2] I am not suggesting that this testimony of the splintered rock is "true" in an absolute sense and that Shembe did indeed have real miraculous powers. Yet for church members it does not matter whether an outsider can discount this story with a rational explanation for why a stone might fall apart as it tumbles downhill, or whether some of the factual details have been blurred through the tale's retelling or embellished by the narrators. What makes the story of the splintered rock, and the countless other examples from church documents that remark upon the superhuman nature of Shembe, significant is that church members believed these tales to be true, whether the story came directly from the mouth of Shembe or from that of a first- or second-hand witness.

My argument in this chapter is that Shembe's biographic narratives are at the heart of his early appeal, and that they sustained the faithfulness of existing members and legitimated Shembe by connecting his biography with biblical and Christian history. The narratives that compose Shembe's biography are replete with visions, aural commands, astral travel, and miraculous events. These thoroughly prophetic accounts of Isaiah Shembe's early life, as Shembe told it, and as church members retold it, generated an aura around Shembe grounded in his prophetic abilities. This aura reinforced Shembe's understanding of himself as God's specially designated prophet for modern times charged with illuminating the path of salvation for God's new chosen people—the members of the Nazareth Baptist Church—and eventually all of humanity.[3] But these biographic accounts are not just prophetic, they are often also Christian. Echoing aspects of the biblical and Christian past is a common legitimating strategy for Christian leaders in order to fold their present into the Christian past.[4] The faith members had in Shembe's prophetic might and divinely charged Christian mission lent legitimacy and believability to his teachings and the worldview he articulated. Shembe's biography, both as Shembe told it and as his church members' have remembered it, reveals a thoroughly prophetic and Christian narrative that constructed and reified their worldview of colonial South Africa as the site for the unfolding of God's cosmic plans for the salvation of his new chosen people.

Explaining the Allure of Shembe's Biography

This chapter analyzes specific testimonies and documents from the church's record, in the chronological order of Shembe's life, that contributed to the church's history and historical memory of the period from Shembe's birth (ca. 1870) to the church's founding (1910). As Mpanza asserted in one of this chapter's epigraphic quotations, there would be no Nazareth Baptist Church without Shembe. Similarly, his biography is inseparable from the history of the church, and this is true whether one was a member on the inside or a contemporary scholar on the outside; at all points in time and from all angles, Shembe's biography is at the heart of the church's history. But how was it that Shembe's words, deeds, and overall biography came to possess such a sense of wonder for church members that it became a cornerstone of the church's historical memory?

At the risk of appearing that I may be suggesting a hagiographic, and not biographic, analysis, I ask readers to attempt to place themselves in the position of the listeners or readers in early twentieth-century South Africa who were listening to and/or reading the forthcoming narratives. Imagine how powerful these stories of fantastic visions of a lightning creature, a putrid corpse, or the heavenly host could be in drawing in potential converts and in sustaining the faith of existing ones.[5] These testimonies circulated throughout colonial Natal and beyond. Most inhabitants of South Africa, as well as parts of Swaziland, Botswana, Zimbabwe, and Mozambique, paid them little attention, but for the tens of thousands who joined the church over the course of Shembe's lifetime, they elicited a sense of awe and mysterious allure that made those individuals seek out Shembe and his church.[6] Once members, their belief in such testimonies directly informed and reinforced what members believed about Shembe, his church, and the worldview he developed and advanced. Such sacralized pieces of oral and written lore actualized the notion, for prospective and current members, that Shembe was a prophet of God living in their midst. These prophecies and sacred narratives are significant because they made Shembe into the prophet and church leader he was, both to himself and in the hearts and minds of his members.

Shembe's biography was not just intriguing, however, but also believable to tens of thousands. These testimonies of Shembe most appealed to a particular sector of the populace, in fact nearly exclusively, and that was those who were already Christian. Shembe was aware of this, as were some of his detractors who accused him of "sheep-stealing." The reason Shembe and the prophetic narratives he told most resonated with Christians was due to the simple fact that Shembe's narrative tropes were often biblical and Christian. Because those most attracted to Shembe and his church were already Christian, they had a familiarity with biblical narratives and could understand and appreciate the evoking of portions of the Christian past in these narratives. Additionally, the content of Shembe's prophecies—including visions of the heavenly host, near death experiences, astral travel, hearing warnings from God to live righteously, and prophetic instructions on how to improve Christianity and please God, among others—are all prophetic claims that can be found throughout Christian history.[7] Such prophetic content fit within what many Christians across history considered likely within prophetic experiences.[8]

The prophetic potentials of Christianity proved to be among the aspects of Christianity that intrigued some of the new and potential Christians in colonial Africa. Enabled by the literacy of Western-educated converts, some individuals recorded the dreams and visions that had sparked their interest in Christianity.[9] These accounts circulated within regions of colonial Africa, highlighting the prophetic undercurrent of Christianity for an emerging generation of African Christians and the leaders who founded Zionist churches. A good number of Zionist churches were created through prophetic inspiration and accentuated this Christian potentiality.[10] These founding prophets, including Shembe, explained their ministerial careers and justified their theologies by insisting they were correcting errant Christianity by legitimate biblical and Christian means. Therefore, while portions of their prophecies and theological admonitions were novel, the form was not. Shembe's early converts, given that they were already Christian, had a basis to find Shembe's prophetic claims and biblical allusions not only alluring, but also perfectly plausible and credible. They resonated with what was possible within Christianity. The fact that Shembe's prophetic claims fit within acceptable Christian bounds, though, does not detract from the extraordinary nature and mysterious allure they could have for members.[11] Having an individual one viewed as a prophet living in one's midst was something most worshipers were, understandably, very likely to view with considerable deference and awe.

Given that Shembe's biographic tropes, both those he personally employed and those ascribed to him by followers, were often biblical and Christian in nature, I further attest that the Zulu nature of the narratives, Shembe's ministry, and the church as a whole, have been given undue emphasis by scholars. Whether to suit nationalist or theological agendas, the "Zuluness" of the church has been exaggerated in an effort to undermine its "Christianness."[12] But Shembe was not a traditional diviner masquerading as a Christian prophet, nor was his church Zulu indigenous religion posing as Christianity.[13] The degree to which the Nazareth Baptist Church can rightly be viewed as a Zulu/indigenous institution is one I examine in greater detail in chapters 5 and 6, but suffice it to say for now that there are unquestionably Zulu elements about these narratives; they were told, retold, and recorded by people who were mostly of that culture after all. For instance, Kolberi the cow is not only named in one of the forthcoming testimonies, but his personality was described and preserved as part of the story. This attention to narrative detail regarding a cow is a product of Zulu culture and the significant place that cattle and cattle-keeping holds in it. Yet the rest of the story involves a creature made of lightning and multiple conversations with Jehovah, which cannot be attributed to Zulu culture, but are not unusual elements within Christian prophecies. Even the very idea that one can have a prophetic conversation with God, that he is capable of punishing you for your sins, and might reveal this via prophecy, all comes from Christianity and the Christian Bible. The fact that a cow holds a reverential place in the story does not render the narrative a mere Zulu archetype. Rather it is a narrative recounted by a man who was asserting he was a Christian prophet, who was a product of Zulu culture, and his cultural background sometimes came through when he narrated his experiences. The overall narrative arc of the prophecies Shembe recounted fit solidly within a Christian prophetic and biblical paradigm, even as he referenced the culture he knew best.

Should the allure and power of these prophetic traditions and biographic narratives still be in doubt to the reader, I add one last, somewhat anecdotal, point concerning the volume of scholarly study of Shembe and the Nazareth Baptist Church. Part of the relatively high volume of scholarly work on the church, when compared to most Zionist churches, must be attributed to the church's size and visibility, their plentiful records, the membership's openness to scholars, and the central place the church had in Sundkler's *Bantu Prophets in South Africa*, a seminal text in the study of Zionist churches. Nonetheless, even for non-members in contemporary times, these prophetic and miraculous tales can possess a captivating allure and suggest an individual with considerable religious genius, as several scholars admit.[14] I too must confess I was not immune to this impulse and these tales did capture my own scholarly imagination, made me intrigued enough to find out more about the church, eventually transforming it into my principle research focus. There does appear to be something most interesting about Shembe and the church's narratives, even for outsiders of another era. Given this, it is not difficult to understand how they might have been captivating to individuals living during Isaiah's lifetime, and how the tales told of him amplified the prophetic aura members ascribed to him.

What follows are not just random biographic bits from Shembe's life, an attempt by members to preserve whatever historical scraps they could recall. Rather these narratives are *the* biographic records from within the church that were recounted by Shembe on more than one occasion, including some interviews with non-members, and preserved in the copybooks and memories of multiple members. When church leaders and members made efforts to recount and preserve the history of their church, the prophetic was heavily favored over the mundane. It seems only sensible that a prophetic individual would have a biography that was equally prophetic. As these accounts circulated among the membership, they reinforced Shembe's distinctiveness, increased the power of his prophetic aura, and inserted him into Christian history.

The Making of a Prophet: The Prophetic Biography of the Early Life of Isaiah Shembe

The church's records reveal a narrative of Shembe's early life, including conception, birth, and childhood, as one shaped by supermundane events. What made these records significant for members was that they demonstrated Shembe's distinctiveness at all stages of his life, even his pre-life through accounts of his mother and his conception. These biographic narratives, therefore, reinforced the prophetic aura of Shembe by providing an account of his early life as one that was not only totally unlike that of all other people, but also divinely guided, as evidenced through numerous supernatural communications. These prophecies were further legitimated by reiterations of Christian history.

Consider, for example, a testimony in the *Acts* with three narrators that describes the life of Shembe's mother, Sitheya, and the supernatural events leading to Shembe's conception. This tripartite testimony claims Sitheya was a morally pure girl because she was guarded by God. When she reached marriageable age, she said she heard a voice telling her not to drink beer or have premarital sex, for she would give birth to the Servant of God. She claimed she was amazed at the voice from the firmament; she knew nothing of Christianity and did not entirely understand the words. This testimony continues that Sitheya's special nature as the future mother of Shembe was further demonstrated one day on the white man's farm where she worked. She and the other female workers had erected wheat bundles. But while they were at lunch a strong wind came and blew over all the bundles except one, that built by Sitheya. This same day, according to these narrators, the voice came to her again and told her not to pollute herself and not to choose a lover, for she would give birth to the Servant of God.

This same testimony continues by recounting how Sitheya became pregnant with Shembe. Shembe's conception began when Sitheya was out collecting firewood with the other maidens. They all saw a beautiful flower, one that surpassed all other flowers on earth in beauty. Sitheya picked it and when she brought it near her face, the narrators insist that the Holy Spirit entered her and went into her womb to wait until the proper time for Shembe's conception. Sitheya remained pure by not engaging in premarital sex, and later entered a polygamous marriage with Shembe's father, Mayekisa. Sitheya had several miscarriages prior to her pregnancy with Isaiah. These narrators explain the miscarriages as the work of the Holy Spirit, who left her womb, thereby killing the fetuses, because the time was not yet right and God wanted Shembe to be the eldest. In the minds of these church members, Sitheya's miscarriages were not personal misfortunes, but part of a plan engineered by God to arrange Shembe's birth in a particular manner. When the proper time came for Shembe's conception, the testimony continues, the Holy Spirit reentered Sitheya and Shembe was conceived. After being pregnant for six months Sitheya had repeated dreams of people in white gowns who told her she would give birth to the lord who would save all nations.[15]

The story of Sitheya and Shembe's conception purposefully echoes that of Mary and Jesus.[16] The Annunciation narrative is one that would have been familiar to those who told and heard Shembe's conception story. The church's narratives do not claim Sitheya was a virgin, as Luke and Matthew do of Mary, but they do assert that she was pure and did not participate in sex until wedded. Similarly, the fact that Shembe's conception was attributed to the Holy Spirit, just like Jesus, is no coincidence. Echoing aspects of the life of Jesus is a common legitimating strategy for Christian leaders. Appealing to the biblical and Christian past roots the present in an ancient and legitimate history, thereby demonstrating this this tale is no contemporary invention. Building connections to the Christian past also made Shembe's biography familiar to his primary audience—Christians. By employing Christian narrative tropes, the reciters of such testimonies proved to members that Shembe was not some average individual who stumbled across the Bible and decided to build himself a following, as some of his detractors suggested. Rather, the bridges built to the biblical past legitimated Shembe within Christian history, which explains his appeal among Africans who had already converted.

Another uncanny story from the Acts, though this one without biblical connections, tells of Shembe's return to life. According to this legend, with multiple narrators, Shembe once fell seriously ill as a toddler, fainted, and was thought dead by his family. Shembe's father, Mayekisa, gathered some neighbors and started to dig a grave. After the grave was finished, a herd boy came from the pasture and told Mayekisa that one of his cattle had died; it simply fell to the ground and perished. A neighbor, Lukhozana Mahlobo, went to consult a diviner about these strange events. The diviner said that Mayekisa should not worry about the death of the cow because its death would bring back the life of his son. Before Lukhozana returned, the women with Sitheya noticed that the blanket over Shembe began to move. They called the men in and, according to these narrators, life very slowly returned to the toddler Shembe and the men filled the grave back in.[17]

These two supernatural accounts were retold and preserved to provide evidence of Shembe's distinctiveness, and form part of a hallowed biography of the church's founder. It is likely that these traditions are a retroactive interpretation of the past, designed to generate a memory of mystery regarding Shembe's early years, and are likely not a direct transcription of the experiences of Shembe's parents and family members. It does not seem likely the average woman would interpret a series of miscarriages as God choosing the correct timing for her eldest born. Shembe's mother also later disagreed with

Shembe's decision to leave her and his wives. This suggests that Sitheya may not have been entirely in support of Shembe's prophetic claims or ministerial intentions, an image of Shembe's mother at variance with the pure child of God portrayed in these testimonies. Despite the embellishments and Christian connections added at some point in the retelling of these stories, these narratives circulated among the membership, and were preserved in the *Acts*, as proof to members, and even prospective ones, that Shembe's conception was supernatural and entirely orchestrated by God. For members of the Nazareth Baptist Church, prophetic traditions like these are historical facts that demonstrate Shembe's distinctiveness and power even before his arrival on earth, much like Jesus. If one believed that Shembe was sent by God and was the most important human of modern times, one would expect there to be extraordinary tales about that individual after all, and testimonies like these provided that sense of wonder by insisting that even Shembe's earliest moments on earth were guided by Jehovah.

The same is true of Shembe's childhood. In a series of first-hand and second-hand accounts, Shembe described three prophetic experiences from his adolescent years that are important for two reasons. By emphasizing the prophetic experiences of his childhood, Shembe demonstrated that his prophetic activity in adulthood was no rupture, but merely a continuity that proved his distinctiveness at all stages of life. Demonstrating this sort of supernatural mystique for all points of their life is a common motif among prophets.[18] These tales certainly contributed to Shembe's prophetic aura. Additionally, these prophecies were critical to Shembe's theological evolution and informed his early thinking about how he defined Christianity and God. Because the life of Jesus between infancy and his baptism as an adult is virtually unknown, these narratives do not make biblical allusions, and instead build up Shembe's prophetic aura independently.

Shembe said his first vision occurred when he was a boy of about twelve. He orally recounted it and the story entered the oralture and literature of the membership. The account below is from a written version of Shembe's grandson, Londa Shembe, recorded in the 1980s, and now archived at the Killie Campbell Africana Library.[19] In explaining the prophetic experience, Shembe recalled how his father had some guests at his home. One of the guests had a small belt on his hat that Shembe liked. He stole it and hid it upon a rock. A short time later the guest noticed his belt was missing and everyone went about looking for it. Shembe left and climbed a hill above where the belt was hidden and described this subsequent visionary experience,

> I saw in the clouds on my right hand side, a red heart which was tied with a string and appeared in the midst of the clouds[.] And a hand appeared near the heart on the right-hand side of the heart. And that hand spoke like a human being, saying "Do you see the heart?" I did not answer it with my mouth but I answered it through my heart

and I said, "I do see it." It said, "This is the heart of the man whose belt you have stolen.["] As the voice said those words, it appeared that there were eyes above the hand and the heart.

The voice said "Do you see the redness of the heart? It is the sadness of the man whose belt you have stolen." I agreed within my spirit and could not utter the words out because of fear. And there appeared two eyes above the heart and the hand: those eyes were the eyes of the man whose belt I had stolen.

Those eyes that I saw were crying but there was no face: it was only the eyes. After that something beat in my chest above the heart: which was sorrow and repentance which is still a wound within me until this day. Within a short time that hand had disappeared, together with the heart and the eyes.[20]

Shembe said this prophetic experience taught him of the grave seriousness and permanence of sin as the act "did not cease to exist in my heart until this day."[21]

Shembe also used prophecy to describe how he learned to pray. As a teen-ager, Shembe worked as a "boy" for Boss Coenraad (on whose land Shembe's father had built his homestead) looking after horses, sheep, and cows. After working for him a short time, Shembe claimed it "occurred" to him that he should go and pray. Shembe described the impulse as an inner voice or inner urging. He went and knelt near a rocky outcrop to the east of Coenraad's home. He had never prayed before and did not know what to say, but then the words "just came to him" and he did not need to think about it. Shembe said that sometimes he sang during prayer and the words to the songs simply came to him as well. He worked for Coenraad off and on for the next few years and Shembe dutifully continued to pray near the rocky outcropping to the east of Coenraad's home. But one day Shembe heard one of the girls who worked for Coenraad gossiping to some other girls that she always found Shembe praying by the rock. From then on Shembe noted that he prayed inside the cattle-kraal to the west of the house, selecting it because the cows liked to sleep there after having been milked.[22] It was from this second prayer location, inside the cattle-kraal, that Shembe claimed to have audibly heard the voice of God for the first time, instead of "hearing" it in his heart. One day, while praying from inside the kraal, Shembe recounted how the sky rent asunder with thunder and lightning. The voice aurally told Shembe to avoid *ukuhlobonga* or Shembe would never see him.[23] Shembe was frightened and ran, and did not know what *ukuhlobonga* was. The next day Shembe asked Mbhinca Mazibuko, another worker at Coenraad's farm, what *ukuhlobonga* was. Mazibuko initially scolded Shembe and told him he was too young to be asking such things. But later that evening Mazibuko told Shembe what it was and asked him what he intended to do with the knowledge. Shembe said nothing about the voice but said, "I'm just asking."[24]

The third instance, and the most famous tale of prophecy from Shembe's early life, one that can be found in many sources, is a tale about a peach tree. The number of times Shembe recounted this tale suggests it was the most powerful prophetic experience of his teenage years. Overcome with hunger when approaching the peach orchard on Coenraad's property, Shembe prayed for permission to take some fruit. Shembe believed he received the response to his prayer, "Climb the tree." So Shembe scaled a tree and began to load his sheepskin with fruit. Suddenly he heard a horse's hooves, followed by a voice saying in Afrikaans, "So these are the footprints of my peach stealers. I wish I could see their owner." The individual behind the voice was none other than Boss Coenraad himself. Noting the rod Coenraad hefted, Shembe was certain a thrashing would be in order and trembled in terror so that it seemed to him even the tree was shaking. Shembe recounted how he heard a voice command him to stop looking down at Coenraad and to look up. He looked up and saw a mountain rising out of the sky and a fireball was shot from its summit. Coenraad passed on without having seen Shembe. Shembe climbed down, moved to the veld, and ate his peaches, but they were not appetizing. Upon finishing Shembe said the voice came to him again saying, "I gave you the chance to steal because it pleases me thus! Know I am always with you." Later in life Shembe pointed to this incident as having taught him several important theological lessons. First, it instilled in him the belief that individuals are each responsible for resisting sin and maintaining their own moral fortitude. Though the voice had told him to climb the tree, it was Shembe who sinned by stealing peaches once in the tree. The world is full of temptations, and it is up to the individual to resist becoming a sinner. God allows the temptations to exist so the worshiper can truly display their righteousness and obedience to God's laws. Second, Shembe also explained how this incident taught him of the omnipresence of God; no sin would escape his notice. Third, just as no sin escapes God's notice, so too do all prayers and pleas for mercy reach him. Despite the scary incident, Shembe described how he was heartened to realize that God answers all prayers and will aid his children even at moments of adversity.[25]

These were not the only prophetic incidents Shembe experienced during his teenage years and later recounted in adulthood. However, this sample suffices to demonstrate their significance to Shembe and his membership and the history they preserved. Whether about stealing peaches or warnings about premarital sex, these prophecies were recounted by Shembe and sustained in the church's documentary record for several reasons. The fact that Shembe was a prophet even before he was an adult is proof for members, to this day, of his distinctiveness and prophetic gifts from early in life. This contributed to Shembe's prophetic aura and lent legitimacy to his powers and teachings. These experiences additionally provided the seeds of Shembe's theological and political understandings of the universe. While it would be some time before Shembe's beliefs and teachings would fully mature, these early experiences began to inform Shembe's faithful confidence that God was ever present and aware of human actions. Therefore, Shembe was convinced that God was not ignorant, unconcerned, or powerless in the face of human suffering. Even if God's plans were not always evident to humans, given God's cosmic vision of the universe, Shembe developed a trust that God had a plan for those who showed the proper adoration and obedience.

Shembe's early prophetic experiences were additionally his first introduction to monotheistic theology. Yet while Shembe believed his early prophecies had a single source, that source remained a bit of a mystery to him. Though the narrators, including Shembe, would retroactively insert the name of God into these prophetic accounts, at the time he was experiencing them, the teenage Shembe was uncertain of the exact source of the voice and visions. Sometime in Shembe's mid-teens, while in the midst of these prophecies and his praying in the cattle-kraal, Shembe made the decision that he must find a way to worship this being who was sending these prophetic communiqués. He did this in two ways that together might be termed a kind of spiritual exploration. The first was to rediscover the religious ways of his ancestors. Shembe had never taken much interest in the rites performed by his family. Shembe said he and his father respected one another on religious matters and nothing was said on the issue. But while learning to pray, Shembe came to feel that perhaps the prophetic voice derived from the Thixo or Unkulunkulu spoken of by his kinspeople. We cannot say precisely how Shembe was involved in Zulu indigenous religion. His early interest in Zulu indigenous religion is understandably not something that gets much mention in the testimonies of Shembe or church members. But in all likelihood Shembe probably participated in some rites and learned as much as he could in order to make a good faith effort to find the source of the voice. At roughly the same time, Shembe found the Wesleyan Methodists and joined in their services. Perhaps, Shembe thought, the voice derived from this God spoken of by the missionaries and their converts. In time, Shembe impressed many Methodist parishioners with his knowledge of the Bible and was said to have memorized the entire book. Thus, some of Shembe's early prophetic activity ran concurrent to his attendance in a Methodist church and with his participation in Zulu indigenous religion.

Two important events occurred during this period of religious exploration. The first was a series of prophetic incidents. Throughout his teenage years, Shembe claimed that he continued to periodically hear a voice telling him to avoid *ukuhlobonga*. But as Shembe approached marrying age, Shembe said the voice began to also tell him not to marry. Shembe recalled one such incident when he was riding one of his father's horses, which stopped all of a sudden, entirely on its own. Shembe recalled how the voice told him, "Don't marry." But interestingly, the voice used the term *ungagani*, the word used for referring to women gaining a husband, and not *ungaganwa*, the word for men taking a wife. Shembe was confused why the voice referred to him in this gender-reversing manner, a confusion the voice never rectified.[26] The second significant moment during this formative time of Shembe's life came during a Methodist service, as recounted by church archivist Petros Dhlomo. The white minister arose and said that Shembe would lead the hymn. As Shembe began to do so, "a mighty spirit came over the people; they vomited their diseases and their poisons out, ...others understood, that the Spirit had come down from heaven. Shembe said, 'Indeed, the Spirit of God has come down over us.'"[27] It was after this Pentecostal-like event, with a supposed outpouring of the Spirit, that Shembe, confident of his own skills as a leader and bolstered by the confidence that derived from his publicly displayed prophetic gifts, began to wander occasionally as an itinerant preacher and developed some regional fame as a healer.

I would posit that this period of religious exploration, bolstered by Shembe's continued prophetic activity, eventually brought Shembe to the conclusion that the Unkulunkulu of his ancestors was the same as the God of the missionaries—the same entity with different names—and the source of his voices and visions. As the key evidence I point to the various sermons, prayers, and hymns composed by Shembe in which Unkulunkulu, Thixo, uMvelinqangi, Zinzilini, God, Jehovah, Creator, and Lord are used inter-changeably. The first three names are typically used in combination with Zulu people and places and discussions of the ancestral past, while the latter are generally used in reference to biblical events and God's salvific dispensation in the present. In short, the name Shembe used for God in his compositions depended on the cultural context and little more. For instance, an oral tradi-tion from the *Catechism of the Nazarites* titled "Shembe's Discourse at Mqeku 20 May 1932" uses the names God, Thixo, Lord, and Jehovah in the course of just five stanzas as the content moves between discussion of ancestral sins of the past and Jehovah's forgiving power in the present.[28] Consequently for Shembe, Christianity and Zulu religion were not two incompatible religions in competition, but religions whose practitioners had chosen two different methods of honoring the same high God.[29]

Having reached what he believed was a clear theological conclusion on the source of the prophecies, and increasingly confident in his own ministerial skills following the Methodist service in which he felt responsible for an outpouring of the Holy Spirit, Shembe began to doubt the accuracy of the Methodists' theology and ritual practice. Shembe's prophetically informed reading of the Bible indicated to him that the Sabbath was clearly on Saturday, baptism was to be by immersion, shoes should not be worn in church, and the

Lord's Supper should be distributed at night. His dissatisfaction with the Methodists led Shembe to begin to attend the African Native Baptist Church, an independent church led by Rev. W. M. Leshega (also written as Lushisha or Lesheya).[30] Leshega appointed Shembe as a reverend of the African Native Baptist Church and Shembe continued to preach and heal, only now with the authority of a ministerial office. Shembe was baptized, by full immersion, by Leshega on 22 July 1906 and received the name Isaiah, the name by which he is most commonly known.

When it came to marriage, Shembe said pressure from his family caused him to defy the voice of God. Shembe's father had died around 1890, leaving Isaiah as the only adult male of the family. Shembe built a homestead on the corner of Boss Coenraad's property, as had his father.[31] The social pressure to care for his mother and family caused Shembe to ignore the warnings of the voice and instead respect his mother's wishes to select his brides. After he married, Shembe said that the rate of prophecies increased as God began telling him to forsake his wives and travel to the east (toward Pondoland) in order to preach there. Shembe ignored these instructions as well and remained married to three women (Nomaloyo, Pikinini, and Noshwalane) and began preparations to marry a fourth (Nyateya). Due to his family obligations, Shembe contented himself with localized preaching tours. Shembe asked the voice, if he went to the east, what would happen to his mother, his wives, his growing family, and his emerging group of supporters?[32] There was no answer for some time.

Shembe's Calling and the Founding of the Nazareth Baptist Church

Just as the narratives of Shembe's early life contributed to his prophetic aura, bolstering members' beliefs about his distinctiveness and their conviction of his God-ordained mission to illuminate the path of salvation, the same is equally true of the years leading up to the founding of the Nazareth Baptist Church in 1910. Shembe described a series of three profound prophetic experiences that convinced him to forsake his wives and family and take up his ministerial calling as he believed the voice of God was insisting.[33] The prophecies themselves involved God's explanation for the deaths of three of Shembe's children, visions of heaven, thoughts of suicide, a lightning strike, a near-death experience, astral travel, and a vision of Shembe's own corpse. As with some of the testimonies concerning Shembe's early life, echoes of Christian prophecy can be found in these narratives as well.

Shembe made abundantly clear that these prophecies had a deep impact on him and determined his ministerial course. This sequence of prophecies was what moved him from occasional itinerant preacher and local healer to church founder and full time minister, and in time, among the most significant Zionist church leaders of Africa. The texts of these prophecies were likewise significant to church members as they explained and justified the founding of the Nazareth Baptist Church while simultaneously reinforcing Shembe's prophetic status. It is little wonder that Shembe told these stories more than once, that they circulated widely among the membership, and that they were recorded in writing on more than once occasion. These prophecies are the most significant in the lore of the church because they establish, for members, that Shembe is both a prophet and the fulfillment of Christian history for modern times.

The first prophetic incident (or more accurately series of similar incidents) Shembe reported in this sequence of prophecies prior to the church's founding concerned the deaths of three of Shembe's children: John, France, and Thulasizwe. Shembe said it began when he was returning from Lake Namhwashu with a team of oxen yoked to a wagon. At nightfall he crawled under the wagon to sleep. Sometime during the night the cattle got restless. When Shembe awoke, he saw a light coming under the wagon as if dawn had arrived. But the light was coming not from the sun, but from a man upon a horse with a red spear in his hand. He had his spear pointed at Shembe and rode away a short time later without saying a word. Again during the night the man returned and did the same thing without saying anything. Shembe recalled how he became quite frightened and could not sleep.

Shembe continued his testimony by recounting how he hitched up the oxen at dawn and started toward home. As he was giving the oxen a break to graze, Shembe said he saw a rider coming up the road. Though he was frightened it would be the same visitor from the previous night, Shembe went out to meet the rider but then recognized the rider as a neighbor, Jim Mkhabela. Jim said he had been sent to find Shembe who must return home right away because Shembe's son John was seriously ill. Shembe reached home by sundown and asked John how he was doing. Shembe washed him and left him with his mother. During the night Shembe reported having another vision of the same rider, this time with an additional rider, both of them pulling a cart. Shembe believed they told him, "You are wanted by the soul of this your son." Shembe went to Nomalaya and inquired about John's status. She replied that he was asleep. Shembe returned to sleep himself only to have the same vision again. This time he shared the vision with his wife and they both became alarmed. They decided to take John to a native doctor. After getting about seven miles from home, John died. Shembe spent the whole night with John's body praying for his resuscitation, without avail.

Just five days after John's burial, France died. A short time later, Thulasizwe died. All three children had been sick for five days before their deaths. Shembe recalled how he prayed, asking what he had done to deserve such severe punishment. He believed he received the response from Jehovah that it was his own fault. When told to leave his wives Shembe had responded that it would be better if they died. But Shembe said God had told him via their supernatural communication that he deemed Shembe's wives unworthy since they were unconverted and impure, so the children died in their places. So distraught was Shembe over the death of his children and the thought of deserting his wives and remaining children that he said he wanted to die. For an entire day he explained how he prayed and pleaded with God to kill him and take him to the firmament. Then he threatened that if God did not take him, he would kill himself. Shembe had every intention of climbing a tree and hanging himself. But before he did, Shembe recalled how he had a vision of a round homestead surrounded by beautiful trees suspended from the clouds. This will be your home, the voice told him. But if you commit suicide you will instead be sent to a cold prison for the duration of your life-span.[34] The vision of the homestead came repeatedly. Shembe said he then returned home and gave up thoughts of suicide. But, he asked Jehovah, what would be gained from leaving his family behind? Shembe believed Jehovah's response was a vision of many people wearing white gowns who were sitting with heads bowed. The voice of Jehovah said these would be the children he would gain if he did as he was instructed.

In his testimony, Shembe recounted that the second incident in this sequence took place sometime later while living at Curwen's farm, after his family was ejected from Coenraad's.[35] Shembe explained how he looked southward toward the Zokhahlamba Mountains, where the Drakensberg Mountains form the boundary with Lesotho. There he saw a lightning flash even though there was no storm, or even clouds, in the sky. At that moment Shembe believed God spoke to him internally, to his spirit, saying, "Do you see this lightning? It will eat your flesh." Shembe said he was very afraid. This was at about 3 p.m. Lightning flashed several more times that day, but the voice did not return. At sundown, near 6:30 p.m., Shembe gathered the cattle of Curwin and his own to be harnessed. Among Shembe's cattle was a very clever beast by the name of Kolberi, who has been described as powder-grey in some variations of the story and black with a white face in others. Whatever his colorings, the accounts agree that Kolberi would typically come to Shembe simply by having his name called, and would then bow his head to be yoked. But on this day Shembe called Kolberi three times and each time Kolberi shook his head and did not move. Another cattle driver, Mnguni, also tried to call Kolberi to no avail. By then the sky had grown overcast and it had begun to drizzle. Shembe took a rope and hit Kolberi upon the back in an effort to get him to move. A bolt of lightning struck down between Shembe, Kolberi, and Mnguni but caused no harm. Eventually the men got all the cattle yoked and headed back to the farm.

Shembe continued explaining how shortly after passing a mission compound, he began to have a vision. In this vision he saw a mighty ball of lightning emanating from the clouds, and at the same time something as small as a fly was flying toward him from the direction of Pondoland. When this small creature arrived it transformed into a huge aerial creature with four wings. Shembe believed God commanded him saying, "Give the prayer of consent!" Shembe replied that he did not know that prayer, so the voice of God then told him what the prayer was. The voice did not speak in Zulu, as normal, but still Shembe said he understood. When he said the prayer it brought him great pleasure and his fears ebbed. Lightning from the giant lightning ball began to flash all about. Lightning struck the ground five times without causing any harm. But the sixth bolt, provoked by the massive celestial four-winged creature, struck Kolberi and killed the ox on the spot. The bolt also burned Shembe on his left side, opening a wound in his thigh that left him unable to walk for three weeks. While healing from the wound Shembe believed Jehovah said to him, "You persist in being attached to your mother, and you do not listen to My voice." A short time later, while being visited by a traditional doctor, Shembe believed God's voice returned saying, "That doctor-priest [sangoma] has the best intention to heal you; but you will never be healed by him, you will be healed by the word of God."[36] The doctor returned a few days later and though Shembe remained seriously wounded, he told the doctor he wanted no more medicines. Shembe paid him one head of cattle for his services and dismissed him. With that demonstration of faith, Shembe claimed he began to heal. From that day forward, Shembe never used any medicine, either indigenous or Western, convinced that this near-death experience and prophetic conversation had taught him that healing came by faith alone.

A short time later, Shembe recalled how he received the greatest vision of his life to date; what was to be the third and final prophetic incident that convinced him to take up the ministerial calling he believed God was commanding. I repeat Shembe's account of this prophecy at length here because of the gravity it had upon Shembe. This is how Shembe later recalled it during an interview with Carl Faye, chief clerk and translator of the Natal Native Affairs Department, on 5 November 1929,

> When I was sleeping, I saw my spirit walking in the firmament; there I discerned people standing, who were clad in long white garments, like gowns. I don't know of what nation these people were; they appeared somehow tawny, like Muslims. All wore hats on their heads; I don't know whether these were made from straw. I wanted to meet with them. I hadn't the strength. I tried hard, but could not reach them although they only stood unmoving...

Then a spirit came out of those people, there, from behind them, and from me there came forth a spirit; and they stood facing one another like this (as two forefingers brought opposite each other). Spirit came forth from their shoulders, while mine came out of my chest. Their form was human-like, and mine too. They drew nigh one another, these spirits, leaving a small distance between them. I speak of spirits, because even if they were of human shape, it was evident that they were not people but spirits. They spoke, the two spirits, they spoke and finished. The other returned whence it had come, mine returned to me, into my chest. It said in my heart: 'Go and tell him, that he is unable to come to us, because he [is] still living in the vile house whence he comes.' Then I had no ears to hear, no eyes to see, but I saw with different eyes, and I heard speech speaking within me. I asked, 'Where is it, this vile house?'

...It said: 'Go and tell him that we shall reveal to him: we shall show him that way'. Then all of them pointed downward, with the same finger (forefinger of right hand) [and pointed at the same spot]. Bolts of lightning leapt from the tips of their fingers, illuminating my body still kneeling down there. I looked and saw my body kneeling there, naked, exuding blood all over as though it were a beaten corpse, dreadful to behold. I saw swarming of maggots in my body.

My spirit went out again and stood before those which came from the congregation; they spoke. Mine returned and said: 'They ask if you see how your body is?' I conceded: 'It is bad'. Then they said, speaking through these spirits: 'If your spirit comes from such a body, it will be unable to meet with us'. ...I said: 'I am not going back into that body'. In the same instant I thought that, my spirit went forth to carry it over.... Forthwith the company pointed down again with their fingers and lightning burst from their fingertips. I felt my spirit moving down from the firmament and returning into my body, and when it arrived there, it entered me from the back.

...In the afternoon of the next day I went out and sat above the homestead, by myself, on a small hill. The voice came to me like a thought, saying: 'Look, come away from women. I wish to speak with you'. I believed in my heart this voice when it spoke. I built a small shelter to the east behind the house of my senior wife, MaShabalala. In that time I felt anxiety toward my wives; I feared them. Even if I seldom went in to them, I would wake up sick at heart, as if I had done wrong. There came the voice again to me, in dream, when I was in my senior wife's house, saying: 'I told you to shun women; I said I would talk to you'. At this stage I told mother that a voice said I should leave women'. Said mother: 'You are insane'.[37]

Shembe was clearly quite shaken by this vision, as likely would anyone be who believed they had a vision of their own putrid corpse. Shembe was convinced that his putridness was due to his impurity from being married and engaging in sex, thereby defying the warnings God had given him many times about being abstinent and pure. Through this vision, Shembe became convinced that his defilement prevented him from communicating with the spirits of the firmament and was an impediment to his calling and divine mission. Shembe believed he was seeing first-hand, in the form of a vision, just how his defilement from sexual indulgence was impeding his spiritual development, inhibiting his ministry, and scuttling his prophetic calling. In the physical world, his connection to his wives, children, and mother tied him to a particular place and obstructed his ability to move about freely, just as the defilement handicapped his spirit in the ethereal realm.

Believing he had little other choice, Shembe gathered his wives, told them they must part ways, and suggested they go back to their relatives. His wives told him he was crazy to listen to the commands of a supernatural voice and shirk his domestic responsibilities and social expectations. Shembe said he would be jealous if they married others while he was still alive, but he understood if they chose to do so. Shembe told those that chose not to remarry that he would feed and clothe them. (In time, two did remarry and two did not.) Late in 1906, Shembe departed and went to the east, toward Pondoland, fully convinced God wanted him to do so. Shembe's decision to become a full-time preacher and healer, then, was entirely driven by the beliefs he had regarding his prophetic experiences.

The course of Shembe's prophetic calling bears commonality to that of other prophets across the globe from an array of religions. He declined his calling for some time, feeling that forsaking his current life would cause too much difficulty for too many people. Although some prophets begin a prophetic ministry the moment they believe they have their first prophetic revelation, being resistant to a prophetic calling is a common theme in the history of prophetic movements.[38] Excessive eagerness on behalf of the prophet might cause some to doubt the prophet's legitimacy or sincerity. Resisting a calling helps the prophet to generate the belief among their community that they are engaged in a holy mission on the community's behalf, not pursuing a ministry of their own design for self-interest. In the end, it was Shembe's genuine belief that these prophetic experiences were real and derived from God that convinced him that his ministerial calling could be resisted no longer.

The course of Shembe's prophetic calling additionally echoes Christian prophecies from other times and places. Conversations with God about one's spiritual and moral purity, visions of heaven and the heavenly host, lightning imagery, a near-death experience, astral travel, and a vision of one's own corpse that will result if one fails to obey, are all common prophetic motifs in Christian history.[39] In using the same Christian tropes, Shembe rendered his own prophecies credible to a Christian audience. Doing so legitimated his prophetic claims, increased the power of his prophetic aura, and connected Shembe's contemporary activity to the Christian past.

After the separation from his family, Shembe left on the ministry he believed God had commanded, heading east toward Pondoland. Somewhere in this stretch of full-time itinerant ministering, Shembe parted ways with Leshega and the African Native Baptist Church over differences of theological opinion regarding interpretations of Levitical laws.[40] In addition to the theological rift that developed between Leshega and Shembe, it is not difficult to imagine that a more self-assured and prophetically imbued Shembe felt he could stand on his own and had no more need of Leshega and his church, though it does not appear Shembe ever articulated his parting in that manner. Following this dual separation, first from his family and secondly from the African Native Baptist Church, Shembe travelled throughout Natal, preaching and healing as he went. A number of member testimonies in the *Acts* tell of the many healing miracles Shembe purportedly performed in these years of traveling ministry from 1906–1910.[41] Shembe made an impact upon people not only through their beliefs in his prophecies and healing, but by preaching too, and gained some converts during his travels. He directed these converts to any local Christian congregation. Shembe said he did not yet know about the divisions of God's people and viewed any congregation as good as another at this time. He never took any money or goods for his healing or preaching efforts, so despite a brief stint as a migrant laborer that ended in 1908, one must assume that he largely lived off the kindness of his converts for food and shelter.

Given the considerably preternatural and prophetic manner in which Shembe explained his biography, one might expect an equally spectacular account of the founding of the Nazareth Baptist Church in 1910. Yet the founding of the church was quite ordinary and unspectacular by comparison. The moment Shembe and church members point to as the founding moment of their church occurred at Botha's Hill (roughly midway between Durban and Pietermaritzburg). Shembe had gained between forty and fifty converts at Botha's Hill and brought them to the local congregation, as had been his habit the last four years. The congregation Shembe and his converts approached was a mission church run by the American Board of Commissioners for Foreign Missions, an American Congregationalist mission body that had arrived in Zululand in 1838. The Congregationalist minister in charge turned the converts away, because those assembled all wore traditional clothing. Following their rejection by the Congregationalist minister, Shembe felt it was his responsibility to care for these converts. He made the decision to cease directing his converts to existing congregations and instead established his own (the name of the church came later). While the exact moment of the church's founding was earthly, the path that brought Shembe to Botha's Hill and the moment of the church's founding, as he explained it and his congregation has remembered it, was one paved by prophecy.

Shembe's Prophetic Aura and Ministry

Shembe's prophetic experiences are unquestionably at the heart of his biography. Surely Shembe's life was not one of unceasing prophecies and miracles, yet it would be easy to gain that impression in reading the church's own narratives. This is the case because the prophetic moments were the ones

Shembe and his parishioners considered to be the most important and these were the ones selected, over other ordinary details, for inclusion in the church's historical narrative of their founding prophet. Prophetic accounts about Shembe's early life were the proof to church members that not only was he the correct person to reveal God's salvific plans, but that he was the only one capable of doing so. Such accounts provided the foundation for a prophetic aura, an aura whose power was legitimated by building connections to the Christian past, and continually nourished by additional prophetic accounts that emerged over the course of Shembe's ministry. While Shembe was alive, church oral traditions first generated, and later reinforced, belief in his prophetic might and divinely charged mission, thereby sustaining Shembe's claims about the church's salvific role in advancing the redemption of Africans. Since Shembe's death in 1935, the tales continue to perform the exact same role, only now to underscore the collective historical memory of Shembe's unearthly status and maintain the church's prophetic course.[42] The frequency and credibility of these tales, for members past and present, established a prophetic aura around Shembe that infused the actions of Shembe with legitimacy and his teachings and the worldview they established with believability.[43]

A prophetic aura is the confidence a prophet and his followers have in the prophet's supernatural power and prophetic might, such that a mystique forms around the individual that bolsters their utterances and teachings and elevates their status.[44] For the membership of the Nazareth Baptist Church, Shembe's understanding of God, salvation, sin, the conquest of South Africa by whites...in short, most anything, was informed by the close relationship they believe he had with God, as evidenced by his ability to prophesy. An individual who embraced the theology of the Nazareth Baptist Church believed that Shembe was an appointed prophet of God, who understood God's will as no other human being had in millennia. If one believed this, then all the teachings, instructions, conclusions, and actions of Shembe became enveloped within a prophetic mystique. A Nazareth Baptist Church member who doubted the theological conclusions of Shembe would be entirely undercutting their faith and theological worldview. Without confidence in Shembe, and faith in his role as a prophet implementing God's will for Africans, little would remain of Nazareth Baptist Church theology. Shembe's prophetic ministry and his prophetic aura existed in a symbiotic, mutually amplifying relationship. Shembe's early prophetic record and allusions to Christian history generated a prophetic aura around him, which lent greater legitimacy and believability to his later prophecies, which increased the power of the aura still further... and so on in a reinforcing manner. This was true during Shembe's lifetime, but the memory continues to the present in the recounting of those prophecies and miracles. Recitation, memorization, and preservation of such stories, and they are plentiful, preserved the historical memory of Shembe and reaffirmed his prophetic status even after his death. It is Shembe, the prophet, who shaped and reified the church's worldview, and his prophetic aura that helped bolster both the faith members had in him and the worldview he articulated.

Isaiah Shembe with a group of women dressed in white, 1930s
Used by permission of the Campbell Collections of the University of KwaZulu-Natal

Shembe was not the only religious founder/leader to be ascribed such a prophetic aura by followers, and a prophetic aura can be found among many prophets. Two African examples, one Christian and one Muslim, will suffice to demonstrate the power prophecy can have upon the biography of a religious leader and the power followers ascribe to them. Because of his demonstrated abilities as a prophet, members of Legio Maria believed that Simeo Ondeto, co-founder of Legio Maria, had the power to cure the ill, raise the dead, exorcise evil spirits, and know what was happening in other places. The powers attributed to Ondeto grew greater over time, so great that his followers began to view him as an African messiah, a redeemer sent by God for Africans.[45] Ondeto's prophet-cum-messiah role generated a prophetic aura that could be described as divine. Even his terrestrial parentage and upbringing were recast into the tale that he was not born but simply "found."[46] In a second example, the prophetic aura of Amadu Bamba, founder of the

Muridiyya Sufi brotherhood (*tariqa*) of Senegambia, has likewise grown stronger over time. Persecution by the French colonial authorities, including two periods of exile, and the recording of his own litany (*wird*) received by prophesy, defined Bamba's initial mystique.[47] Bamba claimed that his miracles were the verses he wrote, and he called himself the servant of the one who is sent by God. Since creation of the brotherhood, however, the prophetic aura of Bamba has been multiplied by his followers, bestowing Bamba with a prophetic aura of personal charisma, virtue, and supernatural ability greater than that he claimed in life himself.[48] In short, a prophetic aura is common to the biographies and memories of prophetic leaders.

The cases of Ondeto and Bamba, like Shembe, indicate that the auras of prophets often multiply over time, growing greater with each prophecy and miracle. The histories of each of these prophets also demonstrates how easily the power of these auras can be preserved in memories that continue to the present, even growing greater as followers continue to ascribe greater power to the founder as generations of worshipers accumulate. The memory of Ondeto's birth gradually shifted with time, taking on divine dimensions, for instance, just as the life of Shembe's mother and his conception had been retroactively recast to add a greater level of prophetic mystique.[49] In addition to demonstrating the power prophetic auras may have, the examples of these three prophetic leaders additionally illustrate the uses of history as a legitimating device. Shembe, Ondeto, and Bamba all established connections to the histories of the respective religions of which they were part, be it Christianity or Islam, to legitimate their movements. Ondeto's performance of healings, exorcisms, and resurrections recreated the biblical past, both Old and New Testaments, in the present. In the case of Bamba, creation of his own litany placed him solidly within Islamic, particularly Sufi, expectations of a charismatic individual worthy of founding a brotherhood. Again, building these historical connections demonstrated that while the prophecies and teachings of these leaders had novel aspects, they were not ruptures from Christianity or Islam, but rather extensions of that past into the present.

In moving my analysis back to Shembe, what follows is a thematic analysis of elements of prophecy from across the time of Shembe's ministry that amplified his prophetic aura, thereby making his explanations of the church's theology and overall worldview more readily credible and believable to members as his ministry transpired. The most direct evidence, quite obviously, for the belief of church members in the prophetic might of Shembe is Shembe's prophetic record itself. Some of Shembe's prophecies were experienced in private, like those he had received as a young adult telling him to forsake his family and take up a ministerial calling. He reported these experiences to his family shortly after they happened, but the prophetic events themselves were not witnessed. The difficulty his wives and mother had in accepting his decision to depart demonstrates the challenge many prophets initially have in convincing others of the validity of their prophetic experiences. But as Shembe's prophetic record grew, two things enhanced the believability of the prophetic experiences he recounted.

The first element was the growing frequency of the prophecies Shembe claimed to have experienced from 1906 onward, the year he left his family and became a full time minister. As the frequency of his prophecies increased and the number of his followers grew, an increasing number of his prophetic experiences became public ones. For instance, the hymns that would one day come to compose the Nazareth Baptist Church's hymnal, *Izihlabelelo zaManazeretha*, were recited by Shembe following prophecies that all bore public witnesses.[50] Shembe described how the words and melody of a hymn would simply "come to" him in a dream or waking vision, as he heard a voice singing the hymn. He would then recite the hymn to his literate followers who would record it in writing.[51] Sometimes the witnesses themselves claimed that they too saw or heard something supernatural. Yet whether or not a witness claimed to have experienced a portion of the prophecy themselves, the witnesses collectively believed that Shembe was indeed a prophetic vessel, and that they were witnessing his reception of a supernatural communication. As Shembe's descriptions of his prophetic experiences accumulated, and the number of witnesses likewise grew, his prophetic aura grew proportionally as belief in each prophetic experience helped engender belief in, and expectation for, the next.[52]

In addition to the growing number of prophecies Shembe claimed to be receiving, a second set of elements that increased the power of Shembe's prophetic aura derived from Shembe's ministry. The healings, miracles, and predictions the church's membership believed Shembe performed all generated a mystique around Shembe that lent greater credibility to his actions and the prophecies he recounted. As tales of these incidents circulated among the membership, they reinforced the prophetic aura of Shembe, thereby granting legitimacy to his teachings and actions during his lifetime, and bolstering the memory of his prophetic status after his death.

The *Acts* are brimming with accounts of miraculous healings performed by Shembe at all points in his ministry. The sheer volume of healing testimonies alone is an indication that Shembe's healing abilities were a key part of members' faith in him and his prophethood. Shembe became such a famous healer in the region that a few scholars have insisted that healing was the principle, if not sole, reason for Shembe's appeal.[53] Healing was certainly important to many early converts, but religious conversion is much too complex to be attributed to a single factor.[54] A few examples on snake bites will suffice to illustrate that the healing power of Shembe was a significant, though not solitary, factor in his early appeal.[55] But more important than the number of converts that healing tales may or may not have attracted, healing narratives kindled belief in Shembe's preternatural powers and amplified his prophetic aura.

The Acts possesses several traditions that involve Shembe healing snake bites at various times stretching from the early 1910s to the mid-1930s. In one such story a young girl was bitten by a puff adder and was brought before Shembe. He sucked blood from her leg and spat it out. According to this story, the girl was perfectly well again and walked away of her own accord. In a second testimony, a girl was bitten by a mamba. Shembe rose and shouted "You mamba! I do not call all of you; I call only the one who [hit] this girl." The narrator of this testimony insisted that Shembe called three more times, and the snake came. Shembe said, "Why did you hit that big girl? Die now, because you hit that girl." According to this testimony, the snake perished and was thrown away.[56] In a third account, describing one of the festivals atop Mt. Nhlangakazi, Shembe prayed that no Nazaretha Christian would die from a snake bite. In his prayer, he requested that if one of the members was bitten by a snake, the poison would turn around and kill the snake instead. Several testimonies in the Acts are from individuals who swear they were saved because of the supernatural protection Shembe gained from God through this prayer. They attest that they were bitten by a poisonous snake and suffered no ill effects. When they went back to the area where they had been bitten, there lay a dead snake.[57] When it came to snake bites, not only was Shembe considered a great healer, but his supernatural power was so great it could heal people from such bites even when he was not around, because these members believed he had implored God to make it so.

As this sample of tales regarding snake bite healings demonstrates, Shembe's healing miracles were certainly a source of discussion among members, entered in the church's historical record, and unquestionably helped to amplify faith in Shembe and his supernatural powers. However, I would aver that Shembe's ability to heal should be properly contextualized within the broader confidence members had in him as a prophetic leader. Members believed he could heal them because he was a prophet; they did not consider him to be a prophet because he could heal. In other words, the beliefs members (and potential ones) had in his miraculous abilities to heal stemmed from their confidence in his prophetic power, not the other way around. Shembe claimed to have had prophetic experiences long before he was a healer; he was not a healer before he was a prophet. In this manner, testimonies about Shembe's healing miracles contributed to his prophetic mystique and supernatural status, but they were not the source of it. Shembe's supposed healing abilities were but one feature in his emerging reputation that had prophecy at its center. Church lore contains comparable testimonies regarding various non-healing miracles and predictions that members ascribe to Shembe.[58]

For Shembe and the members of the Nazareth Baptist Church, Shembe's calling and ministry were no mere occupational choice or conversion experience. Rather, his prophetic experiences and the miracles he performed due to his prophetic status, gave Shembe the firm conviction that he was a prophet charged with implementing God's plan of salvation for colonial Africa. His subsequent actions reflected his own confidence in his prophetic ability and supernatural power.[59] This same confidence occurred among the membership as well, who embraced a biography of Shembe and a history of his early ministry as one laced with supramundane and prophetic events. The remembering, retelling, and recording of these events multiplied the prophetic aura of Shembe, and members' faith in him and the worldview he articulated about their place in colonial Africa. In this manner, Shembe's ministry and his prophetic aura were mutually reinforcing, with each prophecy lending strength to his prophetic aura, and his aura granting legitimacy and believability to his prophecies.

Conclusion

Despite the thoroughly supernatural history of the Nazareth Baptist Church told by Shembe and his congregants, I am clearly not implying that we, as non-members, should believe the prophecies and miracles ourselves. For my own analysis, whether or not we, as non-members in the contemporary world, choose to interpret these events as facts or fairytales is without consequence. What is significant for this study is that this is how Shembe and the members of the Nazareth Baptist Church conceived of Shembe and their congregation's origins. We do need to assume that the leaders and members believed these supernatural events to be true and were acting based upon this faith and confidence in the prophetic abilities of Shembe.[60] To push these explanations aside and instead suggest that I, the scholar, have detected the "real" political, economic, or social resistance within the members' behavior, hidden beneath a religious façade, is to resort to a hermeneutics of suspicion.[61] Such specious logic presumes that historical subjects do not behave with conscious intent and out of genuine personal desires, but were instead just acting religious to disguise their "true" materialist wishes.[62] I find this line of thinking to be an insult to the intelligence and religious sincerity of one's subjects.[63] The founder and members of the Nazareth Baptist Church explained their own history within a prophetically defined worldview, and it is this worldview that needs analysis, synthesis, and explication to understand the church from an emic point of view, not supplanting with academic theories about heroic resistors that support notions of how we think black historical actors should have behaved under colonial and white supremacist conditions.

Portions of these testimonies made purposeful allusions to biblical and Christian history in order to legitimate Shembe and his prophecies through connection to this ancient past.[64] Astral travel, visions of the heavenly host, hearing warnings from God to live righteously, prophetic instructions on how to please God, and near-death experiences all have plenty of parallel in Christian history, but none in Zulu indigenous religion. Some of the elements in the prophecies, it is true, cannot be explained through a Christian paradigm. The heart in the sky, the parable of the peach tree, or the red figure with a spear, for instance, are not explicitly Christian, but neither are they specifically Zulu. Only infrequently, such as the high level of narrative detail given to Kolberi the cow, or in the prophetic warnings to avoid *ukuhlobonga*, do these narratives employ aspects of Zulu culture exclusively. The Zulu "essence" of the church's narratives has been exaggerated by previous scholarship in order to underscore the overall "Zuluness" of Shembe and the church and detract from its "Christianness."

Shembe's early life, calling, and ministry were unquestionably prophetic and Christian, were thought of in that way by himself and church members while he was alive, and have been remembered as such within the testimonies of church members following his death. From the stories explaining his conception, to the aural warnings to be celibate, to the vision of his own rotting corpse, prophecy is the *uhlanga*, the source, for Shembe's biography and the early history of the Nazareth Baptist Church, both as he told it and as the church's membership has remembered and preserved it. This prophetic paradigm imparted a sense of mystery and authority to Shembe that generated a prophetic aura about him, thereby granting legitimacy and believability to his teachings and instructions.

A Prophetic Worldview amid Empire: The History of the Nazareth Baptist Church, 1910–1935

I do what I do merely because I am inspired to do so, as you say, it is given to me by revelation.
    —Isaiah Shembe, Interview with Native Economic Commission, Apr. 1931.

An undated oral tradition in the *Acts of the Nazarites* (hereafter *Acts*) describes an encounter between Isaiah Shembe and a white police officer. The policeman summoned Shembe from a church member's home where he had spent the night (the location is not revealed in the testimony), asking, "Are you the man who interferes with the work of missionaries by entering the Mission Reserves? Follow me; and nobody shall follow us." They retreated into the forest, and witnesses said they were expecting to hear a shot from the policeman's rifle. But what instead happened after they entered the forest, according to the teller of this testimony, was that God revealed the true nature of Shembe to the white man, who began to tremble as a result. The policeman then confessed he had been instructed to kill Shembe. Shembe replied that he should do as his superiors had told him, to which the white man responded, "I am unable to do so, because you are not an ordinary man; you are of divine character." The testimony continues that they left the forest and returned to the homestead. The policeman asked Shembe to move on, but said he would tell his superiors Shembe had already left by the time he had arrived. And so, on this occasion, by the reckoning of this testimony, Shembe's life was spared, and the police agent's deadly ambitions thwarted, through the intervention of Jehovah.[1]

I have previously demonstrated how Shembe's prophetic biography and the history of the early church, and the connections narrators made to the biblical and Christian past, were mutually reinforcing with his prophetic aura; each prophecy lent strength to his mystique, and that mystique granted legitimacy and believability to his prophecies. Yet Shembe's prophetic aura did more than this. The overall mystique that was generated by Shembe's prophetic record and aura likewise legitimated the overall worldview he advanced. Within this worldview Shembe could explain how everything in the lives of church members—from the presence of whites, to the Zulu past, to Shembe's place in Christian history—fit within Jehovah's grand divine plans. While the entire cosmic vision required God's omniscience and omnipotence to fully view and comprehend, Shembe and his congregants believed God was granting glimpses of his divine plans to Shembe via prophecy. The members of the Nazareth Baptist Church held Shembe in such high regard as a specially chosen prophet of God that this same sense of awe lent legitimacy to the explanations he provided about both the supernatural world and the mundane one—in short, an entire worldview. This worldview guided the way in which Shembe and his congregation understood their place in history and interpreted the world beyond their church, including their interactions with agents of the colonial state.

Testimonies like the one above about the policeman are rare in the church's documentary record. Most of the preserved pieces of church lore are inward-looking and concern themselves with the affairs of Shembe, his church, and its members. More rarely do the church's records divulge information about or even acknowledge the world beyond the boundaries of the church. This fact alone is quite revealing about what mattered to Shembe and his congregants. But more importantly for my purposes in this chapter, when the world beyond the church was addressed within church lore, it was subsumed within the church's own prophetic interpretation of the world. In the above tale, an agent of the state with lethal intent, the blessing of his political superiors, and the tacit support of Western missionaries who lodged the original complaint against Shembe, had his scheme ruined by Jehovah who forced him to see the "truth." Even though the witnesses were remembered as being initially fearful, ultimately church members did not interpret the event as an indication of ruthless oppression by a white supremacist state whose police were out to kill their leader. Rather, for them, the event was additional confirmation of Shembe's distinctiveness and might, such that God prophetically intervened and turned the policeman away, so that Shembe would continue his God-ordained mission to preach the correct path of salvation to Africans.

The commitment and faith Shembe and his congregants had to this worldview was resilient and weathered surveillance by, and even occasional intervention from, agents of the colonial state in the church's early decades. An examination of government records indicates that while Shembe and his church came under immediate suspicion and were surveilled by state officials, by the 1920s Shembe and his congregation were cleared of these accusations and permitted to operate with relative freedom. Yet even when the state did directly intervene in church affairs, as it did three times from 1922-1931,

Shembe and his congregation still interpreted these events prophetically and not politically. While we may be accustomed to thinking of twentieth-century South Africa prior to 1994 as a place of totalizing oppression and persistent resistance, this was not the experience of all segments of the population at all times. Through an analysis of the church's history from ca. 1920–1935, I explore how Shembe and his congregation "maneuvered at the margins." Even a white supremacist state like the Union of South Africa produced uneven experiences among the colonized, producing "wide margins for maneuver and negotiation" for individuals and communities like Shembe and his congregants to largely fulfill their religious concerns without a posture of resistance.[2] The infrequency of state interference made the church's prophetic narrative of history all the more believable and convincing for Shembe and his followers, thereby reinforcing their prophetic worldview of their place in colonial Africa. Yet even where the margins closed and direct intervention, even seemingly oppression, was experienced, the founder and congregants of the Nazareth Baptist Church remained committed to their prophetic worldview.

Accusation and Acquittal: Church-State Relations, ca. 1910–ca. 1920

As one would expect to happen to an autonomous black institution in a colonial white supremacist state, Shembe and the fledgling Nazareth Baptist Church came under almost immediate suspicion by district (principally Inanda and Ndwedwe) and provincial (Natal) authorities.[3] They raised their concerns with their superiors at the national (office of the Secretary for Native Affairs in Pretoria) level. What resulted was a minor national dialogue, involving police and various levels of the Native Affairs Department concerning Shembe and his congregation. Government documents reveal that officials from the district and provincial Native Administration sent police officers and administrators to observe the membership of the Nazareth Baptist Church in response to various accusations lodged by government agents, missionaries, Natal's white inhabitants, disgruntled chiefs, and unhappy African husbands. These accusations involved a variety of concerns: political rebellion, "sheep-stealing," getting Christianity "wrong," immorality, taking women from their homes, charlatanism, and even murder.

Of immediate concern to government officials and the white citizens of Natal was the fear that the Nazareth Baptist Church was merely a front for black nationalism and anti-government activity. This fear was a ubiquitous one whites throughout colonial Africa had of black organizations, religious and otherwise, and the Nazareth Baptist Church did not escape such suspicion in its early years. One can see such a concern within the remarks of citizen G. G.

Kessel, when he wrote to the magistrate at Port Shepstone. Kessel said of Shembe,

> He teaches that the people should not listen to the Missionaries. I have reason to believe him to be a Kushite or Ethiopian in doctrine. Teaching the people to be dissatisfied with the Government.... As a Church we are against Etheopianism [sic] & it would be desired by us to have this man leave the country.... [I] think it good for the Government as well as the Church & people that he be silenced.[4]

Kessel expressed a disdain for Shembe and his church on two levels. Religiously, he noted that established denominations were against independent churches, and it would be of benefit to Christianity that Shembe be stopped. Kessel does not make clear which type of Christianity he defended, but the notion that emergent forms of African Christianity were some sort of challenge to "real" Christianity was a widespread sentiment among many Christians, white and black. Politically, Kessel was convinced that Shembe preached discontent with the government. This too was a pervasive belief about independent black church leaders among many whites from across colonial Africa.

The fear that an independent black church was being used as a venue to foment political discord, though grossly exaggerated within the imaginations of many whites, was also not entirely unfounded. Though few, there were some Ethiopian and Zionist churches in various parts of colonial Africa that had been informed by black nationalism and possessed anti-colonial sentiments. This fear was compounded in South Africa in the early 1920s as a result of the tragedy of the Israelites. The Church of God and Saints of Christ (also called the Israelites) was a Zionist church near Queenstown in the eastern Cape, led by Enoch Mgijima. Mgijima preached that judgment was near and predicted a future cataclysmic racial war that only his followers would escape. At Passover of 1920, they held a celebration on Bulhoeks Common, near Queenstown, and then encamped there to await the judgment day they believed was imminent. The Israelites defied all ultimatums issued from the government to vacate the Crown land they were camped on. After a year the South African government sent a large police force to remove them forcibly. The police opened fire with rifles and machine guns, killing 163 Israelites and wounding 129. For decades to come, a fear continued among whites in South Africa that another anti-government showdown and Bulhoek Massacre might result from the continued growth of independent African churches.[5] The fear that the Nazareth Baptist Church might become a similar organization of government defiance and human tragedy was real to many of the inhabitants of Natal and to agents within the native authority.

While such fears were real for many South African whites, and had been nourished by what happened at Bulhoek, there were also some government officials, both police and administrators, white and black, who stated that suspicions of the Nazareth Baptist Church's political activities were based on conjecture, rumor, and envy. The magistrate of Inanda (the district Ekuphakameni was in) wrote, "There appears to be nothing which would justify a conclusion that Tshembe's activities are of a political nature."[6] A white police officer who observed some church services reported that "nothing was preached against the Government."[7] In reference to the 1922 pilgrimage and ritual atop Mount Nhlangakazi, a black policeman wrote, "I kept a close watch upon all that went on at Nhlangakazi but could see nothing wrong."[8] In sum, while some citizens portrayed the Nazareth Baptist Church as a front for anti-government activity, no evidence was ever found (by white or black government agents) to suggest this was the case. The police surveilled gatherings of the early Nazareth Baptist Church, but quickly concluded that it posed no political threat. The fear of the next Israelite movement developing within African churches was greater than the potential, and the majority of Ethiopian and Zionist institutions were just what they claimed to be: independent black churches.

A significant concern expressed by both state and church leaders was that Shembe and the Nazareth Baptist Church operated without European supervision.[9] This, of course, was closely tied to the above fear that the church was a political organization. But it additionally stemmed from two religious concerns. The first worry was that of "sheep-stealing," that is, that Shembe was taking converts away from Protestant churches. It is indeed true that most of Shembe's early converts were previous members of Protestant churches.[10] Shembe himself did not try to deny this and stated in a 1923 interview, "I am afraid many of my followers come from other denominations, consequently those who are left, feel bitter against me, and imagine that I do not follow the Christian faith; but I do."[11] The second related concern was that Shembe and his congregation had Christianity "wrong" and were essentially de-converting individuals away from Christianity. The archived remarks of a white police sergeant and a black minister reveal this concern. In 1921, a sergeant with the South African police wrote to his district officer that "[t]here is no doubt that real Christianity is unknown in these denominations [in reference to the Nazareth Baptist Church and the Zion Apostolic Faith Mission]...of these so-called Christians."[12] A minister with the Norwegian Lutheran mission, Petros Majosi ka Silomo, made the following statement, "They are preaching a doctrine which is in conflict with our teachings...[T]hey tell people that we do not baptize Natives in accordance with the teachings of Christ."[13]

Both this white police sergeant and black minister expressed concern that Shembe's Christianity was in error. Independent black ministers operating without "supervision" was a broad anxiety throughout colonial Africa. For many whites in colonial Africa, including this police sergeant, a black minister that did not have to answer to white ones was fertile ground for revivalist teachings, a bridge back to tradition and "heathenry" that could potentially pull individuals toward black nationalist sentiments, political agitation, and even violence. For ministers, black and white, independent black ministers were a dual danger. They could undermine the mission's reputation and provide an alternative, and potentially more attractive to Africans, site for Christianity. But they could also "ruin" what efforts the Protestant and Catholic churches had made by spreading their "erroneous" notions of Christianity and leading the population down the wrong path. Such a concern clearly stems from a mission's efforts to protect their own interests and what they believed to be "proper" Christianity. For the leaders and members of Zionist institutions, they believed their churches provided a "superior" version of Christianity. Regardless of such theological judgments about what does or does not constitute "true" Christianity, the concern of a lack of supervision helped to fuel political fears of Shembe and his congregation. Such fears prompted state officials to conduct surveillance, but stopped short of interference and oppressive edicts.

Aside from these political and religious accusations, there were also ethical ones leveled against Shembe. Like many new religions, the Nazareth Baptist Church was accused of being a cult (not a "true" religion) and its leader an egomaniac out solely for fame, sex, and money. The magistrate of Nkandhla wrote, "I think there is little doubt but that there is very little religion and a great deal of immorality."[14] Sgt. Craddock wrote in 1921 that "both sexes sleep on the veld and Shembe selects a female, other of his male followers do likewise, and should the slightest resistance take place, the female is regarded as not being a faithful follower."[15] A year later he wrote that, "Shembe does not sleep in the men's compartment during the night, but with 3 girls on either side. He will inform a girl that she has been 'chosen' and that the Lord will visit her during the night and she must not be afraid." Craddock concluded that "local raw natives look upon Shembe's Woman Converts as prostitutes and nothing else."[16]

Charges of sexual misconduct are often made against leaders of new religions. However, often it is the interpretation of the leader's conduct that is at stake between a religious group and political authorities. To take a well-documented modern American example, Wayne Bent (known as Michael Travesser within the church) of The Lord Our Righteousness Church did not deny that he had lain "naked with virgins" or touched a naked teenage girl who needed to "unburden her heart" during counseling.[17] On this count the teenagers involved, Bent, and the state's district attorney prosecuting the 2008 case against Bent of criminal sexual contact and contributing to the delinquency of a minor, all agreed.[18] Yet while the state viewed the events as morally corrupt and criminal, Bent was convinced his actions were either directed by a higher authority, God, in the first instance, or within accepted bounds of alternative healing with the second. Though teenagers had asked him for sex, Bent maintained that he always declined, and therefore no laws had been broken. The prosecutor and jury disagreed with the understanding of Bent and his supporters at Strong City and found him guilty of one count of criminal sexual contact and two counts of contributing to the delinquency of a minor.[19]

Though an ocean, and a century, apart, the case of Wayne Bent and The Lord Our Righteousness Church has comparative value for Shembe and the Nazareth Baptist Church. That Bent had "lain with virgins" and touched the chest of a naked teenager during counseling was something well known to the fifty-some-member community at Strong City. The events would have been difficult to obfuscate, and ultimately Bent and his defense attorney did not deny them, but instead insisted that the instances were not sexual, and therefore not illegal. So in the case of Bent and The Lord Our Righteousness Church, there was a basic set of facts that all agreed upon, with differing understandings between the church and the state. In the case of Shembe and the Nazareth Baptist Church, the charges of sexual misconduct do not appear to have ever been more than conjectures. As anyone who has ever witnessed a Nazareth Baptist Church service or celebration knows, the church, at all points in history, has gone to great lengths to separate adherents by age and gender. Shembe and church adherents believed that the purity of young women was one of the virtues that maintained the well-being of the community.[20] No direct observations of the congregation by state agents substantiated the claims of the magistrate at Nkandhla or Sgt. Craddock. In sum, unlike the case of Bent, there was no set of agreed-upon facts that acquired different rhetorical spins. There were only accusations without any evidence.

Other contemporary observers of Shembe, in fact, suggested that the unethical behavior was coming from Shembe's accusers for spreading unsubstantiated rumors and accusations. A contemporary of Craddock, Chief Native Commissioner of Natal C. A. Wheelwright, dismissed Craddock's allegations as based on mere hearsay or conjecture and not reliable.[21] A Native Constable, Dhlamvuza Dhlamini, reported his own observations in 1923 saying, "Tshembe pitched a tent, and made the women and girls sleep on one side, and the men on the other...The whole following was well behaved during the whole time...The morals appeared to be good and Tshembe himself took particular trouble to keep the sexes apart."[22] Lastly, reporter Nellie Wells wrote in 1929 that "in no other religious community have we found the value of a woman's virtue reverenced or cultivated as under Shembe's domination."[23]

So, either Shembe was sexually exploiting his congregation's young women, but he disguised it so skillfully that it escaped the notice of observers, no witnesses ever came forward, no legal cases were filed or investigated, and all his congregants kept the secret. Or, and this seems the much more likely scenario, Shembe had several accusers who did their best to discredit him, and he and the male members of his congregation were not sexually exploiting young women. One must also remember that Shembe claimed to have had several powerful prophetic experiences related to God's insistence that he be abstinent. Therefore, in Shembe's mind, sexual misconduct would only bring the wrath of God. He had been prophetically warned about sexual impurity on many occasions and believed he was struck by lightning for his sexual defiance. In short, accusations of sexual misdoings by Shembe or his adherents seem unfounded as verified by some direct observations preserved in archival documents, the absence of witnesses and court cases accusing Shembe of such, the church's long-standing concern with gender segregation and the purity of young women, and Shembe's prophetic confidence that God nearly killed him for his sexual defiance earlier in life.

The charges of sexual misconduct were interconnected with gender concerns. In 1915 the magistrate at Port Shepstone wrote of the "mischievous propensities" of the church and referred to Shembe as a "scurrilous fanatic"; the magistrate's primary evidence for such "depraved activities" was based on the perception that fathers and husbands were losing control over their wives and daughters.[24] This charge was also echoed by some chiefs. Chief Mlokotwa and Chief Jiyana made separate statements that Shembe and his congregation were demoralizing the women of their wards.[25] In another statement, Setshebe Mbhele ka Ndadano said he was being evicted from the Denver Zear farm because his wife was no longer attending the mission church, but was instead attending services of the Nazareth Baptist Church, and doing all of Shembe's mending and washing.[26] In this way, the charges of sexual misconduct against Shembe can be seen as a contestation of gender politics and the renegotiation of social and gender roles in early twentieth-century Natal. The predominance of women in the early history of the church was not well received by many husbands and fathers who were interested in controlling the labor and mobility of women. Religious choice, and the social impact that came with it, was not a decision many African men were yet willing to accord to women.

Even mysterious deaths were attributed to Shembe and his church. Craddock, in a report to the police district commandant in Durban, wrote that "Strange deaths have taken place at the camps from time to time."[27] Craddock did not explain the number or circumstances of these deaths, but it is unlikely he was lying about it. Once Shembe had developed a regional reputation as a great healer, many people came to him, often with incurable conditions and deadly ailments that traditional or Western healing methods had failed to address. The *Acts* is filled with tales of healing by all of the church's central leaders. Given the number of gravely sick, even dying, people who came to see Shembe, it is hardly a surprise that some died coming to, at, or departing from, church gatherings. Craddock mentions only one case involving a deceased Indian man whose wife could not obtain a death certificate because her husband had already been buried by the time she arrived herself. Given that Craddock was otherwise a bit cryptic about the strange deaths, perhaps he only knew of one but was attempting to use this single case to convince his superiors of the public danger Shembe posed. But a few deaths from the chronically ill does not seem so strange, ultimately. Any place the gravely ill gather certainly has the potential to be a site of death.

Among the individuals who attempted to discredit Shembe and his congregation with the police and native authorities, Craddock's efforts were assuredly the most sustained. It appears it was his serious and quite numerous accusations of un-Christian teachings, sexual exploitation, and mysterious deaths that were the catalyst for a reexamination of Shembe and the congregation of the Nazareth Baptist Church in the early 1920s. In response to the dire allegations made by Craddock, district magistrate McKenzie sent an indigenous police agent to observe the church. That agent, Native Constable Zulu, reported nothing political or immoral in the January festival atop Mt. Nhlangakazi in 1922, suggesting Craddock's claims about the 1921 annual festival were exaggerations, perhaps even purposeful misrepresentations. Zulu's 1922 report prompted McKenzie to write to the native commissioner for all of Natal, Wheelwright, dismissing Craddock's claims and advising that suppression of the movement would be unwise.[28] Craddock's second letter of 1922 expressing the same "grave" concerns now began to seem a bit hollow and raised some question about his credibility.[29] Commissioner Wheelwright wrote to the secretary for Native Affairs in Pretoria, in 1922, informing the national office that Craddock's claims were based on conjecture and hearsay, and "that the great difficulty has been to obtain a hold of concrete facts." Given the lack of evidence against Shembe and his congregants, Wheelwright felt that permission should be granted to the Nazareth Baptist Church to continue their pilgrimage to Nhlangakazi, and instructed the magistrate of Ndwedwe (the district Mt. Nhlangakazi was in) to inform Shembe that the pilgrimage would be allowed after a petition for permission had been submitted.[30]

The reports of political subversion, corrupt Christianity, immorality, and the like, proved not to be of interest to Natal's top official for native affairs, C. A. Wheelwright. The accusations lodged over the course of the 1910s and into the early 1920s proved groundless in his mind, based upon the report of his own observer, and the fact that his office had not received "complaint from parents or guardians." So by the early 1920s, the lack of formal complaints and factual evidence had proven the earlier accusations as efforts to discredit Shembe and his membership. No political conspiracies or wrongdoing could be located, and the church appeared to be exactly what it claimed: a prophetic Christian church. From the early 1920s onward, Shembe and the Nazareth Baptist Church were allowed to operate with a relative religious freedom. Surely Shembe and his congregation were never in a position to operate in total freedom, yet neither was the church harassed or purposefully under-mined by state officials. The surveillance of the church by police and officials tapered off and a general lack of concern replaced it. This relative laissez faire attitude to the Nazareth Baptist Church which had developed within the Native Affairs Department allowed Shembe and his congregants to develop and administer their church without being forced into a posture of resistance.

Shembe was aware of many of the accusations leveled against him and his church, not least because government agents asked him to respond to some of them. In a 1923 interview in the magistrate's office at Ndwedwe, with Magistrate Charles McKenzie, two other government officials, and six local chiefs assembled, Shembe addressed the charges of fraud and personal aggran-dizement by stating, "I never ask for money...[M]y followers would lose faith in me." He spoke to the concern with immorality by asserting that, "It is untrue the sexes sleep together. The morals of my followers are I think better than in other places."[31] As I illustrated above, some government observers supported Shembe's assertions on these matters in their own reports. McKenzie even noted in the interview transcript that the story Shembe told of his life coincid-ed with that reported by the assistant chief native commissioner.[32]

Yet it was politics and the fear of the Israelites, not charlatanism or immo-rality, that dominated government concerns in the early years of the Nazareth Baptist Church. Given the number of times Shembe addressed the issue of politics in interviews and sermons, it seems he had an awareness of the gravity of the government's political concern with black churches. We cannot know of the degree to which Shembe developed this cognizance himself or whether it was produced by questioning from government agents, but it seems logical that both sources were informing Shembe's awareness of Natal's political climate. On the one hand, Shembe was being asked pointed questions about his political position by government agents in a clear demonstration of the government's concern. Yet on the other hand, it does not take great levels of acumen and insight to imagine that a white supremacist state might be concerned about independent black organizations. Shembe was assuredly an intelligent enough man for us to safely assume he had the requisite wisdom to appreciate the delicate political position of himself and his new church. Leav-ing no room for doubt about the government's ultimate concern with black churches, McKenzie, in the 1923 interview, explained to Shembe what happened to the Israelites at Bulhoek two years earlier. McKenzie stated that he did not feel that Shembe's organization was similar because "it is shown you are submissive to the Laws and I feel you will continue to do so" yet he was also concerned because Shembe was in "much the same position as the leader of the Israelites." McKenzie made clear he was not trying to suggest that Shembe was "in any way working against the Authorities," but telling the story of the Israelites was clearly an invitation to Shembe to respond and offer his political views.

Shembe gladly did so, placing his political views within Christian (by citing biblical obedience to civil authorities) and prophetic (by explaining how God had revealed the purpose behind the presence of whites in South Africa) paradigms. He also made clear that he did not possess a revolutionary political agenda or even a subversive theology. Shembe replied to McKenzie, "God has given me certain work to do amongst my people. I therefore realize that God has also placed the Authorities over us, and those who disregard or defy the Government, disregard the Will of God." He additionally explained that the presence of whites in South Africa was a material and spiritual gift from God. God saw that blacks were naked and blind, so, "He sent Europeans amongst us, and now we are clothed and can see." To combat whites, therefore, would be an offense to God, suggesting one did not appreciate these gifts. Shembe additionally cited the Bible during the interview to support his church's obedience to the state. Shembe noted Romans 13:1-6 to McKenzie as evidence that God wants his people to obey those placed over them, including submission to the law and willing payment of taxes.[33]

Were the political sentiments Shembe shared with McKenzie and the others assembled at Ndwedwe in 1923 a crafted response that offered up what Shembe thought the government agents and the chiefs wanted to hear? In other words, was he cunningly "playing politics," and becoming the agreeable and subordinate black church leader he thought whites and traditional authorities wanted him to be? I contend that no, Shembe was not performing from a "public" or "hidden" transcript of resistance by playing the role of a compliant and submissive black minister.[34] Rather, Shembe was revealing his genuine political convictions, convictions that were neither resistant nor acquiescent.

On the question of resistance, we must remember that the postures of the dominant and subordinate can come in a variety of forms and guises, manifested across a range of strengths, degrees, coverages, and shifting self-interests. It would be a gross generalization to presume that every individual in some sort of subordinate role was mired in a constant feeling of hegemonic oppression, and was therefore on a constant quest to find means to resist by any and all methods, public and hidden.[35] The quest for the universal and perennial resistor says much more about nationalist and postcolonial scholarly fashion than it does historical actors. Not all historical actors living within every colonial state at all times and all places felt they were oppressed and therefore had to resist. Black church leaders who did possess a black nationalist or politically resistant posture, like John Chilembwe, Enoch Mgijima, or Simon Mpadi, either found it difficult to conceal or had no interest in doing so.[36] Shembe, on the other hand, never once expressed his views of the world, publicly or privately, through a lens of hegemonic oppression and the need for resistance. So either Shembe was a resistor, but no trace of it reached the documentary record of the state or the church, and no hint of it has ever been turned up through the collection of oral data over the decades. Or, and this appears to be far more likely, Shembe was not a resistor and the documentary trail we have of his thoughts, both from government (public transcripts) and church sources (both public and hidden transcripts), is a genuine reflection of his political ideology.

As evidence of this, I point to the fact that Shembe provided the same insistence upon obedience to political authorities as good Christian behavior befitting God's prophetic plans in his preaching and correspondence when government officials were not about, and when he no longer had a reason to presume he was being monitored. Consider a dictated missive to Chief Mambuka Mthiyane of 4 December 1932 in which Shembe reiterated important teachings he had shared with the chief in person the day before. He firstly told the chief to obey and fear the laws of Jehovah. He then proceeded to remind the chief that, "You must not go behind the back of the government in the Law." The chief should "drive the tribe that you rule before you (Colossians 3:22; 1 Timothy 6)" insuring that they respect the government and pay their taxes, "because for the time being the Whites have been instructed that they should rule us."[37] In an undated statement titled "The Command-ments of Shembe, Servant of Suffering" (it is unclear whether the remarks were originally a sermon, public guidance to a congregation, or a letter), Shembe preached similar remarks as those he included in the letter to Chief Mthiyane. Amid instructions about the proper behavior of ministers and the care of widows and orphans, this statement includes remarks about obedience to the political authorities saying, "Love your kings not on your faces but in your hearts. If they tell you to pay your taxes...you should give whatever they request. And when the request becomes too burdensome, kneel before them and humbly say: 'Our lords, we deserve this yoke of taxpaying.'"[38]

While the provenance of "The Commandments of Shembe" is unclear, the nature of the letter to Chief Mthiyane is evident. These instructions to this chief, both oral and written, were not made in the presence of government agents, or any white citizens of Natal. Shembe was not under such careful sur-veillance when he dictated the letter in 1932 that he had any reason to assume his letters were being intercepted. Nor do government documents provide any indication that such a thorough level of surveillance was ever considered for Shembe, let alone executed. If Shembe had been concerned that his actions were being watched so carefully, he easily could have made the remarks to the chief orally alone, and not provided opportunity for his missives to be subject to inspection. The fact that Shembe placed what could have remained oral in writing, suggests he felt free to correspond with his flock without worry of interference. A hounded individual is generally not one who is inclined to produce a paper trail for fear that anything might be misconstrued or used against them. There is, then, solid reason to assume that Shembe produced this document with the assumption that the information would stay within the church. This, therefore, means it is a genuine window into Shembe's thoughts and not a recorded "hidden" transcript of resistance written in code to avoid detection or craftily play politics as a submissive black man.

One can conclude, then, that Shembe's statements, whether public or private, can be taken at a relative face value and reveal his honest thoughts about the state and why he believed God wanted him and his followers to be obedient. Shembe's political comments were always grounded in his prophetic worldview and how they fit with Jehovah's cosmic plans. Shembe taught respect to the authorities because he sincerely believed that is what God wanted of his new chosen people as a means of exacting penance for their ancestral sins and ultimately actualizing their salvations. Reading the remarks as covert resistance would do a disservice to Shembe and his congregation who did not see a need for such coded behavior or have a political position that even needed a disguise.

Yet the political views Shembe articulated in interviews, his preaching, and his missives, were not an expression of acquiescence either, for two reasons. First, the very notion of acquiescence connotes nationalist assumptions about what Shembe "should" have done to support the "struggle." In this view of South African history, the only response to hegemonic white oppression was to be part of a united non-white, political response. By this notion, that which did not manifest as resistance and clearly advance the undermining of the white state was therefore the antithesis, or apolitical acquiescence.[39] However, those two positions, resistance or acquiescence, do not exhaust the options available to the colonized (or subordinate of any kind).[40] It was perfectly possible to operate within the many possibilities between these archetypal behaviors, as well as alternate between political positions. Moreover, an emphasis upon resistance or acquiescence also presumes a political determinism, as though politics and the colonial state was the most dominant feature of life for everyone in a colonial situation.

Second, viewing the leader of the Nazareth Baptist Church as politically acquiescent also misses the prophetic dimension, that which was most central to Shembe's thoughts and actions. Given Shembe's intense conviction that he was a prophetically appointed servant of God, Shembe's political perspective should be seen as his expression of faith in the cosmic plans he believed God had revealed via prophecy. Shembe was assuredly not ignorant of the political context of early twentieth-century Natal and South Africa; he and his congregants lived in it after all.[41] However, the most important thing in Shembe's life was living in accordance with what he thought was God's will as he had been prophetically commanded. If Shembe's prophetic revelations had told him to resist all authorities, there is a very good chance that is what he would have done, as have other prophets and their communities, like Mgijima and the Israelites. But his prophetic guidance had informed him that white control of South Africa was part of God's cosmic plans. Whites brought the gospel to South Africa, thereby introducing Christianity to Shembe, and ultimately providing for Africa's salvation as Shembe spread his prophetic messages. While whites were not as critical an element in this plan for Africa's salvation as Shembe was, they were, nonetheless, a necessary ingredient. Fighting them meant fighting against God's salvific designs. With this prophetically revealed knowledge in mind, political obedience was what Shembe preached in recognition that obedience to the authorities appointed by the ultimate authority, Jehovah, was required to support the unfolding of God's plans for Africans. Shembe and his church advanced a prophetic and theological response to the conditions of colonial South Africa. Empire was not determining their fate, as they saw it; God was.

View of Ekuphakameni, undated
Used by permission of the Campbell Collections of the University of KwaZulu-Natal

Not only were whites responsible for bringing the gospel to South Africa, as Shembe believed he had been prophetically informed, they were also the agents that would bring about the atonement of Africans. For instance, in "Shembe's Prayer in Remembrance of His Nation" Shembe referred to the curses of the Zulu kings Shaka, Dingane, Mpande, and Cetshwayo that continued to plague the Zulu nation. But with the arrival of Shembe, the redeemer the church's membership believed had been promised by prophecy, the Zulu could now embrace true and accurate worship of Jehovah. While the stain of ancestral sins still marred the Zulu, they now had the means of removing that stain. This prayer concludes with Shembe reporting a prophecy he received one day, while mourning for the nation, where he thought he heard thunder. However, it was not ordinary thunder, as the voice of God informed him, but the thunderous sound of the footsteps of the kings entering Ekuphakameni, a clear sign via prophecy that the atonement of ancestral sins had begun.[42] In another prayer titled "A Prayer for the Day of Dingane," Shembe notes the ways in which Zulus suffered at the hands of white Afrikaners on that day of battle, but notes that it was all part of the plan of Jehovah to atone for the sins of the Zulu nation.[43] Such sentiments are mirrored in hymn 67 of the church's hymnal that refers to God's chastisement because of the sins of their fathers, and names the Zulu paramounts Dingane, Senzangakhena, Shaka, Mpande, Cetshwayo, and Dinizulu.[44]

Such a dispensation is not reserved for the Zulu, however, even if the sins of the Zulu nation were greater because of the conquests of the Shakan era. Hymn 116 calls on the contemporary king of the Zulu, King Solomon (who married one of Shembe's daughters, Zondi, in 1926) to honor Jehovah at Ekuphakameni. This hymn proceeds to call on the Baca and Pondo, and later all nations, to the proper worship of Jehovah.[45] While the Zulu have more to atone for than others, Shembe's prophetic message was for all of God's "brown people," and one day all of humanity.

The evidence could go on, as references to the sins of the ancestors and the need to embrace proper worship of God are peppered throughout many of Shembe's compositions. Suffice it to say that atonement was a key concept for Shembe that provided a foundation for his political position, and he believed he had been prophetically instructed on its need. The good news for the Zulu and other Africans, as the congregation saw it, was that Shembe had been appointed God's special prophetic messenger and the path of spiritual and moral liberation was now illuminated before them. Such liberation, however, required suffering, and it was God's plan that that suffering come at the hands of whites in a racist South Africa. The suffering would be alleviated in time, and African land would be returned to them when God had determined that the period of atonement was sufficient.[46] Through this prophetically revealed guide of the past, present, and future, empire was readily subsumed into the dominant prophetic narrative told by Shembe. The fact that Shembe's theology and his understanding of his prophetic instructions were agreeable with the authorities in native affairs was a beneficial side effect of Shembe's political perspective and not his goal, which persistently remained oriented around his supernatural communications and the worldview they revealed.

State Interventions of the Nazareth Baptist Church, 1922 to 1931

Starting in the early 1920s, some state officials, like Magistrate McKenzie and Commissioner Wheelwright, began to challenge accusations coming from other agents of the colonial government, Sgt. Craddock most notably. As they did so, surveillance of the church gradually tapered off and Shembe and his church operated with a relative degree of freedom. Yet despite the state's growing tolerance, colonial agents did interfere with the church on three occasions from 1922–1931. These three interventions had the potential to be harmful to the church's operation and growth, and therefore could have posed a challenge to the church's overall worldview and political position. It would not have been unreasonable for Shembe and his congregation, in the face of direct interference, to develop an enhanced secular awareness about the consequences of a colonial white supremacist state, thereby lessening the strength of their worldview. But ultimately the state did not challenge, undermine, or politically radicalize the worldview embraced by Shembe and his congregants. In all three instances Shembe did not see the state's interference as oppression in need of political defiance. Even when the state angered him, he saw the actions of the government agents involved as sins against Jehovah, as the colonial officials were sinfully derailing God's plans for modern Africa, and not as oppressive acts against him and his congregation. The church's response in all three cases was to await prophetic instructions from God on how to navigate the situation the government had created so that God's plan of atonement and salvation for Africans could be sustained. The politics of empire was subsumed in all three instances into the church's prophetically underpinned worldview.

The first such instance came in 1922 when the state insisted Shembe secure permission for his annual pilgrimage to Mt. Nhlangakazi. From 1916–1921, Shembe had gathered his followers at Mt. Nhlangakazi with seemingly little trouble, suggested by the fact that there are no government records from this period concerning the pilgrimage. In 1922, however, Commissioner Wheelwright had instructed Shembe to request an official permit to assemble, a permit that had not arrived by the time the pilgrims had begun to gather at Ekuphakameni for their walk to the mountain. Today the church attributes the hold-up of the permit to the leaders of other Christian churches who resented Shembe and his growing congregation. At the time, Shembe blamed himself and his followers for an unknown transgression that had caused God to withhold the permit. He suggested fasting and praying to discover why God was angry and denying permission through the local native court. Amid their fast, a member of the Nazareth Baptist Church came forward, the son of Magobongwana Macineka of Ntanda, and reported having a dream the previous night. In this dream he described seeing "an angel standing in the sea, who had a sharp sword in his hand. He lifted up his foot and stepped in the sand. Then the sand ran away into the forests, and a broad track opened up."[47] Shembe believed the dream was a sign the congregation had been granted divine permission to begin their trek to the holy mountain via a wilderness route. The group left Ekuphakameni along a path through the grass and forest, neglecting the main road. When they reached Emaqadini, they were met by a court messenger who provided the permit. In the minds of the faithful, Shembe's command to fast and pray was answered with a dream that provided divine directions on how to reach the holy mountain, and in time, the officials at Ndwedwe, as agents of Jehovah, provided the permit along the way.[48]

Archival records of 1922 and 1923, however, demonstrate that the local native authorities may not have been pleased with Shembe's alternative route through the wilderness. While the church may advance a memory of a prophetically illuminated path in 1922, government officials quite likely viewed it as sneaking about. Concern from the local chiefs, perhaps in conjunction with Shembe's failure to secure a permit before beginning the pilgrimage in 1922, may have prompted the interview meeting between Shembe, Magistrate Chas. McKenzie, and six chiefs from the Lower Umzimkulu, Verulam, Pinetown, and Ndwedwe districts on 15 January 1923 (the same interview discussed in the previous section). McKenzie explained that one of the purposes of the meeting was to alert Shembe to the complaints made against him, including the pilgrimage, and allow him a chance to respond.

In the interview, the magistrate passed along the chief's complaints that the pilgrimage had an "unsettling effect" upon women and girls who left their homesteads to attend the pilgrimage "causing much annoyance and inconvenience." The chiefs further disapproved about diseased individuals travelling through their lands to Mt. Nhlangakazi for healing. On the first count, Shembe admitted that his membership had more female congregants than male. But he made clear that the pilgrimage was not mandatory and he did not force anyone's attendance. He also stated that if a "husband or father should come for his wife or daughter, I would not refuse to let her go," but that no such demand had ever been made. On the second count, Shembe reported that he did not take those suffering from infectious diseases to the mountain, only those with longstanding ailments, but he did appreciate that some came of their own volition.

An additional set of accusations derived from various complaints the magistrate had heard from "what people say" about Shembe. These criticisms concerned Shembe charging people for shaking his hand, not segregating congregants by gender when they slept during the pilgrimage, offering burnt offerings and generally behaving in an un-Christian manner, and lastly, purposefully holding services near other churches. Shembe assured Magistrate

McKenzie that all these grievances were unsubstantiated rumors. To prove that all these complaints, both those from the chiefs and those from the general populace, were unfounded, Shembe invited the magistrate to send two officers to observe the upcoming 1923 pilgrimage.[49]

The magistrate did indeed take Shembe up on this invitation, though he sent one officer, not two as Shembe has suggested. Native Constable Dhlamvuza Dhlamini was sent to observe the 1923 pilgrimage. He spent two weeks with Shembe and his congregation (including ten days on the mountain and the commuting time between Ekuphakameni and Nhlangakazi), and reported to the magistrate's office at Ndwedwe on 31 January to report his observations. Dhlamini did state that he thought Shembe's healing claims were simply fraudulent, as no ill person looked any better over the course of his observation period. Yet just like Officer Zulu in 1922, Dhlamini concluded in 1923 that, "The whole following was well behaved during the whole time, and there was nothing we could take exception to."[50] Police observers in 1922 and 1923 both agreed that the Nazareth Baptist Church's annual pilgrimage to Mt. Nhlangakazi was law-abiding and morally acceptable. Shembe did agree that from 1923 onward he would make request for a permit to assemble his congregation on Mt. Nhlangakazi, before the pilgrimage began.

Did Shembe purposefully attempt to skirt the government's order for a permit in 1922 with his off-road route? If he did, can the action be understood as non-violent resistance and political commentary? His selection of a wilderness course might suggest Shembe wished to thumb his nose at the command. Yet the government allowed the 1922 and subsequent pilgrimages to continue, indicating that if the state saw it as a political act, it did not trouble them greatly. Three elements from the point of view of Shembe and his congregation also suggest the 1922 pilgrimage should not be interpreted politically, but would be best understood prophetically.

First, the odds are not very high that the pilgrims would have avoided detection, and surely Shembe and his congregation were aware of this. Church membership was not huge at this point, yet scores, perhaps even hundreds, of pilgrims would quite certainly have caught the attention of local inhabitants. The chiefs had complained of Shembe and his congregants crossing their territory the previous year and it is not likely that even a wilderness route would escape attention in the era's densely populated African reserves. Second, Shembe never made any remarks to indicate he found the government's request unreasonable or sinful, nor did he indicate he had covert intentions with the 1922 pilgrimage. As a matter of fact, he had been complying and had requested a permit; the permit had simply not arrived by the time they wished to begin. Third, given the congregation's sincere conviction that God communicated his prophetic desires to them with regularity, it would not be a stretch of logic for Shembe or his congregation to believe a dream from God was suggesting they go through the forest.

What at first blush might appear to be an attempt to skirt the law, perhaps even an act of civil disobedience, may, in fact, simply be the church putting their faith into action by obeying a prophetic dream. The correctness of the prophetic interpretation was likely affirmed for Shembe and his congregants when a government agent provided the permit en route, thereby proving, in their minds, that the prophetic wilderness route was the right course of action. The state's seeming compliance with God's prophetic instructions enabled the members of the Nazareth Baptist Church to view the whole incident as prophetic in nature, where the officials of the state were the agents of God. In this manner, the entire 1922 pilgrimage and the drama surrounding it, within their imaginations, were but part of God's plan that both the congregation and the native authorities were a part. From the point of view of Shembe and his church's membership, political obedience was not simply a matter of complying with colonial officials. It was additionally a matter of everyone, their congregation and state officials, complying with the desires of Jehovah. While they obeyed the edicts of the state, state officials also obeyed God. When both obeyed God, the conditions for African salvation, as Shembe prophetically understood them, became actualized.

The second incident of state intervention in the church was generated from emerging national health policies. In the 1920s, the Public Health Office of the Union of South Africa promulgated a number of compulsory vaccination and public health projects. Inanda district in Natal was targeted in 1926, making smallpox vaccination compulsory for all non-Europeans there.[51] When the district surgeon came to Ekuphakameni in July 1926 to vaccinate the members of the Nazareth Baptist Church, those assembled simply refused. Of the more than 200 people gathered at Ekuphakameni, just one family was willing to be inoculated. After Shembe's near-death experience from a lightning strike, he believed God had told him that all medicines, whether traditional or Western, were forbidden, and healing would come entirely through faith. For this reason, Shembe and his congregants refused the vaccinations, convinced that taking medicine in any form would be a grave offense to God. Moreover, they felt the faithful had no need for immunizations as their proper faith in God kept them safe, as they felt Shembe's near-death prophecies had revealed. The state doctor left having vaccinated just one family. In response to their refusal, the court at Verulam suggested Shembe and his congregation be fined £25 sterling. If they refused to pay the fine, an imprisonment of six months was ordered. Pastor Mlangeni appeared before the court as a representative, and Shembe too later appeared before the Verulam court.

Shembe was furious about the vaccination issue. Court officials attempted to scare him, suggesting his death could be imminent without the smallpox vaccine and told Shembe that "dogs will lick up your blood." Shembe responded to the threat by saying that his time had not yet come. Shembe then angrily continued, "Tell those, who have installed you to this office, that you have soiled this dominion, which Jehova has given them." This remark reveals that Shembe's anger was principally religious in nature. He felt the officials of the state were clearly offending God by forcing medicines upon God's chosen people, something they had been prophetically warned against. Shembe's statement implies that state officials should have known better than this, and that they had ruined the opportunity (rule over South Africa) that Jehovah had provided them. So angry was Shembe that the state might ruin the church's covenant, that while on a trip to Pondoland, Shembe consulted with George Champion. In 1926, Champion was Transvaal secretary for the Industrial and Commercial Workers' Union (ICU), and would become national secretary a year later. It seems likely Shembe called on Champion for his political and legal skills in standing up to the state, something Shembe had no experience with. Champion initially declined to write a letter, indicating it was illegal to defy the state in this way. But a testimony in the *Acts* reports that Champion later sent a letter to Pietermaritzburg recording the following words of Shembe, "Jehova says, that the Government soiled this dominion, because they fight with me now, who has been sent by Jehova." This remark, like the earlier one Shembe made to a court official, indicates that Shembe's outrage, and his congregation's defiance of the vaccination order, came not from a sense of oppression or political subjugation, but from a feeling of theological outrage and moral disgust.

This sense of religious distress is even more palpable in a later portion of this same testimony. Following his consultation with Champion, Shembe continued to Pondoland and from there sent a message to Ekuphakameni. Shembe commanded that [first name unknown] Dladla and his family be expelled, both from the church and from their homestead on church grounds, for being vaccinated. Dladla's family was then evicted and "the soil of his fields was carried away by the maidens and thrown into the Umzinyahti river." A short time after, the congregation embarked on their annual pilgrimage to Mt. Nhlangakazi. More than once during their pilgrimage to the mountain, Shembe made the remark that due to Dladla's evil, he was not sure if they would return. While atop the mountain, Shembe had everyone remain inside their tents and pray, as he believed the voice of God and a visit from an angel had instructed him to do. They were to await the arrival of the heavenly people. One evening Shembe and the pastors climbed higher to pray. While there, Shembe reported having a vision of a large army of soldiers with wagons of fire. He interpreted this as the heavenly people they had been awaiting. The next day Shembe held a service where the congregants reported that many individuals were healed and a demon was exorcised from a girl. As a result,

Shembe and his membership believed the congregation was made whole and granted forgiveness for the covenantal transgression of the Dladla family for taking medicine.[52]

At first blush, legally mandated vaccinations might seem oppressive and any reactions against it an overt and clear form of resistance. Shembe was indeed angry about the whole affair, but his anger at Dladla and his family for their wickedness was as great, perhaps greater, than that aimed at state officials. Though Shembe did consult with one of the region's best-known political organizers, George Champion, when he expressed his anger to the Verulam court it was to call the state's agents sinners who were ruining the dominion they had been appointed to rule. He did not engage in acts of political or legal defiance. Even when he used the famed black nationalist Champion as an intermediary, Shembe's theological anger is clear. The solution to the whole matter, for the church, was asceticism and atonement via Shembe's prophetic instructions. Shembe and his congregation fervently prayed, as they felt they had been prophetically instructed to do. When Shembe had a vision of a fiery heavenly host, it was a sign for them that the period of atonement for the sins of Dladla, the district surgeon, and the Verulam court was sufficient.

The government encountered enough resistance and collective refusal nationwide that it backed off mandatory vaccinations, and did not take the step of forcing them upon entire communities at this time.[53] The members of the Nazareth Baptist Church were not the only ones to object; some other individuals objected on political and racial grounds. For instance, some non-whites claimed they were being "dipped" like livestock in the government's anti-lice campaign, before they were allowed into urban areas, and the ICU protested the practice.[54] As a result, the Nazareth Baptist Church and others who had objected were granted a reprieve from the vaccinations.[55] For the ICU, the national health measures were racially informed and they lodged a political response. Shembe and his congregation also refused to participate, yet they saw the state's edicts as a sinful derailment of Jehovah's plans, not as oppression by whites. For Shembe and his congregation, their outrage about the vaccinations was principally fueled by the fact that a vaccination would violate their covenant with Jehovah to abstain from all medicines. When some among them were vaccinated, Shembe embarked upon a plan of prayer and atonement to remediate the situation. In this case, Shembe refused to obey the state, but his refusal was propagated by faith and moral outrage, not racially informed political protest, as it was for the ICU.

The third instance of state interference in the church came over land in 1931. The state's growing tolerance, even perhaps fondness, for Shembe and his church is evidenced in the multiple land purchases he secured in the 1920s. The land where Ekuphakameni was constructed was obtained in 1914, and Shembe added to the church's properties across the 1920s. In 1923, he purchased Inanda farm from the Inanda Wattle Company.[56] The purchase was originally opposed by district commissioner Barrett, but he changed his mind later, saying that the purchase would act as an anchor for Shembe and permit the state to observe that he continue to remain law-abiding.[57] Six years later, in 1929, Shembe purchased 881 acres in Umzinto district on the south coast of Natal with the permission of Governor-General Lord Athlone. Similarly, in 1931, Shembe's purchase of New Hanover went unobstructed.[58] These purchases were allowed despite the fact that they were outside of a native reserve and therefore technically not permissible under the 1913 Natives' Land Act, that restricted African land ownership to roughly 7% of South Africa. That Shembe was allowed to skirt the land act on multiple occasions is a clear indication of his growing favorable opinion among state officials at the local and provincial levels. Shembe's ability to purchase land despite such a formidable legal challenge as the land act reinforced the belief in Shembe's distinctiveness and power among his followers.[59]

While the state allowed Shembe to purchase land on multiple occasions, thereby facilitating the construction of temples in numerous parts of Natal, the state also forced Shembe to destroy some. In July 1931, the Native Affairs Department issued a command to close several temples within three months. The targeted temples had been built on land donated to the church by chiefs. The closure of these particular temples intimates that the state preferred to have Shembe build temples on land purchased through the white economy. Perhaps this was the state's means of monitoring the geography of the church, or perhaps the state was fearful of independent black institutions, even those it liked, operating in the heart of "wild" Zululand administered by chiefs. In response to the order, Shembe contacted his lawyer in August, a Mr. Dickson, asking for his guidance. The guidance Shembe requested, however, was not on how to fight the edict or defy the state, as Shembe noted he did "not wrangle with obstinacy." Rather, the guidance he requested was whether or not his lawyer felt it wise to request permission to have the names of the temples written on stones because,

> I believe a white Lord will come from [Europe], who does not fight God and who wishes that God be praised in Zululand.... This lord will sit on the seats of the rulers who destroy these places. He will restore these places, and will ask for their names. It will be good for him to find all the names of these places written down by me while I am still alive. I ask permission to write them on stones, and to erect them at all these places. Please advise me as to whether you agree or disagree. I will listen to what you say. My conscience tells me to do it: but I wish to obtain permission from the government.[60]

This statement of Shembe's is quite revealing. It demonstrates that Shembe viewed the actions of the government as wicked because they "fight

God," and believed they would be displaced by the future white lord who did not fight God. Shembe did not interpret a rather devastating command for his fledgling church—dismantling of some temples—as colonial oppression. Nor does it appear Shembe even took the edict personally or saw himself or his church as being targeted. Rather, Shembe's understanding of the government edict was that it was a sinful act of state officials who were defying God. What to the outsider might appear as a political act perpetrated by a white suprema-cist state upon a black church was, to Shembe, a theological act against God. Such an interpretation clearly informed the sort of response Shembe found appropriate to the situation. While an oppressive action might suggest a response of political defiance or legal wrangling, a theological act required an equally religious answer. Shembe provided such a response in the form of a prediction. What Shembe does not make overtly clear in the letter is whether or not this prediction is his own, or whether he is passing along words that he believed he received from God. However, given that Shembe's other predic-tions were inspired by some form of prophetic communication, it seems safe to infer a supernatural communication in this instance as well, even if Shembe does not state so directly.[61] To fulfill the prediction, Shembe desired to write the names of the temples upon stones and erect them at the sites of the destroyed temples.[62] Yet even though his conscience told him to do it, he still sought legal counsel on the matter and wanted to obtain the government's permission to do so. Even as the government demanded the dismantling of some of his temples, Shembe still asserted a religious response and saw the acts of the government agents as sinful ones aimed at God, not himself or his church, even as it had negative repercussions for his church.

In all three of these instances—the pilgrimage permit, the vaccination con-troversy, and the destruction of temples—Shembe and his congregation advanced a theological and prophetic interpretation of the state's actions. In the first instance, requirement of a permit was viewed as part of Jehovah's plans for both the church and the state. Even if the members could not entirely articulate what those cosmic plans were, or how the permit fit within the plans, the veracity of the dream prophecy convinced them that their faith in such an interpretation was correct. In the latter two instances, Shembe understood the state's actions as sinful and an offense to God as they were derailing God's plan for the redemption and salvation of modern Africa as it had been prophetically described to him. Despite the harmful consequences for the church, Shembe did not view the vaccination controversy or even the destruction of some temples as political oppression, but as the sinful actions of some agents of the colonial state who were "fighting God." The state's direct interventions in the Nazareth Baptist Church ultimately did not pose a chal-lenge to the church's prophetically shaped worldview.

Maneuvering at the Margins: The History of the Nazareth Baptist Church, ca. 1920 to 1935

There is little denying the suspicion, surveillance, and occasional intervention by agents of the native authority upon the members of the Nazareth Baptist Church in the church's early years. State records make this clear as do the church's own traditions.[63] However, starting with Native Commissioner Wheelwright's dismissal, in 1922, of earlier accusations, suspicions of Shembe and the Nazareth Baptist Church began to subside, and counter-narratives began to emerge. Rather than wild "natives" engaged in political and immoral acts, the members of the Nazareth Baptist Church came to be seen by whites— both colonial officials and the general public—as a safe and fascinating group of Zulus. In spite of the three direct state interventions surveyed in the previous section, the space at the margins of empire increased for the congregation of the Nazareth Baptist Church over the course of the 1920s and 1930s. The government's retreat from surveillance, even if contemporaneously interspersed with occasional direct interference, made a prophetic narrative of the Zulu past and South Africa's present all the more believable for members as they were not forced into a posture of resistance through constant challenges to their worldview.

The changing opinion of the Nazareth Baptist Church among Natal's white population can be witnessed in the attention it gained in the English-language press that was principally local, but international in one case. The first such press attention of Shembe and the Nazareth Baptist Church began in the late 1920s. The first mainstream news article was a 1927 article head-lined "Herd Boy Turns Healer." The article stressed Shembe's healing abilities, his strength of character, and his strong belief in his divine mission.[64] Consider another article from 1929 in the English-language newspaper *District Notes & News* that praised the church as an example of how Africans "may be raised up without becoming exotics, or mental and moral snobs."[65] An article even appeared in *The Illustrated London News* on Shembe and the Nazareth Baptist Church in 1930. This article stressed his asceticism, hard work, and knowledge of the Bible. It appears the *Illustrated London News* article was based on the writings of Nellie Wells, who served as a special representative for the *Natal Mercury*. Wells had known Shembe since 1923 and had employed some of the wives he renounced. She wrote reports of the July festival in 1927, 1928, 1929, and 1930.[66] In a letter to the magistrate of Ndwedwe, Lugg, Wells wrote that Shembe's welfare system had attracted the interest of government and mission authorities. Wells noted Shembe's disinterest in politics and nationalism, highlighting the fact that Shembe turned out members of the ICU (Industrial and Commercial Workers' Union).[67] Shembe's renunciation of an organization known for militant unionism and black nationalism likely proved popular with the government and further dispelled the previous suspicions about political intrigue.

What began to develop in the imagination of Natal's white population over the course of the 1920s and 1930s, as the press attention and the handful of government reports of the time reveal, was a picture of Shembe and the Nazareth Baptist Church as the perfect example of cultural assimilation. They were not raw untamed "natives," yet neither were they *kholwa* (converts/believers)—black Christian "imitators" of whites who grew "uppity" and demanded their rights. Shembe and his followers, as white Natalians saw them, occupied a position somewhere in between. They were Christians, yet they practiced strange rites and danced for worship. They were hard-working and industrious, yet they were not political agitators. They were Zulus, but were not striving to be black ladies and gentlemen and attempting to supplant the positions of whites. In short, they were the new African; one that had given up some of the ways of the past but had not entirely embraced white culture, and thus remained separate from it. This goal of limited assimilation was supported by segregation laws passed in the 1920s. Wells presents this view in her 1929 news article stating, "The celebrations at Ekuphakameni during the month of July are an exposition of how the Bantu may be raised up without becoming exotics, or mental or moral snobs."[68] Wells also wrote that two hundred white Durbanites had observed the festival that year, a practice that continued through the 1930s and 1940s. If the popularity of the newly "domesticated" July festival with white Natalians is in doubt, one need look no further than one of the Durban Publicity Association's advertisements for the "Shembe Festival, Inanda," which contains a history of Shembe and the movement with directions on how to get to Ekuphakameni.[69]

The congregation of the Nazareth Baptist Church attracted its first academic attention in 1935 when Esther Roberts conducted fieldwork for her M.A. thesis titled "Shembe: The Man and his Work." Roberts describes Shembe's most striking characteristics as "his tolerance and his appeal to people in various stages of development...from 'raw' Natives...to the sophisticated town boys."[70] Roberts quotes Shembe as saying, "God is like the centre of a wheel; the Europeans, Bantu, Indians and Coloureds are on the outside edge. They are separate from one another, but they are all the same distance from God and He loves them all equally."[71] Clearly this is a statement that many whites would have found palatable in a segregated society, and perhaps even encouraged. Shembe is saying that all are equal before God, but yet can exist separately. This story of a wheel of races is not repeated elsewhere. It is unclear today whether this was Robert's own interpretation of Shembe's teaching or remarks, or whether this was a one-time statement by Shembe that was not preserved, or perhaps later expunged, in the church's own lore.

The timing of Roberts' study reflected the tenor of her times. It would have been virtually unimaginable for a student to have written a master's thesis on the Nazareth Baptist Church a decade earlier. It was only after the 1920s, when there was a shift in the way Shembe and the Nazareth Baptist Church were perceived by the authorities and the general public, that an academic study became a feasible project. The same could be said for attention from the press. The image of the Nazareth Baptist Church had become domesticated. It was now seen as appropriately safe and tame.[72] The church was no longer perceived as a covert political organization but merely a quaint church filled with strange practices and curious dancing that whites could safely observe on the weekend. Additionally, whites saw it as a good model for the way in which other Zulus should assimilate. That is, assimilate somewhat, but do not assimilate so much that you will threaten the positions of whites. Whites did not perceive Shembe and the Nazareth Baptist Church's adherents as a threat to the status quo not only because they were perceived to be generally apolitical by whites, but also because they were just Zulu enough to remain outside the mainstream white culture and economy. This made them better than a "pure" Zulu who was wild, unruly, and pagan, and better than a Western-educated Zulu elite who was too Western and too well educated to remain content in a segregated society. An article in *The Illustrated London News* referred to Shembe as a "restraining influence" and whites liked it that way.[73] In the end, this worked to the benefit of the congregation of the Nazareth Baptist Church as well, as they were largely free to worship as they saw fit and were not subject to constant surveillance and harassment. This was not by design, but rather was a beneficial side-effect of Shembe's prophetically-informed political perspective that left the unfolding of modern South Africa in God's hands.

The growth of Shembe's reputation as prophet, healer, and church leader was as great among Africans as it was whites. As Shembe's reputation grew, it began to draw in a new source of converts. By the late 1920s, converts from Zulu indigenous religion, as opposed to the almost exclusively Christian converts from earlier, also began to join the Nazareth Baptist Church. For these converts, allusions to biblical and Christian history were less of a draw than they had been for the first generation of converts; Shembe's prophetic allure began to take on greater significance as a draw for new converts. Shembe also garnered the attention of King Solomon kaDinuzulu, since 1916 the official Hereditary Paramount Chief of the Zulu. It may be that the growing number of converts from Zulu religion was what attracted the interest of the king. The king may have perceived them as remaining more Zulu than the converts of other Christian churches, and therefore a source of political support. Solomon also appeared interested in Shembe's endorsement of traditional values such as *hlonipha* (respect/deference) and the purity of maidens.[74] King Solomon's interest in the Nazareth Baptist Church was considerable enough that he even married Zondi, Shembe's daughter by his first wife Nomaloyo, in 1926. King Solomon attended a number of services at Ekuphakameni in the late 1920s.

Ultimately Solomon had an ambiguous relationship with the Nazareth Baptist Church, and his interest entirely waned by the early 1930s. While attendance at the services was a chance for Solomon to enhance his paramountcy and appear among a large cross-section of Zulu-speakers, his presence there also lent legitimacy to Shembe. In the later years of his life, Solomon seemed hesitant to attend services of the Nazareth Baptist Church and have his presence be mistaken as endorsement of Shembe. Shembe had a different notion of *hlonipha* which informed a different vision for the future of the Zulus.

Isaiah Shembe on horseback and a group of children robed in white, 1935
Used by permission of the Campbell Collections of the University of KwaZulu-Natal

While Solomon interpreted *hlonipha* as according proper respect and deference to traditional authorities, Shembe understood the virtue as granting proper respect to God.[75] Any changes in South Africa, for Shembe, would be in accordance with God's will, not agitation through politics or the embrace of traditional authorities. For Shembe, obedience to God's laws and proper observation of the Sabbath was what constituted *hlonipha* and would be the only hope of redemption. By this notion of *hlonipha*, traditional authorities were of relevance in serving as leaders of ancestral redemption and as models of Godly obedience, but not as political figures. Shembe invited Solomon to lay the foundation stone for a new building at Ekuphakameni (after Shembe claimed he was prophetically instructed by an angel to invite him), just as King Solomon, son of David, had done in Israel. Solomon did not answer the invitation. Shembe interpreted this as a possible repeal of God's blessing on Solomon and said he would not be surprised if a king from a new house was soon installed, just as Saul had been displaced by David (1 Samuel 16). The brief friendship between Shembe and Solomon appeared over. So instead Chief Manqamu Mbonambi laid the foundation stone.[76]

As the church grew, Ekuphakameni, as the physical center of the movement, began to take on greater theological importance. Hymns, prayers, and *izibongo* (praise poetry) paid tribute to the greatness of Ekuphakameni. In "Shembe's Prayer in Remembrance of His Nation," God is referred to as the God of Ekuphakameni who is inside the gates of Ekuphakameni. The prayer goes on to tell that Shembe claimed he awoke from the sound of thunder one day, but was told by a voice that it was not thunder but the footsteps of the kings entering Ekuphakameni.[77] Presumably this refers to the kings of the Zulu, as the earlier portion of the prayer refers to the curse of the ancestors, but perhaps it additionally refers to the kings of Israel. This would conform to the belief that Ekuphakameni was the New Jerusalem. Socially, it became a refuge for orphans, widows, the handicapped, or other people unable to fully support themselves unaided, who, Shembe taught, should be well treated according to James 1:27.[78] Testimonies in the *Acts* say Shembe never turned anyone away, even *isangoma*, or indigenous priests. The church has always had more members than it has had land to support them, so most members have made their own living separate from the church. Despite this, the church has a long tradition dating to the late 1910s and early 1920s of having church members settled on church property, largely self-sufficiently. While no teeming metropolis, Ekuphakameni was nevertheless a modest settlement that managed to sustain itself and absorb widows and orphans. Many villagers sold handicrafts for extra income, but church members were forbidden from taking domestic work (a significant source of income for African women at the time) because they would be forced to work the Sabbath and to handle impure foods. The design and purity of Ekuphakameni reflected the fact that it was thought to be the city of the saints, the future city of God, and the New Jerusalem.[79]

Roberts reported upon the ethnic composition of the Nazareth Baptist Church in 1935, noting members came from a variety of ethnic groups: Zulu, Xhosa, Pondo, Tembu, Swazi, and Basuto, as well as fifty Indian members and 150 Coloured. Congregations could be found as far away as Rhodesia (Zimbabwe) and Bechuanaland (Botswana). Roberts wrote that the Nazareth Baptist Church had thirteen temples in 1935: two at Umtwalumi, one at Umzumbi, one at the Cape, one at Inyoni, one at Gingindhlovu, two at

Umtentweni, three at Empangeni, one in Northern Zululand, and one at Nongoma.[80] By the late 1930s, the church had somewhere in the neighborhood of 20,000 to 30,000 adherents, perhaps as many as 40,000.[81] Then, as now, most members were Zulu and most temples in Zululand, yet from the church's early decades, as the above list indicates, the Nazareth Baptist Church has always had members from a variety of ethnic groups and temples in multiple nations of southern Africa. Shembe viewed his prophetic message as one for all Africans, and later all humanity. Zululand is where his ministry began, the place where the membership believed God selected his chosen prophet, Shembe, because that was where the need for atonement was the greatest.

By the 1930s, Shembe began to tell people on a number of occasions that he would not live much longer because God was going to take him home soon.[82] Prior to his death, Shembe had demonstrated an understandable concern in having his church continue past his lifetime. After the death of his eldest son, Benjamin, in 1934, Shembe asked Jehovah whether the Nazareth Baptist Church would last after he was gone. Shembe was delighted to receive the prophetic response that it would continue to grow. Shembe predicted that the next leader would be more powerful than he, but warned his son Galilee to be wary of false prophets who would try to take control of the church.[83] Adherents of the Nazareth Baptist Church believe that Shembe knew when his death was approaching because of his prophetic power; this did not seem an odd thing for a prophet to know. Shembe never gave a precise day and time for his death, but merely said he knew that his death was imminent. When Shembe felt his time was near, he lay down on the ground while fasting and poorly dressed. When his son, Galilee, came to visit him, Shembe said he was tormenting his flesh to ensure that his soul went to heaven, for he was leaving the earth soon. But he did not know whether God would then put his soul at Ekuphakameni or Mt. Nhlangakazi. Shembe died a short time after this conversation with Galilee, on 2 May 1935, at 9 a.m.[84] Galilee attributed his father's death to salt-fever, the reabsorption of his own sweat from working too hard. Roberts attributed his death to a fever contracted while standing in a river for three hours baptizing people on a cool day. And finally, the local press blamed his death on blood poisoning caused by the bite of an insect.[85] The exact cause of Shembe's death remains uncertain, but it may be that a lifetime of asceticism and fasting had also taken its toll on Shembe's approximately 65-year-old body, as confirmed by a white doctor who examined him.[86]

Following Shembe's death, some followers claimed the sky thundered like a charge of gunpowder, while others said the news was so distressing it made them want to run into the woods and commit suicide. But Shembe had left careful instructions for the execution of his will and funeral. His body was brought on 4 May from Mikhaideni, where he died, to Ekuphakameni, where Shembe instructed he should be buried, even if others wanted to bury him in

Zululand. He was buried on Sunday, the 5th, not on the 4th, which was a Sabbath. His funeral was well attended by all races and well covered by the local press. Shembe had ordered that people should not weep at his funeral because he said he came alone to this earth, and would leave it alone. While no one was seen wailing in the manner of traditional Zulu funerary practice, many people could not hide their tears. Shembe was praised by the singing of "He is holy!" and a service was conducted by Rev. B. J. Hlatshwayo. Shembe was placed in an L-shaped grave, wrapped in two cattle skins, and buried with his notebook.

For a prophetic church like the Nazareth Baptist Church, however, Shembe's physical death did not diminish faith in his prophetic power. The members of the Nazareth Baptist Church believe that as an eternal spirit, Shembe has powers that extend beyond his bodily death.[87] They believe that the spirit of Shembe arose to heaven and resides with Jehovah; there is the likelihood that he will be sent to earth again to act as God's messenger at some time in the future. Members of the church believe their founding prophet continues to influence the course of the church's history, largely by directing his progeny, but also by assisting members. This is beyond dispute to members and accepted as simply true as a demonstration of Shembe's prophetic aura and might, even after his physical death.

Adherents of the Nazareth Baptist Church describe Shembe as a presence who gives guidance and approval to personal decisions. Some members claim to have received dreams inspired by Shembe.[88] One church member, a Mrs. Manqele from KwaMashu, reported in 1991 that everything she did was because Shembe appeared in her dreams and instructed her to do so.[89] Another woman, with the pseudonym Tam, reported Shembe appearing to her in a dream in the late 1970s. In the dream, Shembe taught her basic English literacy with use of a blackboard. When she awoke the next morning, to her amazement, she had basic literacy skills, thereby allowing her to keep her job as a housekeeper and nanny.[90] In another such testimony, Josiah Mthembu recounts how he was suffering from a disease in his shoulders that was crippling and blinding him with pain. In a dream, he saw Shembe laying hands on people and healing them. When Shembe got to Mthembu, he struck him in the shoulders with his staff. Mthembu reported that he was healed and had not even suffered a cold from that time onward. The time of Mthembu's dream is not clear from his story, but he did state it was after the time of Isaiah's death.[91] As these examples illustrate, dreams of Shembe may guide individuals but do not comment on larger church matters. A member who declared they had a dream of Isaiah (or another central leader) who told them to reform church rule X or do away with practice Y would be met with great skepticism. It is believed that these are matters that God would reveal only to members of the Shembe family because only they have the prophetic strength to receive it and understand it properly.[92]

Perhaps nothing exemplifies the church's belief in the postmortem power of Shembe better than hymn number 220 in the Nazareth Baptist Church hymnal. The church hymnal explains that the hymn "enveloped" Galilee Shembe in January 1938 at the annual festival atop Mt. Nhlangakazi. Though the hymn was Galilee's, the envelopment was caused by Isaiah, making this hymn (and number 223) a prophetic one inspired by Isaiah atop Nhlangakazi following his death.[93] This explanation clearly reinforces the belief that Isaiah was spiritually resurrected and serves as a prophetic guide to his progeny.

Yet ultimately, the Nazareth Baptist Church has steered a rather conservative course with Shembe's postmortem powers. While church members may legitimately claim inspiration from Shembe on personal matters, Nazareth Baptist Church theology does not allow anyone other than the central leadership to know the direct will of God. Those who claimed grander inspiration, beyond personal matters, from one of the Shembes or God, would be regarded as having received a false prophecy. Knowing the will of God is believed to be the privilege of Shembe's sons and grandsons, who regularly receive inspiration from Isaiah and God, often mediated by Isaiah or the Holy Spirit. The power of Shembe is thought to be so great that it has continued beyond his physical death and advises members on personal affairs and his progeny on sacred matters. In this manner, the early history of the church under the leadership of Isaiah is remembered as a thoroughly prophetic history, the prophetic power of which continues even after Shembe's death.

Conclusion

While Shembe and his congregation came under immediate suspicion by Natal's district and provincial native authorities, and were surveilled by various state officials, by the 1920s Shembe and the members of the Nazareth Baptist Church were gradually cleared of the accusations and permitted to operate with considerable freedom. The state's relative laissez faire attitude regarding Shembe and his church produced "margins to maneuver" that allowed Shembe and his congregants to largely fulfill their religious concerns without a posture of resistance. When the state directly intervened in church affairs, seemingly closing those margins, Shembe and his congregation still interpreted these events prophetically and theologically, and not politically. While the state's actions impacted the course of the church's history, it did not derail or even seriously challenge the prophetically-defined worldview of Shembe or the membership of the Nazareth Baptist Church. Nothing shook Shembe's resolve, or his congregant's faith in the same, that he was a prophet chosen by God who was fulfilling the will of Jehovah in colonial Africa. Within

Shembe's explanation for contemporary conditions, it was the will of Jehovah that whites rule South Africa, in order for Africans to engage in penance and atonement for their ancestral sins. To fight whites meant fighting God and his plans, and ultimately derailing one's chances for salvation. This political position was neither resistant nor acquiescent, but prophetic. The prophetic worldview of Shembe and his congregation was capable of subsuming empire, and every feature of the universe for that matter, into their explanation of the world as they believed God was prophetically explaining it to Shembe. Maneuvering at the margins of colonial Natal provided the room for the production and maintenance of a prophetic narrative of why colonial Africa was as it was.

Prophecy, Theology, and the Identity of the Chosen

The City of the Nazarenes
is where we are going.
It shines more than
the sun and the moon.

The leader of it
is only one;
it is only Jehovah,
the Lord of all might.

Let it be known to all the nations
of the world;

—Izihlabelelo zaManazeretha, hymn 10, verses 1-3

Narrator Daniel Dube, in an undated testimony from the *Acts of the Nazarites* (hereafter *Acts*), recounts a prophetic vision of Isaiah Shembe. In the vision, Shembe described how he saw pieces of straw flying all over the earth, and a very bright spark amid them. According to the testimony, Shembe asked Jehovah what the vision meant. Shembe believed God gave him the response that the pieces of straw "are people, and this spark, which you see, is you." As the vision continued, some of the pieces of straw came toward the spark, and all which did so began to burn brightly. The bundle of radiant straws increased in size, first to the size of a hand, then to that of a ball, and kept growing. The light gradually radiated outward until it lit up Africa, England, India, and all inhabited places on earth. Dube continued the testimony by explaining that this prophecy of Shembe's is an indication that "The nations on earth, who had been waiting for the Lord, have now heard, that he is at Ekuphakameni."[1] According to this testimony, regarding a visionary and aural prophecy, the light of salvific truth was radiating outward from Ekuphakameni, through the teachings of Isaiah Shembe. With the passage of time, all humanity would be drawn to this truth and the light of salvation would shine upon the whole world.

This chapter explores two interrelated aspects of the theology of the Nazareth Baptist Church hinted at in Dube's testimony: the church's theophanic sites and their soteriology. Both contributed to the identity Shembe and his congregation ascribed to themselves as a unique community of the chosen. While their sense of identity was not unique in the sense that many other Christian churches, past and present, have made claims to be God's new chosen people, their identity was unique within their own minds, as they truly believed they were the one and only chosen people of God with the only proper message of salvation. The belief in their chosenness was a true cornerstone of how Shembe and his congregation defined themselves, and also informed how they related to the world beyond the church.

The belief of Shembe and church members that they were the elect, in possession of the most sacred sites on earth and the only true message of salvation on the planet, provided the bedrock of their communal identity, an identity that was so significant that it transcended the other forms of communal identity available to them. The two theophanic sites of Ekuphakameni, the New Jerusalem, and Nhlangakazi, the church's holy mountain, coupled with the church's soteriological theology, generated a religiously based identity for Shembe and his congregants, an identity that trumped political or national ones. While whites had thrust political identities upon Africans by redrawing the map of colonial-era Africa, Shembe and the members of the Nazareth Baptist Church produced their own map of South Africa, based not on national boundaries and colonial authority, but on who was within the borders of salvation that rippled outward from the church's headquarters and their holy mountain. From these sacred epicenters emitted the "correct" message of salvation that linked up the various temples and congregations throughout southern Africa into a sacred community of the chosen, and eventually even transcended colonial boundaries and colonial regimes by connecting congregations in Swaziland, Botswana, and Zimbabwe with those in South Africa. On this map that could not be hung on any wall, generated by a prophetic cartographer, the political world of white South Africa was eclipsed by the religious world of the Nazareth Baptist Church's map, that contained the holy ground tread upon by the congregation of the Nazareth Baptist Church, the ancestral kings, the heavenly host, and even God himself.[2]

This notion of identity, defined by who was and was not within the bounds of the chosen, likewise transcended ethnicity. At first blush this may sound like a surprising assertion for a church that had a majority Zulu membership, used the Zulu language, and was highly concerned with the sins of the Zulu ancestors. The significant Zuluness of the early church, however, was not an exercise of ethnic chauvinism or exclusivity. Rather, Shembe explained that the Zulu had the greatest level of ancestral sin to atone for, due to the violence involved in the building and maintenance of the Zulu empire. For this reason the Zulu were the starting point for God's renewed message of salvation, and that was why a prophet was selected among them. But, Shembe continued, the Zulu were not the endpoint of God's plans, and the message of salvation was not intended to be theirs alone. The Zulu were the first to be granted the possibility of atonement and salvation as part of God's new chosen people, but Shembe provided many indications that the message of salvation was one to be spread to all the nations. Just as in the vision of the spark, Shembe desired that the "light" of his message would radiate outward from Ekuphakameni and Mt. Nhlangakazi, eventually shining on all the earth. In this manner, the community of the chosen, though beginning with the Zulu, was an identity grounded in faith, not ethnicity. In Shembe's lifetime, the concentric circles of radiating light had not spread much further than the Zulu and neighboring peoples, but it was the goal of Shembe and his church that their message eventually reach "all the nations under the sun."[3]

Theophanic Sites

Shembe developed two sacred spaces in the early history of the church, Ekuphakameni, the New Jerusalem, and Nhlangakazi, the holy mountain, both of which church members believed to be sites of theophanic wonder. These places were no ordinary pieces of land, nor were they simply places to assemble for worship, but the two terrestrial places most favored by Jehovah. When God visited earth or prophetically communicated to Shembe, he did so most often, but not exclusively, at these two sites, which changed them from mundane land to prophetic spaces that were blessed with the presence of God. In this manner, Shembe's notion of a sacred space was novel to South African Christianity in two fashions, and outside Protestant and Catholic norms, though not entirely without parallel among Zionist churches. The sacred spaces of his church were firstly natural, and not architectural, as is most common to Protestantism and Catholicism. Though temple structures were built on both locations, worship was generally conducted in the open, and this was particularly true for the two annual festivals, when the structures could not accommodate the number of worshipers. Secondly, and more importantly, the Nazareth Baptist Church's sacred spaces were theophanic, places where the divine realm met the human one. For congregants, both sites served as symbols of their chosenness and their elect status with Jehovah, which reaffirmed their faith in Shembe, the worldview he constructed, the relationship to the state he advocated, and the path of salvation he preached. Ekuphakameni and Nhlangakazi, as sacred sites of theophany and prophecy, and ritual spaces for the communal expression of faith, were physical and theological symbols that reinforced first Shembe's, and then the congregation's, prophetic understanding of the world and their church's place within it as the hub of Christian truth and the sacred home of the saved.

Ekuphakameni: The New Jerusalem

After Shembe made the decision in 1910 to no longer direct converts to existing congregations, but instead retain them as his own congregants and build a church, among his first goals was the purchase of land. Shembe's son, Galilee, told of the hardships he and his family faced while his father was saving every coin for the land purchase.[4] Shembe's first land purchase was enabled by a young male church member of the Gwacela family. Seeing the fasting and physical hardship Shembe was enduring to save money, the young man said, "Father, I feel very sorry when looking at the great suffering of our father, I have got a small place near the lower end of the school of Ohlange, which I had bought. However, I did not yet pay it off completely to the Whites. I offer it to God."[5] Through personal savings and donations from his converts, Shembe managed to come up with the remaining twenty pounds sterling for the thirty-eight acres at Inanda, on the outskirts of Durban. The transfer occurred in 1914, shortly after passage of the 1913 Natives' Land Act that forbade Africans to purchase or lease land outside African reserves. Yet this plot of land was not turned over to the state, and the Natal government allowed the transfer to Shembe. Rev. Leshega of the African Native Baptist Church, contrastingly, was denied the right to purchase land, suggesting Shembe's church was palatable to the state in a way some other African churches were not.[6]

Upon the thirty-eight acre plot at Inanda, Shembe created his own biblical Zion, the model city of God, that he named Ekuphakameni (the exalted place). In an interview with Carl Faye, chief clerk and translator of the Natal Native Affairs Department, on 5 November 1929, Shembe stated that the name "just came to him."[7] Shembe used the verb *ukufiga*, to arrive, in describing how the name came to him. In the use of this verb was Shembe's connotation that the name was simply a spontaneous idea, akin to the idiom of a "light bulb moment"? Or, was Shembe suggesting that the name "came to him" in the same fashion that he had received other prophecies? Either connotation could be validly interpreted from Shembe's use of the verb *ukufiga*. However, it appears Shembe was indicating the latter, that the name Ekuphakameni was prophetically inspired, as he portrayed many other prophetic experiences similarly. In describing how he learned to pray, for example, Shembe claimed that the urge to pray simply occurred to him. Despite having never prayed before, Shembe reported that the words of prayer "arrived of themselves," without thought. Shembe described the prophetic arrival of the church's hymns similarly. In other words, just like the name Ekuphakameni, the words of Shembe's first prayer and all of the hymns, simply arrived to him without conscious effort of his own. Additionally, Shembe utilized the same verb, *ukufiga*, in describing all these occasions.[8] Thus it is accurate to refer to Ekuphakameni as a prophetically inspired name. Such a supernaturally derived name would only be fitting for the place the members of the Nazareth Baptist Church believed was the New Jerusalem, Jehovah's new Zion, the place of refuge for God's new chosen people, and the site of the church's most important annual gathering each July. For Shembe and church members, Ekuphakameni was a site of theophany—a place where God came to earth and revealed himself, as demonstrated by the many hymns Shembe claimed to have prophetically received there. No other place on earth was as sacred to Shembe and the early Nazareth Baptist Church.

With the founding of Ekuphakameni, a formal congregation began to form, as opposed to the temporary supporters Shembe had had as an itinerant preacher. The church's demographic growth in its early years was steady, but modest. The church had, after roughly a decade, about four hundred members in 1921.[9] Shembe continued to perform wandering mission tours, and these itinerant efforts attracted converts from beyond the area of Durban. New temples/homes were founded and additional properties were added to church land holdings to accommodate the growth in converts. Some of Shembe's bids for land were denied by regional colonial authorities, but enough were accepted for the church to spread to various parts of Natal.

In the 1920s, Shembe began appointing a priesthood to assist him with itinerant preaching and the overseeing of the regional temples. The earliest priests, who were ordained at Mt. Nhlangakazi, were Johannes Mlangeni, Petros Mnqayi, and Amos Mzobe. Mlangeni became Shembe's right hand man and acted as Shembe's power of attorney; he finalized land purchases and often traveled with Shembe.[10] He and Shembe had a falling out when Mlangeni married a woman whom Shembe told never to marry, because of her guilt, to which she had agreed. Shembe and Mlangeni later mended their personal relationship, but Shembe did not allow Mlangeni to return to his priestly duties. Mnqayi and Mzobe both left the Nazareth Baptist Church with a group of followers to found their own churches. Both later returned and were allowed to rejoin the church after they were purified, but neither were allowed to act as pastors again.[11] Shembe ordained some additional individuals in the late 1920s and early 1930s: Melthaph Shozi, Hornet Mbatha, Benjamin Hlatshwayo, Esfanela Mpofana, Simon Mngoma, Eliot Ngcobo, Ezra Mbonambi, and Jeremiah Thabethe.[12] These men shared the fact that they were already Christians upon joining the Nazareth Baptist Church, had little formal education, religious or otherwise, and did not request to be pastors but were selected by Shembe, as he felt the Spirit told him to do. The Nazareth Baptist Church's early priesthood, then, was prophetically generated, as

Shembe claimed the ordination decisions were not his own, but those of the Spirit.

As the membership, priesthood, and land purchases grew over the course of the 1910s-1930s, a patchwork of congregations emerged in Natal with Ekuphakameni as something of a literal geographic center, though not perfectly so. Ekuphakameni's significance as a symbolic epicenter of the church assuredly increased as the church grew demographically and matured ecclesiastically. Various member testimonies attest to the importance and power of their New Jerusalem in the church's early decades. The three testimonies below are but a sample, but suffice to illustrate this significance.

In one such testimony from Selina Nomahashi Mpanza, she recalled how she came to be in charge of filling the water basins for the birds at Ekuphakameni. Shembe had discharged another girl from the job because she had lazily filled the basins without washing them first. He scolded the errant girl, telling her, "These birds of this place are people; they pray in the morning and in the evening, during the day and also at night. And they do not pray before they have taken a bath."[13] Mpanza's testimony reveals Shembe's conviction that the birds that inhabited Ekuphakameni were not avian creatures at all, but people who deserved good care. It is unclear whether Shembe meant this metaphorically, that the birds, with their song, prayed like people, or whether he meant this literally, that the birds were actually humans, perhaps deceased ones, come to bless the holy city with their songs of prayer. Given that Shembe also believed that angels lived at Ekuphakameni, guarding and blessing the new Zion, there is a good chance that he meant the statement literally, believing the birds to be supernatural creatures.

In a second testimony from 1932, this one from the *Catechism of the Nazarites*, church elder and former minister Petros Mnqayi describes the power Ekuphakameni had to cleanse apostates. When those who had left the church to join the schismatic movements of Ezra Mbonambi and Amos Mzobe returned, asking to be reinstated, Mnqayi recounts that Shembe did not know what to say or do about them. Mnqayi suggested that they be cleansed at Ekuphakameni. Shembe agreed with his proposal, Mnqayi conducted a ritual cleansing of the apostate members at Ekuphakameni, and they were allowed to rejoin the community. Shembe later instituted this practice as law for all returning members.[14] This testimony demonstrates the belief Mnqayi and Shembe had in the power of Ekuphakameni, the only place that could purge apostates of their offense against God for leaving the chosen congregation.

Finally, a third undated example from the *Catechism* records a sixteen-verse prayer said by Shembe at Ekuphakameni. Each of the verses implores Jehovah to continue to provide blessings to Shembe and the chosen at Ekuphakameni. Each verse ends identically with two lines stating "Let Jehovah be praised at Ekuphakameni. Praise Jehovah, Amen!"[15] This prayer displays the special covenantal relationship that Shembe believed existed between God and the congregation of the Nazareth Baptist Church, a covenant symbolized by their holy city of Ekuphakameni.

Ekuphakameni, as the New Jerusalem, transformed the geography of Natal during South Africa's white supremacist era. While the political map may have been dictated by whites, the church generated their own map of southern Africa, with their holy city as the epicenter of a sacred geography. Members believed that Ekuphakameni was a model city of God, the most sacred site on earth. That sacredness radiated outward to other temple locations and transformed the landscape of South Africa into a geography of salvation grounded upon faith in God's cosmic plans for a future day of political and salvific liberation through atonement, obedience, and faithful adoration of God. Within the bounds of the sacred city and the congregation's temples, the laws of Jehovah, not the laws of the South African state, reigned supreme. In this manner, the political world of white South Africa was trumped by the religious worldview of Shembe. Ekuphakameni, as a sacred site of theophany and prophecy, and a ritual space for the expression of faith, was a physical and theological symbol that reinforced the membership's sense of "chosenness" and what they believed was their God-given mission to preach the correct message of salvation to the world.

Mt. Nhlangakazi

The second most sacred site within the Nazareth Baptist Church was Mt. Nhlangakazi (the place of the great/big reed), and like Ekuphakameni, it was considered a site of theophany—a place where God revealed himself and his wishes.[16] The church's holy mountain was, therefore, an intensely prophetic site that played a central role in the formulation of Shembe's theology and the church's worldview. Shembe's first prophetic experience involving Mt. Nhlangakazi concerned the command to go there, a story recounted at the start of this book. Shembe climbed the mountain in January of 1915, shortly after the founding of Ekuphakameni in 1914. An array of oral traditions within the Acts has recorded the lengthy prophetic experience, or more accurately series of experiences, of Shembe while atop the mountain for the first time.[17]

This assemblage of traditions is largely consistent in what it records of Shembe's recounting of the experiences. Shembe reported being subjected to an extended temptation akin to that of Jesus in Matthew, chapter 4. Shembe had been fasting, and like Jesus in Matthew 4, the tempters supposedly hoped to take advantage of his bodily weakness in order to condemn his spirit. Unlike Matthew 4, where it was Satan doing the tempting, in Shembe's account the tempters were a variety of spirits who live on the earth, and an ultimate diabolical impetus from the Devil was not suggested in the stories. The terrestrial spirits did reveal malevolent intent, however. Some spirits merely asked if Shembe was waiting from them, in an effort to lead him off the mountain and therefore astray from the righteous path of God. Other spirits more overtly asked if they might take possession of him, to more effectively divert his ministry. Each asked if Shembe was waiting on the mountain for them. Each time Shembe insistently responded, "No! I don't know you."

After Shembe resisted this series of supernatural tempters over the course of eleven days, on the twelfth day Shembe claimed to have received a visionary experience of God himself, accompanied by the saints of heaven.[18] Jehovah stood before him with a vessel in his hand, and from the vessel gave Shembe the heavenly meal of communion and then anointed him with the oil of grace. This event brought about Shembe's transfiguration. After his transfigurative moment, Shembe believed God told him, "Today, I give you all the authority to go all over the earth and to preach the message of the Nazaretha Church to all the nations under the sun.... Go now and teach all nations the way of God that leads to heaven, and baptize them in the name of the Father and of the Son and of the Holy Spirit. Today, I make a covenant with my Brown people."[19] Following his anointing and charge, Shembe reported that Jehovah provided him with all the instructions he would need to teach all the nations and show them the proper path to salvation. Among Jehovah's instructions was the directive to construct the Ark of the Covenant, an additional sign of the chosenness of those who belong to the Nazareth Baptist Church. And lastly, it was amid these instructions that Shembe believed he was also assigned the task of turning Mt. Nhlangakazi into a site of pilgrimage with the command, "Never fail to come here to the mountain Nhlangakazi; whatever may happen, never fail to come to this mountain."[20] The significance of Mt. Nhlangakazi for Shembe and the membership of the Nazareth Baptist Church began with this transfigurative experience in 1915.

The next year, 1916, Shembe climbed the mountain as he believed he had been commanded the year before. A portion of the congregation had accompanied him on the pilgrimage but stayed behind at the Bhedazitha temple when he ascended the mountain. The prophetic command of a year earlier left open to interpretation whether the directive to come to the mountain was to Shembe alone or to all the faithful, so Shembe prayed on the matter for illumination. According to an account from the Acts, one day during the 1916 visit, the sky became overcast and a terrible storm rolled in. All the congregants took shelter, except one maiden named Hannah Mkhabela, who sat down in the rain. After the storm had passed, the pilgrims emerged and asked Hannah why she did not take shelter from the downpour. She replied that God had commanded her to stay put, and had then told her that the congregation should bring a ram as an offering when they want to ascend the mountain. The matter was reported to Shembe the next day, who called for Hannah, and she recounted her experience to him. Following her story, Shembe asked two individuals (Rev. Mnqayi and Alice, the women's leader) if they believed the tale. They said they did not know. Shembe responded that he believed the prophecy was a true one, because he had been praying on that very matter. However, Shembe felt a ram was too expensive of an offering for God's humble chosen ones, so Shembe changed the offering to five shillings. Hereafter, the congregation made the pilgrimage up the mountain each January along with Shembe.[21]

This occasion was a very rare one, when a member of the congregation claimed to have received a prophecy directly from God, yet Shembe did not dismiss it as a false one. Shembe (and the central leaders after him) maintained a very tight control over direct prophecies from God.[22] In this particular case, though Shembe did not receive the prophecy himself, he did, nonetheless, control it and mediate its interpretation. The congregation looked to him to judge the prophecy's genuineness, first of all, based on the belief that Shembe was the one best positioned to judge a true from false prophecy. Second, Shembe assumed, and publicly stated, that he was the cause of the prophecy. He stated that it was his query to Jehovah, via prayer, that spurred the prophetic message. Shembe thereby inserted himself into the unfolding of this prophecy, lessening Mkhabela's significance, and heightening his own by attributing the reason for the prophecy to himself. Hannah Mkhabela was then transformed to a simple messenger who relayed information to the person who started the sequence, Shembe, who was also the only one who could measure the accurateness of the information. Third, Shembe modified the prophecy! In adapting the prophecy Shembe not only displayed that he was the impetus and correct recipient, but also that he had the power to interpret and even alter the prophetic command. The offering portion of the prophecy was retained, but reduced, through Shembe's mediation.

From that point forward, the annual pilgrimage to the holy mountain, from 9th–25th of January, was performed by both congregation and central leader. Each January pilgrims gathered at Ekuphakameni and then walked, in song and prayer, the roughly 30 kilometers to Nhlangakazi (and back again upon conclusion). The church's Ark of the Covenant was brought with them. The Nazareth Baptist Church viewed the pilgrimage as an opportunity for the central leader and the membership, in the presence of Jehovah, accompanied by the Ark, to demonstrate that they were fulfilling their covenant with God. If they were not, members believed that such would be revealed by God at this holy site, he would admonish the membership or leader for their transgressions, and right the course of the church. For Shembe, Mt. Nhlangakazi was simultaneously a site of theophany, among the chief locations where he believed he regularly received prophetic instructions from God, and also a personal spiritual refuge, a place where he could wander off for solitude and contemplation, bask in the presence of God, and stand again in the place of his transfiguration.

Shembe composed, and orally transmitted, a list of ten rules for pilgrims to follow while on the mountain. Church secretary Petros Dhlomo later recorded those rules in writing for the *Acts*, during the era of Galilee's leadership. The rules revolved around two major issues: (1) treating the site with the proper hallowedness, by avoiding noise and sleeping in camps segregated by gender, and (2) preserving the site, by praying, sleeping, and relieving one's bodily functions in designated places "so that the mountain may remain as clean as they found it."[23] The faithful were additionally instructed to wear their white gowns at all times while on the mountain, even during sleep. Dhlomo's written version simply lists the rules, without narration, so it is not clear if these rules derived from prophecy or Shembe's own religious imagination. Given the mountain's significance and sacredness to Shembe, it would not be surprising if Shembe had attributed his generation of the rules, at least in part, to prophecy, but this cannot be known for certain.

The sacredness of the pilgrimage, and the sense of divine awe the holy mountain had for Shembe and the church's members, is revealed amid an array of miracle stories from the *Acts*. To the faithful the stories reified both the strong presence of Jehovah at the mountain, and the prophetic power of Shembe. One tale recounts how the mountain came to have plentiful water. The pilgrims had been drawing the water they used during the pilgrimage from the Umdloti River. But one day Shembe "knew" water had sprung forth under a tree-fern upon the mountain. He sent pastors with a tin container to find it. The pastors located the spring, gathered water from it, brought it to Shembe, and he drank. From that day on, pilgrims reported finding plentiful water on the mountain, a convenience attributable to Shembe's extraordinary knowledge.[24] The eastern and northeastern portions of South Africa are the wettest parts of the country. While far from tropical, the region's climate is hardly arid either, particularly during January's rainier summer conditions. The presence of water can therefore be readily explained rationally. But it was not the existence of water that was the amazing part of the story for the witnesses, but rather that Shembe had the uncanny insight of exactly where a spring had burst forth from the ground of the mountain.

Two church members, Esther Zungu and Sindile Cebekhulu, recounted wondrous stories involving snakes, snake bites, and healings on Nhlangakazi. In one story, Cebekhulu recounted how a snake went up the trouser leg of a young man, crawled all the way up his leg, came out of the top of his pants, but never harmed him. The snake's course and the young man's fortune were attributed to "the work of Shembe." In another incident told by Cebekhulu, a young woman was not so fortunate and was bitten upon the foot by a puff adder, a venomous species of viper. The bite was reported to Shembe who knelt in front of the girl, placed his mouth upon the wound, sucked out the venom, and spit out the blood. Zungu told a story where a girl had been bitten by a snake and brought to Shembe for healing. He told some individuals to retrieve his knitted shirt and tie her leg with it. The members did so and the maiden recovered "through the God of Ekuphakameni." In the two tales where individuals were bitten, Shembe administered first aid of the era based on the nature of the snake's toxin. A puff adder's cytotoxin destroys tissue by affecting the localized area. In Shembe's time, in many parts of the world, suction of the toxin was considered the most appropriate treatment.[25] The story from Zungu does not disclose the type of snake that made the bite. Shembe's decision to apply a tourniquet suggests it may have been a mamba, as limiting the spread of the mamba's neurotoxin is the best treatment. While non-members may be inclined to see Shembe's actions as sensible applications of first aid techniques based on the type of toxins involved, for members of the Nazareth Baptist Church such events were evidence of Shembe's miraculous, God-bestowed healing powers that he employed to protect his flock. Such testimonies from the *Acts* within the minds of congregants, reinforced Shembe's might, his ability to heal, and also his mastery of the environment and its creatures, so that no harm would befall God's chosen people while upon the holy mountain.

In one last undated example from the *Acts*, Phasika Mhlongo recounted how the congregation received supernatural visitors during their time on the mountain. According to Mhonogo's testimony, while Shembe was preparing the Lord's Supper, Mhlongo and other members saw a maiden come down from the firmament. At the conclusion of the Lord's Supper, Shembe said his heart had been made pure by the maiden.[26] Mhlongo reported that another heavenly apparition was seen on a different occasion. This visitation occurred while they were assembled at the temple at the base of the mountain. Church members reported that "a wonderful boy, whose body was covered with stars, was standing in front of the congregation."[27] Mhlongo's narratives of Mt. Nhlangakazi reveal the belief he had, and he asserts was shared by others, that the heavenly host approved of their worship on the mountain.

It is evident from these testimonies from the *Acts* that Shembe and church members believed their holy mountain to be a special place of divine mystery and theophanic wonder. It was a place where God displayed his divine power and revealed his desires to Shembe and the faithful. It was additionally a place that displayed the power of Shembe as God's anointed messenger, the recipient of God's theophanic visits, and the expounder of the means to salvation. Like Ekuphakameni, Mt. Nhlangakazi brought the divine world down into the mundane world for Shembe and his congregants. Doing so simultaneously affirmed the special role of Shembe as God's anointed messenger, while it also imbued the geography of Natal with a sense of sacredness. This topography, based on those who were within the boundaries of the saved, transcended the political map created by whites. Within the bounds of the sacred city and the holy mountain, and the network of temples connected to them, the laws of Jehovah reigned supreme. While this map was meaningless to the colonial authorities, it symbolized the prime identity embraced by Shembe and his congregation as God's chosen ones, who believed it their duty to preach the only correct message of salvation.

Soteriology

The soteriological theology developed, taught, and reified by Shembe was doubly significant for Shembe and his congregants. First, Shembe's theology of salvation, built upon proper observation of a Saturday Sabbath and adherence to God's laws, provided church members with a theological plan of action for achieving salvation at the personal and local, and eventually continental and global, levels. This path of salvation had been illuminated through the prophecies Shembe received, and reinforced the distinctiveness of Shembe and his teachings. Given that this was the most true and accurate message of salvation on the planet, as members saw it, their own faith in Shembe's soteriological teachings also bolstered beliefs about their own elect status as God's new chosen ones.

Second, and mutually reinforcing with the first, the soteriological theology Shembe developed, and members embraced through faith, required a period of suffering in order to redeem Africans, the Zulu particularly, for the moral offenses to God committed in their ancestral past. Within this worldview of Shembe and his congregation, it was part of Jehovah's cosmic plan that black South Africans be ruled by whites for an indeterminate time to provide this atonement. Shembe taught, and members endorsed the belief, that nothing could be done about white control of South Africa so long as atonement was needed, except to express love for God through correct observation of the Sabbath and God's laws. Such loving acts of worship not only displayed the proper obedience Shembe and the members of the Nazareth Baptist Church believed Jehovah desired, but were also an expression of faith in God's cosmic plans for Africans. That plan required atonement at the hands of whites, but offered far greater rewards through temporal elect status as God's chosen and the heavenly reward of eternal salvation, gained through proper worship and atonement. Displays of political resistance, conversely, would be expressions of doubt, even hate, against God, his salvific plan, and his prophetic communications to Shembe that explained the plan. The soteriological theology Shembe articulated not only subsumed white supremacy and the conditions of colonial Africa within this divine plan of atonement and salvation, it required it.

Shembe's soteriological theology, with its strong emphasis on obedience and redemption, was even more convincing when combined with the period of atonement and white rule. Weathering white supremacy became a sensible option for church members when joined with the greater goal of placing faith in Jehovah's cosmic plans for redeeming the Zulu, Africans, and humanity, as this course contributed to one's salvation. In short, the soteriological theology taught by Shembe, and subscribed to by the membership, provided a key part of the intellectual reinforcement of Shembe's overall worldview and the place of the Nazareth Baptist Church's congregation within colonial Africa.

The Sabbath

Worship at Ekuphakameni and pilgrimage to Mt. Nhlangakazi were, for members, signs of their chosenness as God's new elect, who were the first to receive benefit of God's new dispensation for Africans through Shembe. While worship at these sacred sites could bless the worshiper and place them in the presence of God, these actions would not, however, grant salvation. According to Shembe, salvation could not be bestowed from the grace of Christ, through one's faith, good works, or a combination of them, as these elements do within most other Christian theologies. Shembe insisted, initially based upon his biblical exegesis and later blessed by prophecy, that other Christians were in serious error in their soteriological theology. This was no facile difference of theological opinion, according to Shembe, however. By Shembe's measure, other Christians were so gravely mistaken they were offending God with their erroneous observation of the Sabbath and had no chance of salvation. It was proper observation of a seventh-day Sabbath, Shembe made clear, that allowed the sinner to one day enter heaven.

Shembe's conviction of a seventh-day Sabbath was supported by his biblical analysis prior to founding the church, and a vision he had in 1913, shortly after doing so. Shembe's initial conviction of seventh day Sabbatarianism developed during the period when he was striving to learn more about Jehovah and Christianity, and was attending services of first the Methodist Church and later the African Native Baptist Church, in order to do so. Improper observation of the Sabbath was among the critiques, in addition to the wearing of shoes on church grounds and erroneous sacramental rites, that Shembe leveled at existing Christian congregations, including the Methodists and African Native Baptists he witnessed. This means he reached this theological conviction sometime in the early 1900s, and likely no later than 1906, when he had the series of prophetic experiences that convinced him to take up his calling. No record exists, to my knowledge, of Shembe stating when he reached the conviction of seventh day Sabbatarianism with greater precision than this general time frame.

Shembe's strident theological commitment to seventh day Sabbatarianism was among the chief biblical conclusions he reached that signaled to himself, and to others, including the ministers in the Methodist and African Native Baptist churches he parted ways with, that he was a theologian in his own right who was developing a theology that deviated from that of the Christians around him. When Shembe struck out on his own as an itinerant preacher in 1906, he did so because he believed he could ignore the command to do so no longer, after the death of his children, being struck by lightning, and having a vision of his putrid corpse. Yet he did so with some theological convictions already in place, including a staunch belief in the correctness of seventh day Sabbatarianism. When Shembe founded the Nazareth Baptist Church in 1910, the church immediately instituted observance of a seventh day Sabbath. Just a few years later, in 1913, Shembe believed he received a vision in which God informed him that he was pleased with the church's Sabbatarian observance. This vision not only reaffirmed Shembe's conviction on the proper day of the Sabbath but was also a prophetic indication of its key salvific role. Following this prophetic experience Shembe was firmly convinced that the Sabbath was the "test of true obedience to God" and the most vital element in the worshiper's salvation.[28]

Shembe's soteriology, with seventh day Sabbatarianism at its heart, was a development of both prophecy and biblical interpretation, with each reinforcing the other. From the perspective of church members, particularly from 1913 onward, this made the doctrine one that could be believed without a shred of doubt. For starters, Shembe received a direct prophecy on the matter. This alone would make this theological article a most believable one. Additionally, church members believe that Shembe, due to his prophetic relationship with God, was capable of making an informed interpretation of scriptures as no other human could. Londa Shembe recorded a "Grave Book" tradition of his grandfather titled "The Biblical Chapters Concerning the Sabbath."[29] In the tradition, Isaiah Shembe cited the following verses of scripture in support of a Saturday Sabbath: Isaiah 58:13,[30] Deuteronomy 5:12,[31] Exodus 16:25,[32] and Exodus 35:1-3.[33] That all these verses emphasize the importance of observing the Sabbath in the eyes of God seems clear, even with a casual reading. Yet whether or not these verses indicate what day of the week the Sabbath must fall upon is surely a debatable matter, as numerous Sabbatarian debates over the course of Christian history can attest. To non-seventh day Sabbatarian Christians the intended day of the week of the Sabbath may seem cryptically indicated in these verses, and any day of the week may seem as suitable as another to assign as the Sabbath. For Christian supporters of seventh day Sabbatarianism, such as Seventh Day Baptists, Seventh Day Adventists, and the Nazareth Baptist Church, their interpretation of such verses hinges upon a contextual understanding of the "seventh day." Seventh day Sabbatarianists support the notion that Jesus followed the Pharisee position on Sabbatarian observation and remained a staunch observer of seventh day Sabbatarianism throughout his life. Whether or not Jesus maintained such a ritual practice is ultimately a matter of opinion and belief, and no historical facts can be brought to bear on the debate. One cannot conclusively demonstrate from biblical verses alone what day of the week in the Julian or Gregorian calendars was intended to be the Sabbath, or at least an ordinary person cannot. For members of the Nazareth Baptist Church, Shembe was no normal individual and his interpretation of the Bible was no common understanding. His exeget-ical efforts, rather, were those of a prophet and the most distinctive being of earth in the last two thousand years. Shembe's biblical interpretation, then, as he and his followers saw it, was as perfect as was possible for a human. This alone made Shembe's Sabbatarian theology a trustworthy doctrine for church members. When supplemented with the 1913 prophetic blessing, it produced a theological doctrine that members believed illuminated the path of salvation all the way to heaven.

Correct Sabbath observance was understood by Shembe to include follow-ing the prohibition on work outlined in Exodus 35:2-3. The definition of work included the drawing of water, the lighting of a fire, or the preparation of food of any kind, whether over open flame or not. A recorded testimony in the Acts of church member Aaron Magwaza illustrates how seriously Shembe took the prohibition on work during the Sabbath. Magwaza's testi-mony tells of a visit by Shembe (date unknown) to the village of Eden outside Pietermaritzburg, in the Natal Midlands, where a church member named Martha Lujiji had gathered wood on the Sabbath. When the local women's leader, Emely, called the transgression to Shembe's attention he stated that Lujiji was "already dead...there is no forgiveness for breaking the Sabbath law," an indication that Lujiji had forfeited her chances of salvation through her offensive actions.[34] The gravity with which members have treated the Sabbatarian prohibition on work is observable even today. As church members begin to gather on church grounds prior to a Sabbath service it is common to see congregants snacking on raw foods, like fruit, in adhering to the outlawing of the preparation of food on the Sabbath. A church member who adheres to such strict Sabbatarian restrictions believes they are demonstrating their love for God and paving the way for their salvation.

The same "Grave Book" tradition of Isaiah ("The Biblical Chapters Con-cerning the Sabbath"), written by Londa, also reveals Shembe's soteriological teaching that proper Sabbath observation is the most significant of God's laws, and breaking of the Sabbath is the only unforgivable sin.[35] According to this tradition, Shembe cited the biblical verses of Exodus 31:14-16[36] and Numbers 15:32-36[37] as evidence for the mortal gravity of proper Sabbath observation. Both biblical excerpts refer to Jehovah commanding the death penalty to individuals for the breaking of the Sabbath. Though there have been some moments of violence during leadership transitions, to my knowledge, no one in the history of the Nazareth Baptist Church has been executed for breaking the Saturday Sabbath. As noted above, Shembe did not himself discipline Martha Lujiji for breaking the Sabbath because she was "already dead." Presumably, then, Sabbath-breakers would be dealt with by God, and justice, corporal or otherwise, did not need to be exacted by the community. While Shembe apparently did not see it as his duty to exact punishment for Sabbath-breakers, he did see it as his moral obligation to spread God's message about the Sabbath, given that its observance held the key to salvation. Hymn 212, in the church hymnal, for instance, states in verse two, "The Sabbath is the key, the gates may be opened." Later in the same hymn, verses four and five express that God's word is, "in all worshipers" who should "murmur and exclaim" about the Sabbath and God's mercy.[38] The hymn's reference to gates is a bit of word play on behalf of Shembe, as gates likely refer to both the gates of Ekuphakameni and the gates of heaven, as the opening of the first can lead to the opening of the second. More importantly the hymn reveals that the key to opening both gates is the Sabbath. The gates remain locked to those who lack this key and critical salvific ingredient.

Preaching the message of seventh-day Sabbatarianism provided Shembe and the church with soteriological purpose and urgency, a message of salvation to preach in South Africa, and then outward from there until it eventually reached all of humanity. The leaders and members of the Nazareth Baptist Church believed they were the only Christians who properly adored God as he wished, a fact they had affirmed through prophecy and Shembe's uncanny biblical exegesis. The church has historically taken this soteriological role seriously and has viewed this charge by God to be greater than the ebbs and flows of the everyday mundane world; more significant than any political development. In Shembe's era, this made his prophetic charge to spread this news greater than any of the machinations of the colonial state or a white supremacist society. For members of the church, the correct message of salvation, grounded in proper Sabbatarian observation, could be gotten nowhere else but within the sacred bounds of the Nazareth Baptist Church. Belonging to this group was evidence of one's chosenness and an indication that the worshiper was on the correct path of salvation. For adherents, there was no greater membership than belonging to the community with the one and only proper dispensation for eternal life.

God's Laws

Following proper observance of the Sabbath, Shembe pronounced that a critical secondary ingredient in demonstrating proper adoration to God was living in accordance with God's laws (also called commandments in church documents). Unlike violation of the Sabbath, breaking of these other laws could be forgiven. Therefore, unlike the Sabbath, adherence to God's laws alone will not grant or eliminate the possibility of salvation, according to the soteriological theology Shembe constructed. Nonetheless, one's love for God meant that one should strive to adhere to God's laws at all times, and obedience to the laws was considered an act of adoration itself. Like the Sabbath, the church's theology regarding God's laws underscored the collective belief of the membership in the correctness of their theology and worship, and in their status as the chosen of God in need of redemption on their way to salvation.

Shembe's interest in adhering to God's laws is even revealed in the name he gave his congregation. In naming it the Nazareth Baptist Church Shembe declared that all verses of the Bible referring to nazarites [nazirites][39] now referred to his followers. The nazirites of the Hebrew Bible were individuals (Samson and Samuel being the most famous) who took a set of ascetic vows, codified in Numbers 6:1-21, either for a set time or permanently. One was first expected to separate.[40] Shembe instituted that separation by two means. The first was through the creation of Ekuphakameni, as the New Jerusalem enabled the purity of the church's membership through its holiness. The second was through the *umnazaretha* (uniform), which will be discussed in the next chapter. Once separated through these two means, Shembe insisted that his community of the chosen must follow the vows of the nazirites, which required that one abstain from all products of the grapevine (grapes, raisins, wine, and wine vinegar), refrain from shaving off one's hair or beard, and avoid corpses and graves. As Shembe further explained, however, these nazirite prohibitions from Numbers 6 were just one of many laws for God's new chosen people to follow.

The earliest pieces of church lore, from the hymnal and "Grave Book," though, do not contain a full compendium of God's laws that worshipers must follow. Given the importance that observation of the laws had in the theology Shembe's formulated, had such a document existed, it is difficult to imagine it escaping preservation altogether. Surely some dutiful member, concerned with adhering to the laws, would have written down such an essential compilation in their copybook that would have found its way into the *Acts* or one of the notebooks preserved outside of the church's archive, had such a vital list of laws existed. Several factors suggest that such a document was not lost, but never existed during Isaiah's time as central leader to begin with, in oral or written form.

Why did Shembe not compose such a list of all of God's laws, in the fashion of Leviticus 11-23, given the laws' importance, a significance he continually emphasized? The answer to this question lies with the fact that

Shembe expounded upon the laws in an ongoing manner over the course of his ministry. He expounded upon some laws as situations arose. This appears to be the case, for example, with one of Shembe's explanations about laws for ministers. In "The Law governing Leaders who want to be married," Shembe explained that God allows a minister to take a second wife, but only provided that the first wife agreed, and that obligations to two spouses would not detract from ministerial duties.[41] The date when these words were spoken was not recorded, but the content suggests that expositions of God's law, like this one, were provided as situations occurred. Until the church had ministers, and until one of those ministers raised the question of plural marriage, there was no need for the teaching. In other cases Shembe spoke about a law when prophetically prompted to do so. With new situations arising that needed rulings, and new prophecies unfolding throughout Shembe's ministry, a compendium of the laws would have been quickly eclipsed and in need of constant revision. This is likely the explanation for why no guidebook of the laws was produced during Isaiah's era; it was a work in progress.

In addition to the fact that a compendium of God's laws was a work in progress during Isaiah's era, there may have been several additional reasons why Shembe followed an inferred approach to the sum of the laws, rather than providing a detailed cataloging akin to Leviticus. First, some of the laws may not have needed underscoring for a southern African audience and might explain Shembe's silence on some particular laws. The consumption of snakes, for instance, was already considered culturally repugnant among the Zulu, so there was scarcely a need to recodify a law on the consumption of snakes that had little danger of being broken among a Zulu-majority membership.[42] Second, some of the laws may not be documented within the hymnal or "Grave Book" material composed by Shembe because he felt there was no need to re-record something that was already sufficiently addressed in the Bible. I have not uncovered any remarks of this sort attributed to Isaiah to bolster this point. Indeed, it would be a bit odd for him to have produced remarks upon actions he did not take. But it does not seem a great leap of logic to presume that Shembe trusted that the Bible was perfectly capable of conveying some of the laws, and that he, therefore, did not need to re-codify them.

The fact that some of these laws are recorded a second time (first within the Bible and second within the "Grave Book" or hymnal) suggests that these are the laws that most concerned Isaiah. For instance, he was emphatic that wearing shoes was not permitted on church grounds. This law is specially highlighted in hymn no. 60, verse 8, which states, "And those who enter with shoes; In the house of Jehovah; Turning it [in]to [a] house of games; In breaking the commandments."[43] (The prohibition on shoes was later preserved in the Acts and the Catechism as well.[44]) Shembe did not claim direct prophetic inspiration for a reiteration of this commandment, but he did remind his congregants that God had originally issued this command via prophecy to Moses and Joshua, and cited Exodus 3:5[45] and Joshua 5:14-15[46] as scriptural evidence for this injunction. The 1970 "Reminder of the Statute," from the *Catechism*, recorded the following words of Shembe on the subject, "According to God's commandment, a man is not allowed to wear footwear in a holy place. Those who enter Jehovah's house wearing footwear turn it into a house of play, and are thereby breaking the commandment. Those who wish to enter a holy place must wear nothing on their feet."[47] Whether Shembe's understanding of footwear being indicative of play and a lack of reverence came from his own moral imagination, his biblical exegesis, or a prophetic communication is not clear within these preserved pieces of church lore. Given that the Bible verses above do not seem to suggest a connotation of play, it is possible the connotation was prophetically gained.

While no full digest of the church's laws of God can be found in Isaiah's "Grave Book" material or in the hymnal, even in the absence of such a compendium, one can safely affirm that Shembe's definition of God's laws embraced the full set of laws outlined in the Old and New Testaments. Shembe viewed God's laws as having biblical origins, which were then being highlighted or supplemented by his prophecies. Shembe did not see it as his role to supplant or replace biblical laws. The embrace of the totality of biblical laws is even evident at a general level. A survey of those laws that were recorded and preserved in the various pieces of Nazareth Baptist Church written lore reveals laws about food, blood, sexuality, and the body, the very same themes that dominate the biblical laws. This fact was made more overtly at multiple points in the "Catechism" recorded in writing between 1963 and 1970. Within this "Catechism," response no. 31 states that one must "keep all these commandments because the One who made them, made them so that they are all kept."[48] Within the same document, question and response numbers 33-35, 50, and 52-54 explain that Moses was the author of the first Testament, Jesus the second Testament, and now Shembe was needed to revive God's laws because humanity was no longer keeping the laws. The "Catechism" makes clear in the church's doctrine that the laws were a continuous whole across human history, communicated by three prophets: Moses, Jesus, and Shembe. Though recorded well after the time of Isaiah, the sentiment is consistent with Isaiah's remarks about the laws.

Despite the fact that the Nazareth Baptist Church observes a seventh day Sabbath, adheres to biblical laws, and views themselves as the new nazirites, it would be inaccurate to describe Nazareth Baptist Church theology as Judaic. Typologies were fashionable in the scholarship on Zionist churches in the 1950s–1970s, and terms such as Hebraist and Judaic could be found within these typologies of African Christianity.[49] Terms such as Judaic were an effort by Westerners to make sense of the heavy emphasis on the Old Testament that could be found within many Zionist churches. While it is indeed the case that Zionist churches typically grant greater emphasis to the Old Testament than can generally be found within Catholic or most Protestant theologies, a term like Judaic, that emphasizes "Jewishness," conveys the implication that Zionist churches were less Christian than the Christianities known to such Western authors. Yet a strong emphasis upon the Old Testament is a perfectly Christian option with both historical precedent and biblical justification.[50] Inclusion of this theological possibility does not necessarily make a church more Jewish than Christian.

The term Judaic, then, when applied to Zionist churches, elevates one theological issue, a church's position on the Old Testament, to the point of categorizing and representing the entire church, thereby decreasing the church's "Christianness." For this reason alone it could be an inaccurate term. But there are additional reasons why the label Judaic does not suit the theology or identity of the Nazareth Baptist Church. First, Shembe's knowledge of God's commandments came from his experience with the Christian Old Testament, not the Jewish *Tanakh*. In other words, his experience with such laws is through the Christian interpretation and translation of such biblical verses. There is no evidence Shembe was exposed to the *Tanakh*, rabbinical commentary on the *mitzvah*, or even to Judaism. Second, Shembe's implementation of what he understood to be God's laws was a distinctive interpretation based upon his own exegesis and prophetic experiences. The soteriological theology of the Nazareth Baptist Church was not based upon a wholesale importation of Old Testament laws, but upon Shembe's mediating experiences as a prophet and church leader. The underscoring of particular laws and silence upon others illustrates Shembe's particular understanding of God's laws. Third, at no point did Shembe or the early membership of the Nazareth Baptist Church identify themselves as Jews. The Nazareth Baptist Church does indeed hold a sincere belief that they are God's new chosen people with a new covenant, but they do not identify as Jews.[51] They see this covenant as a new grace bestowed by God upon Africans in the twentieth century, not a resuscitation of the previous covenants between God and Moses, Abraham, Isaac, or Jacob.

There is little doubt, however, that Shembe understood the observance of God's laws as part of this covenant and the second most critical ingredient of worship, following proper Sabbath observance. Taken together, observation of a Saturday Sabbath and adherence to God's laws provided individual members and their church with a place within God's plan for ancestral atonement and contemporary salvation for Africans. Members believed nothing could be done about white control of South Africa so long as atonement was needed—nothing, that is, except expressing love for God through correct observation of the Sabbath and his laws. Such acts of adoration were an individual and collective expression of faith by Shembe and the church's faithful in God's prophetic explanation of the universe and Africans' place in it. The soteriological theology Shembe articulated subsumed white supremacy within this divine plan of atonement through a dutiful obedience to God's laws in modern times. African liberation, in the form of divine pardon and personal salvation, would come through faith in Jehovah's limitless wisdom, prophetically shared with Shembe, and preserved in the soteriological theology of the Nazareth Baptist Church.

The Identity of the Chosen

Taken together, the theophanic sites and soteriological theology of the Nazareth Baptist Church generated and reinforced a religiously based identity for Shembe and his congregation.[52] Their belief that they were the elect in possession of the most sacred sites on earth, provided the bedrock of their communal identity. This identity that was so significant that it transcended other options of communal identity that existed in colonial South Africa, including political and ethnic ones.

Within the worldview of Shembe and his congregants, the colonial state and its agents were necessary parts of Jehovah's plans for atonement. Colonial rule was, therefore, a necessary stage in Africa's history that must be endured to bring about their absolution. This belief, taught by Shembe and embraced by the members of the Nazareth Baptist Church—that colonial rule was part of Jehovah's plan that would bring about individual and communal salvation—was the chief reason why Shembe and his church refused to adopt a resistant political stance even amid conditions of white supremacy and imperial over-rule. Yet the colonial state had almost no impact upon how Shembe and his congregants defined their identity.

Whites had imposed new borders upon South Africa, generating an array of new local, provincial, and national identities prescribed by new political boundaries. The identities of some Africans were directly molded by the state's new map of South Africa. Some educated elites and labor organizers, for instance, began to shed ethnic identities in favor of regional, racial, or pan-African ones united in a desire for reform of, and later abolition of, the national political and economic colonial system whites had created. In this manner, being from the eastern Cape, Natal, or South Africa began to take on meaning for some non-whites living in colonial South Africa. Such was not the case for Shembe and his congregation, however. The state's notions of identity surely impacted the daily lives of many members of the Nazareth Baptist Church, perhaps in their jobs, as they interacted with whites, or had to deal with colonial officials or bureaucracy. But within the boundaries of the church, a different identity was transcendent. Shembe and the members of the

Nazareth Baptist Church possessed a different mental map of the boundaries that composed southern Africa. Their map was not informed by political boundaries or colonial control, but on who was within the perimeter of salvation that rippled outward from the church's New Jerusalem and holy mountain. From these two theophanic epicenters emitted the "correct" message of salvation that created a network of temples and congregations throughout southern Africa that were united into a sacred community of the chosen. The church's map subsumed all political boundaries and replaced them with soteriological and theological ones based upon who was and who was not within the boundaries of the chosen elect and following the will of Jehovah.

This map likewise subsumed, but did not set out to obliterate, ethnic distinctions. The Nazareth Baptist Church has always had a majority Zulu membership and for this reason alone has had a strong Zulu cultural character. There is also evidence to suggest that Isaiah Shembe was personally culturally comfortable as a Zulu. Zulu was the language he always spoke, and it remained the *lingua franca* of the church throughout his lifetime. When Shembe instituted *ukusina* (dance worship) as a sacrament, he used a modified form of Zulu dance. From Shembe's point of view there was nothing wrong in using, or even being proud of, Zulu culture. Within Shembe's thinking about ethnicity and race, every people and culture were part of God's creations. Therefore, one could still be proud of one's Zuluness or blackness even as one embraced the greater identity of being among the chosen. Reporter Nellie Wells observed Shembe preaching a warning to parishioners that they not forget their blackness, Westernize, and behave like whites, as embracing Western culture had nothing whatsoever to do with salvation. Wells recorded a statement from Shembe that, "It had taken the Lord [a] long time to make a black man, and a very long time to make a Zulu. We ought to respect the Lord's distinctions. He does not make mistakes."[53] As this remark reveals, as Shembe saw it, there was nothing wrong in being Zulu, Sotho, black, Indian, British, white...as all distinctions among humans were the product of Jehovah's creation. This pride, or at least lack of shame, makes it easy to understand why some observers and authors have viewed Shembe as an ethnic revivalist and his church as a nationalist refuge.[54] Yet despite Shembe's clear personal and ecclesiastical usage of Zulu culture, and his admonition that acculturation would not produce salvific results, it would, nonetheless, be a mistake to view Shembe or the Nazareth Baptist Church as ethnically nationalist or chauvinist.

The soured relations between Shembe, the Zulu paramount, and the royal house's ethnic revivalist ambitions demonstrates that Shembe's notion of Zuluness did not embrace any sort of ethnic nationalism or revivalism. King Solomon kaDinuzulu had taken an initial interest in Shembe and the Nazareth Baptist Church in the 1920s, perhaps seeing the church as an opportunity to gather additional popular support. The king even married one of

Shembe's daughters, Zondi, in 1926. Shembe too viewed the king as a friend and invited Solomon to build a house at Ekuphakameni so that his counselors might stay there and "learn how to govern the country and the people." This would enable everyone to learn the rules of respect, stop fighting, be considerate and compassionate, and then "Whites will no longer have any work to do on behalf of the people, and the Brown people will rule themselves...because they will have received the power from God."[55] The king did not build a house at Ekuphakameni, and unsurprisingly, resented Shembe's critiques of his behavior. As the 1920s progressed Solomon's visits to the church evaporated and relations between the king and Shembe fully soured by the late 1920s. For Shembe, such critiques of Solomon's ethics were perfectly appropriate and necessary, for if the Zulu people were going to be redeemed, the king needed to be a model of correct morality and proper adoration of Jehovah. Shembe attempted to steer the king, the royal house, and indigenous officials to his moral agenda and theological vision of South Africa. He had no interest in theirs and Zulu nationalists were disappointed to find that Shembe and the Nazareth Baptist Church was no source of ethnic nationalism and could not be employed for a revival of ethnic politics. The failure of King Solomon and his nationalist supporters in the intelligentsia to direct Shembe's efforts toward their own is a clear indication that Shembe's ambitions, political ideology, and notions of identity did not match those of avowed Zulu nationalists.[56]

The failed attempt to involve Shembe in an effort to create a Zulu national church further demonstrates that he and Zulu nationalists had quite different notions of identity. Though it never gathered much popular support and also failed to gain the backing of King Solomon, a group of Zulu nationalists, in the 1920s, had attempted to create a Zulu national church, even toying with the idea of naming it "Shaka Zulu's Church."[57] While a Zulu national church never materialized, the 1920s ambition to create one was "aimed to restore the political legitimacy of the Zulu royal house and formed part of the resurgence of Zulu nationalism."[58] Supporters of a national church had hoped to adopt and transform the Nazareth Baptist Church into the Zulu national church, but their efforts to co-opt Shembe and build a national church never materialized.

Not only were Shembe's overall goals for the Zulu at variance with those of Zulu nationalists, he was just as disposed to be innovative in his understanding of Zulu culture as he was to embrace it.[59] For instance, Shembe's usage of the Zulu concept hlonipha (respect/deference) was quite different from how most Zulus understood the notion. For most Zulus, particularly those with traditionalist or nationalist leanings, hlonipha was understood as a political concept, one which meant granting proper respect and deference to traditional political authorities. Shembe also understood the term to imply respect and deference, but he redirected that respect away from earthly figures and toward Jehovah. Within the notion of *hlonipha* Shembe preached, it was the responsibility of all of the chosen, from the most humble individual to the Zulu king himself (and Shembe too) to accord the proper *hlonipha* to God through proper observation of the Sabbath and obedient devotion to God's laws. These were the ingredients of redemption according to the soteriology Shembe articulated. Not even the Zulu paramount was above the need to grant Jehovah proper *hlonipha*, as Shembe saw it, and this difference of political and theological opinion contributed to the souring of relations between King Solomon and Shembe. Traditional authorities, by Shembe's notion of *hlonipha*, were of relevance in serving as leaders of ancestral redemption and as models of Godly obedience, but not as political figures. As Shembe's Christian redefinition of *hlonipha* indicates, he was certainly not averse to significantly modifying Zulu culture. For this additional reason, it would be erroneous to cast him and the members of the church as Zulu nationalists and neo-traditionalists engaged in a valiant struggle of cultural resistance against a crushing wave of Westernization.[60] Shembe was just as likely to promote changes in Zulu culture as he was to preserve it; cultural preservation was not among his goals.

In addition to modifying Zulu traditions, Shembe also encouraged the spread of non-Zulu culture. As evidence, one need look no further than his very promotion of Christianity itself. While Shembe and his followers assuredly indigenized Christianity, even within their view, Christianity was a foreign religion brought by whites. Far from resenting whites for this "cultural imperialism," Shembe was grateful for it, and built this gratitude into the church's theology and worldview. This gratefulness can be seen in the words of reporter Nellie Wells, who in the course of producing a video documentary of Shembe and the Nazareth Baptist Church from 1930–1934, also recorded a set of written notes for the film. In these notes Wells made the observation in her own words that "Shembe says all white people bring an aura of light, and with other natives affirms that evil spirits and darkness flee as Europeans advance."[61] Though this remark is not in Shembe's direct words, it is a powerful sentiment nevertheless, that displays gratitude to whites for dispelling superstition and bringing the light of Godly worship to South Africa. Blacks owed whites, as Shembe saw it, a degree of gratitude for introducing the worship of Jehovah to Africans, whose sinful ways sorely needed introduction to the Bible and God. Quite obviously, Shembe rejected the forms of Christianity practiced by whites and was convinced his prophetically informed version was superior, yet nevertheless he felt that Africans needed to be grateful to Europeans for the initial introduction. Shembe's encouragement of the Bible, baptism, communion, abstinence from alcohol, prohibition of consumption of pigs and chickens, outlawing of pre-marital sex, and the list could go on, were all new practices that were either without indigenous precedent or counter to them. In sum, given Shembe's often novel take on Zulu culture, and his promotion of non-Zulu culture, it would be more accurate to see Shembe's use of Zulu culture as using that which was most familiar to him in building his church, and not as cultural resistance or support of a nationalist revival.[62]

This distinctive and hybrid approach to culture by Shembe lent itself to an equally novel approach to identity. For Shembe, the identity that mattered most was that built upon faith and one's inclusion among the chosen. This identity was a new one—new because it reflected the belief of Shembe and his congregation that a new dispensation from God had arrived to humanity via Shembe—that transcended ethnicity. At the moment of his transfiguration atop Mt. Nhlangakazi, Shembe believed Jehovah had informed him a new era had arrived for Africans by stating, "Today, I make a covenant with my Brown people."[63] While the Zulu were the starting point for God's renewed message of salvation via Shembe, the message was intended for all "brown" people, as they were all part of God's new covenant. Therefore all Africans had the potential and opportunity to join the new community of the chosen.[64] While the church had a majority Zulu membership during Isaiah's leadership, the church's trans-ethnic message of salvation for all Africans did have some appeal beyond the Zulu. Esther Roberts made particular reference to the ethnic composition of church services she witnessed in the 1930s, noting there were Zulu, Xhosa, Pondo, Tembu, Swazi, Basuto, Indians, and Coloureds in attendance.[65]

There are, then, remarks of Shembe preserved in church records that reveal his belief that Jehovah wanted him to spread a renewed and newly modified message of salvation to Jehovah's new chosen "brown" people. But what of the rest of humanity? The statement Shembe retold from his transfiguration appears to be, at first glance, a bit ambiguous on this count. For while the statement does make clear Shembe's conviction that God had established a covenant with all blacks, a portion of the same testimony that precedes mention of the covenant said, "Today, I give you all the authority to go all over the earth and to preach the message of the Nazaretha Church to all the nations under the sun.... Go now and teach all nations the way of God that leads to heaven...."[66] Yet can a commission be both exclusionary and universal simultaneously?

In the case of Shembe and the Nazareth Baptist Church it appears the answer to the above question is yes, and this record of Shembe's transfiguration is in congruence with the church's overall theology and worldview. Shembe believed God created a covenant with blacks because they were the ones most in need of redemption, and God had imposed white overrule as a form of punishment to advance that atonement. For Shembe, then, the covenant was a symbol of God's promise to firstly bring about the redemption of

Africans, and then secondly provide them the opportunity for salvation through the soteriology taught by Shembe. As Shembe and his congregation saw it, "brown" people were Jehovah's new chosen people, but in time, all of humanity would be welcomed to join the community of the saved in possession of the only proper message of salvation. While "all the nations under the sun" did not need the same atonement Africans needed, all nations did need the "correct" message of truth radiating outward from Shembe and the church's holy sites. The peoples of other nations had a less urgent need, and this is why, according to Shembe's explanation, he appeared among the Zulu so the truth could begin to spread from that part of the world first. As Shembe viewed it, then, the church's identity was an evolutionary one that began with the Zulu, had then spread to the neighbors of the Zulu, but would one day encompass the earth. Like in the vision of the spark discussed at the beginning of this chapter, Shembe desired that his church's teachings and soteriological theology radiate outward from Ekuphakameni and Mt. Nhlangakazi and shine upon all nations. Zululand was an originating point, not an ethnically exclusive endpoint.

CHAPTER VI

Sacrament, Ritual, and Identity

You amaNazaretha are no longer soldiers of the blood; you are now soldiers of God. When an army will attack you, you will put on your white gowns and go out to the open.

—Isaiah Shembe, Mt. Nhlangakazi, 1932

Abednego Josiah Mthembu, in an undated testimony from the *Acts of the Nazarites* (hereafter *Acts*), explained how a healing miracle and recurring dreams of white gowns prompted his conversion from the Catholic Church to the Nazareth Baptist Church. As a young man, while working at the Marine Hotel in Durban, a co-worker and friend, Enos Mchunu, asked Mthembu to help him take his mother to Ekuphakameni. Her crippled feet had left her unable to walk and she was going to Ekuphakameni in the hope that Shembe could heal her. The two young men helped mother Mchunu, via train, taxi, and wheelbarrow (she playfully referred to Mthembu as her "motor car" for pushing her in the wheelbarrow), reach Ekuphakameni. Mthembu thought to himself, "If this woman will be healed here, then I shall join this church." The young men returned to work while she stayed behind and lived in the women's quarters. Sometime later, Mchunu told Mthembu that his mother had been healed. The two young men returned to Ekuphakameni. Mthembu describes his surprise to discover that mother Mchunu was indeed healed and could now walk. Despite his earlier vow, Mthembu did not convert at this time. As more time passed, Mthembu recounts in this testimony how he began to receive recurrent dreams about people in white gowns. The dreams served to remind him of his vow, and Mthembu closes his testimony with the words, "Then I chose the lord of Ekuphakameni."[1]

For Shembe and the members of the Nazareth Baptist Church, including Mthembu, their white gowns were more than attire for church or markers of Zionist affiliation, but a sacrament, one instituted by Shembe based upon a number of visions he claimed he had of the heavenly host wearing identical attire. The previous chapter analyzed how Shembe's theology regarding the church's two theophanic sites, and his soteriological theology, produced an identity for Shembe and his congregants firmly grounded in their collective belief that they were God's new chosen people. The church's holy sites and theology of salvation were not, however, the only elements that supported the congregation's identity of being Jehovah's chosen ones with a commission to preach the correct message of salvation. The sacramental theology Shembe developed also reinforced this identity.

Beginning in his years as an itinerant preacher and stretching into the early decades of the church, Shembe established a sacramental theology composed of four sacraments: baptism, communion, *ukusina* (dance worship), and *umnazaretha* (uniform). The first two are familiar to most variants of Christianity, while the latter two are entirely unique to the Nazareth Baptist Church. As with the rest of the church's theology, their sacraments were deeply informed by the prophecies Shembe asserted he received, though each was prophetic to varying degrees. Shembe's status as a prophet imbued all the decisions he made on these sacraments with a sense of legitimacy and truth for worshipers, regardless of the number of direct prophecies he received on the matter, or even whether he received any at all.[2] The aura of Shembe's prophetic might legitimated his theological conclusions for himself and his congregation, whether direct prophetic inspiration was absent, as it was with communion, or voluminous, as it was with the *umnazaretha*. Regardless of the degree to which a sacrament was legitimated by direct prophetic inspiration, Shembe's prophetic aura, or most commonly a combination of the two, all the sacraments were ritualistic celebrations for worshipers of their chosenness in the eyes of God. Such communal events bolstered the faith of members, affirmed the teachings and worldview of the church, and enhanced the membership's sense of community and identity.[3]

Lord's Supper

Of the four sacraments generated by Shembe for ritual observance in the Nazareth Baptist Church, the Lord's Supper was informed by prophecy the least. The documentary trail of the Lord's Supper within the church's own records is sparser than one might imagine something as important as a sacrament might be. Unlike baptism (see the next section), for which Shembe retold and members preserved a number of prophetic and miraculous tales, far fewer tales were preserved regarding the church's formation of the Lord's Supper. The relative sparsity of testimonies within the church's own documentary record can be attributed to the lack of prophetic events surrounding this sacrament, making tales of its mundane genesis less attractive for retelling and preservation. Recounting and preserving Shembe's more ordinary, and less prophetic, theologizing does much less to reify Shembe's distinctive prophetic status and the community's sense of chosenness, thereby dampening the motivation to preserve such plain history. The Lord's Supper Shembe created was, however, "exotic" to those who observed the church. These handful of observer reports, when combined with a few testimonies from the church's *Acts*, allow reconstruction of Shembe's development of this sacrament, even with a leaner documentary record when compared to other aspects of the church's theology.

Shembe's earliest development of a sacramental theology for the Lord's Supper was part of a bundle of theological conclusions he developed while involved with the Methodist and African Native Baptist churches in the early 1900s. The practice of communion within these churches was among a number of critiques Shembe leveled at both churches. A testimony from Petros Dhlomo within the *Acts* explains that Shembe was upset by the fact that these churches performed communion during the day, when he believed God wanted the sacrament performed at night.[4] Dhlomo's testimony cited John 15:10,[5] Matthew 26:20,[6] and 1 Corinthians 11:23[7] as evidence for why communion must be a nighttime ritual. The biblical citations ostensibly derive from Shembe, yet this cannot be corroborated with evidence outside of this sole tradition of Dhlomo's. Yet whether the citations originated with Shembe, or were added to this tradition at a later date, the descriptions of the last supper of Jesus in Matthew 26 and 1 Corinthians 11 do make clear the original was an evening event. For Shembe, this was apparently evidence enough to insist that proper reenactment of the Lord's Supper required a nighttime ritual, something the Methodist and African Native Baptist congregations were ignoring. This critique, in conjunction with their failure to remove shoes on holy ground and their improper baptismal rites, contributed to the ideological rifts between Shembe and the leaders of these churches. When Shembe received the series of prophecies in 1906 that constituted his prophetic calling and began to work as an itinerant preacher, he brought with him a number of theological convictions, including when communion should be properly performed.

Many stories of Shembe performing miraculous healings and baptisms are preserved in the *Acts* from his years (1906–1910) as an itinerant preacher. Yet no testimonies are preserved regarding his performance of the Lord's Supper during these years. To a degree this is logical, for the goals of any itinerant minister are to produce conversions and generate enough excitement for their religion to sustain it before moving to the next location. Though there is no reason an itinerant preacher could not perform communion, this sacrament generally has a greater congregational and performative orientation than the itinerant preacher's goals allow. Healings and baptisms, on the other hand, are well suited to individuals or families, thereby aligning with the itinerant preacher's goal of laying the seeds of their faith before moving on. The lack of testimonies regarding communion during these years, when combined with the general strategy of an itinerant preacher, does suggest that Shembe's performance of communion during these years was infrequent. If more than infrequent, it is possible the remembrance and recording of Shembe's early communions was neglected in favor of the more fantastic conversion moments, healing miracles, and baptisms. The former seems more likely, that the records are roughly proportionate to the frequency of Shembe performance of communion during these years, that is to say, rare. The former seems even more likely when one considers that infrequent distribution of communion was standard practice for Shembe even after the founding of the church in 1910.

Shembe insisted that the Lord's Supper was to be performed on special occasions, not every Sabbath. Within the early Nazareth Baptist Church, the Lord's Supper was performed at least two times per year, during the two main church festivals in January and July, and on occasional Sabbaths when Shembe felt the membership would benefit from the penance and strengthening of faith he associated with the sacrament. The infrequency of the Lord's Supper within the Nazareth Baptist Church does not appear to be prophetically motivated, or at least there is no record indicating Shembe claimed to have received any sort of prophetic communication on the matter. The infrequency may have been practically motivated, as the particular ritual practice Shembe instituted required greater preparation and dedication than would be possible for a weekly rite.

Shembe generated a highly ascetic and penitential form of the Lord's Supper. The abstemious nature of the church's sacramental practice was something noted by two observers of the ceremony. A reporter (simply cited as N. W.) for the English-language newspaper *District Notes & News* noted in a 1929 article that members of the church had been fasting in preparation for holy communion. John Dube made note of the same in the 1930s.[8] The supplicating nature of the rite can also be observed in the text of the "The Statute of the Lord's Supper" within the "Catechism." According to this statute, worshipers must "abstain from all things that are forbidden...and must not do things which go against the rules," for the entire month prior to the Lord's Supper.[9] Adhering to God's laws ought to be a central concern of dutiful church members anyway, but the leaders and members of the Nazareth Baptist Church believed that disobeying God's laws prior to distribution of communion would leave the worshiper too polluted to receive it. Additionally, for a full two weeks before the distribution of communion one must confess and atone for one's sins through a thorough self-examination. The confession is internal and need not involve a minister. One's heart must be pure and not filled with anger or envy.[10] In addition to the purity of spirit, one must be bodily pure as well at the time of the ritual, having no diseases or wounds, and women must not be menstruating.[11] Such an ascetic and penitential rite, that requires a week of fasting and sexual abstinence, two weeks of introspective spiritual purifying, and a month of dutiful observance of God's laws produced a sacrament for which an occasional frequency seems the only practical possibility.

In addition to the nighttime distribution and the infrequency of the rite, Shembe also insisted that foot washing must precede the ritual. As with the nighttime celebration, this theological conclusion was one Shembe had reached in his years as an itinerant preacher and was among the factors that caused him to leave the Methodist and African Native Baptist churches. Shembe cited John 13:14-15[12] as evidence for why he should humble himself,

Isaiah Shembe washing the feet of male followers, undated
Used by permission of the Campbell Collections of the University of KwaZulu-Natal

as had Jesus, in performing this part of the ritual for parishioners.[13] However, there were apparently limits upon the degree to which Shembe felt it his duty to physically, as opposed to ritually, cleanse the feet of members. Dube recorded his own observations of a communion service where Shembe chased away people who had grimy and cracked skin on their feet saying, "Go and wash yourself! Do you think that I should wash off all this filth? Go and learn to keep yourself tidy."[14] Shembe was noted for his impeccable grooming and sharp appearance. His reaction might initially appear to be fueled by personal disgust that individuals had made their physical cleanliness his responsibility.

However, recall that physical purity was among Shembe's concerns in following God's laws. So while repulsion appears to have played a role, Shembe was likely also disgusted by such flagrant neglect of a member's dedication to maintaining their purity, as he believed God desired. Despite such potential for repulsion, either from dirtiness or witnessing the sinful neglect of a member's purity, Shembe remained convinced that footwashing prior to the Lord's Supper was his duty.

So sources make clear that Shembe's theology of the Lord's Supper insisted upon nighttime distribution, asceticism, and footwashing. But what did Shembe think and teach regarding the sense in which Jesus is present in communion? The words of Jesus from Matthew 26:26-28, "this is my body" and "this is my blood," have proven to be among the more elusive and controversial in Christian history of the last several centuries. Two testimonies from the *Acts* describe how Shembe mocked two theological positions on the presence of Christ in communion: transubstantiation and transignification. While Shembe was not terribly forthright about his own thoughts concerning the theology of the presence of Christ in communion, his position can be inferred through these critiques.

The first, transubstantiation, is the belief that "through the consecration of the bread and wine there comes about a conversion of the whole substance of the bread into the substance of the body of Christ our Lord, and of the whole substance of the wine into the substance of his blood. And this conversion is by the Holy Catholic Church conveniently and properly called transubstantiation."[15] Though not entirely without controversy, this position has dominated the Catholic Church since the ninth century, remains a possibility within Anglicanism, and is embraced within some forms of Lutheranism. There was a sizable enough presence of all of these denominations, particularly the last, in eastern South Africa that it is possible Shembe learned of this doctrine directly from pastors or members of these congregations. He may also have become aware of it from other denominations, like perhaps the Methodists during his time with them, who attempted to instruct Shembe on the "errors" of this position of their denominational competitors.

Regardless of how Shembe learned of transubstantiation, a testimony from the *Acts* reveals his disdain for it. On a trip (date unknown) to Amanzimtoti, just south of Durban, a group of people from the community came to greet him and his entourage, including two pastors, one of whom was the famous nationalist and pastor Petros Lamula.[16] Shembe happily greeted the pastors, indicating that he had questions for them about their theology, yet normally did not have the opportunity to speak directly with ministers. Shembe told them he had heard that they administer the flesh and blood of Jesus during their communion and he was troubled by this teaching. He asked them whether this was true, and if so, he deridingly asked, "Did you make biltong, or where do you take his flesh? And do you fill his blood from the fridge?"[17] Shembe made similarly mocking remarks during a trip to Ntanda (date unknown). The remarks presumably emerged in dialogue with ministers or parishioners from an unknown congregation, and Shembe tauntingly asked, "Who has cut the flesh of Jesus on the cross which we eat in the Lord's Supper? And if it has been cut, is it not yet finished? And does this blood, which we drink, not get finished?"[18] These two testimonies leave little doubt that Shembe was no endorser of transubstantiation, and his jeering accusations of finite supply and cannibalism were not unlike critiques some Protestants historically leveled against Catholics.

The same testimony from Amanzimtoti, however, indicates that Shembe did not subscribe to transignification either. Transignification is the belief that the bread and wine change their significance through the sacramental liturgy, but the change to bread and wine is subjective, not objective. The change is within the worshiper, who now perceives the bread and wine differently, and is not the result of actual change in the two items.[19] One of the ministers, Rev. Lamula, in the story from Amanzimtoti above, provided a response to Shembe's taunting about making biltong and keeping the blood refrigerated. Lamula answered, apparently patiently at that, that no, his church did not

Feast of the Passover, undated
Used by permission of the Campbell Collections of the University of KwaZulu-Natal

believe in transubstantiation, but rather they consumed bread and wine to signify the flesh and blood of Jesus. Shembe rejoined by saying, "What do you mean by 'signify?' Because if it is a symbol, it says that Jesus has not yet come. But if he has come, it is no longer a symbol. When we sit in the village of Ekuphakameni, and look at the women, who rejoice by excelling in display, then this is not a symbol. Rather, it is reality."[20] Mdluli's testimony concerning this conversation between Shembe and Lamula appears to reveal that Shembe did not see the Lord's Supper as a symbolic memorialism of Jesus either.

Shembe's use of the term Lord's Supper over both Eucharist and communion may be an indication of his own theological proclivities, and a means to distance himself from the terms most commonly used in the churches who subscribed to transubstantiation and transignification. The testimonies above indicate that Shembe mocked a literal understanding of real presence as held by transubstantiation, and rejected a symbolic presence as maintained by transignification. Yet these two positions do not exhaust the theological possibilities of how Jesus may be believed to be present in communion. If Shembe believed the Lord's Supper contained a real, and not symbolic, presence of Christ, yet rejected the notion of a real physical body and blood, that leaves one likely explanation, that he believed Jesus was present in the Lord's Supper in a noncorporeal, or spiritual, manner. This appears to be the theological position he articulated at Amanzimtoti and Ntanda, in the testimonies above. Following his criticism of transubstantiation, Shembe responded by saying that his congregation, "will no longer use this flesh and this blood. Rather we will eat sorghum bread and drink water from heaven."[21] A reenactment that was not symbolic, "Rather it is a reality."[22] This position is not unlike the concept of pneumatic presence held by most churches from a Calvinist tradition. Given the prominence of the Dutch Reformed Church in South Africa, it is possible Shembe had indirect exposure to their teaching, particularly early in life while living on the farms of Afrikaners. Yet arriving at a theological position between transubstantiation and transignifaction is not so profound that Shembe would have needed any intellectual assistance in coming up with the notion of spiritual presence. It remains possible, therefore, that Shembe arrived at this theological position independently.

As the discussion of the Lord's Supper has revealed thus far, Shembe's theology on this sacrament was largely inspired by his biblical exegesis. However, where the theology concerning the Lord's Supper intertwined with God's laws, the Nazareth Baptist Church's theology of communion can be considered prophetic. Because prophecy underscored some of the laws about purity, especially those surrounding the nazirites, which included abstaining from the products of the vine, the church's communion may, in this way, be considered prophetically informed, albeit indirectly so. Members of the

Nazareth Baptist Church believed the sacrament of communion Shembe established was in perfect accordance with God's wishes and embraced observance of God's laws, and this was so because Shembe was a prophet. By generating the "best" and most "accurate" form of communion on earth, Shembe bolstered the faith of members in him and the theology of the Nazareth Baptist Church.

The ascetic and penitential nature of the Nazareth Baptist Church's communion ritual served to bolster the faith of individual worshipers, and ultimately their confidence in the overall soteriological theology Shembe had constructed. Preparing for the Lord's Supper compelled worshipers to be even more mindful of observing God's laws and maintaining their purity, with the ultimate goal of securing one's salvation. Coming together to perform the ritual provided communal reinforcement of the conviction that the members of the Nazareth Baptist Church were God's new chosen people, led by the most important human on earth. The church's sacramental theology, and ritual enactment of the same, was a communal demonstration to members that they were on the correct path of salvation. They were, therefore, within their own worldview, not victims of a wicked white supremacist colonial state, but a chosen elect engaged in a penitential rite, and had first God, and then Shembe, to thank for it.

Baptism

Like the Lord's Supper, Shembe's theology of baptism emerged early in his years as a minister, during his time with the Methodist church. Galilee Shembe reported that his father had requested the Methodist minister to baptize him by full immersion, but was denied this request. Yet Shembe was fully convinced that the Bible indicated baptism was to be performed by this method only. Citing John 3:23,[23] which describes John the Baptist practicing baptism by immersion at Aenon, likely a tributary spring of the Jordan River, and Matthew 3:13-17,[24] Shembe insisted that baptism must be by full immersion, and a natural water source must be used.[25] The water source must be moving (i.e. have an outlet) to guarantee that no evil spirits could be trapped inside.[26]

Following the Methodist preacher's refusal to baptize him by immersion, Shembe began to attend services of the African Native Baptist Church, led by Rev. Leshega.[27] Leshega was likewise convinced that baptism was to be by full immersion alone. Finding Leshega's theology of baptism acceptable, Shembe was baptized by him on 22 July 1906. Two records, one in the *Acts*, by Dhlomo, and another in John Dube's biography of Shembe, recount the event, ostensibly in the words of Shembe. In the testimony by Petros Dhlomo, Shembe's baptism is recalled in a manner that draws parallel with the baptism of Jesus, as recorded in Matthew 3:13-17. The Gospel of Matthew states that as Jesus arose from the water the heavens parted and the spirit of God descended upon Jesus. Dhlomo's testimony similarly recounted that after Shembe's immersion, "the Spirit of the Lord worked power through him and poured over him prosperity, blessings, and talents."[28] John Dube wrote that Shembe told him that after his baptism his powers to exorcise and heal were strength-ened.[29] It seems evident from these accounts that first Shembe, through his oral account, and later the members, through written preservation of that testimony, are unquestionably attempting to demonstrate Shembe's distinc-tiveness, might, and close relationship with God, through the mystery of his baptism. Yet while the account of Jesus' baptism in Matthew further states that the voice of God affirmed he was pleased with his son, Jesus, Shembe stopped short of such an assertion. While Shembe's baptismal tales purposefully recreate portions of the baptismal story of Jesus, to generate Christian legiti-macy and demonstrate the power of Shembe, they do not contain claims by Shembe of divine status. Shembe asserted he was anointed by the Spirit, granted blessings, and had his prophetic power strengthened, but he did not declare divine pedigree, as the Gospel of Matthew does of Jesus.

It was with the beliefs about, and the memory of, his own supernatural experience of baptism, and a strong conviction in the accuracy of his biblical exegesis on the matter, that Shembe generated the Nazareth Baptist Church's sacrament of baptism, after parting ways with Leshega and the African Native Baptist Church. Not only did Shembe believe that immersion was the way God wished baptism to be performed, but he additionally believed that any other method provided a false baptism that arrested the spiritual growth of the convert. This is demonstrated by an account from the Acts. When Shembe came to Groutville in the Umvoti Reserve in 1913, interested converts came to greet him and receive baptism. The American Zulu Mission's black pastor confronted Shembe, saying "You should not preach here, because all the people are already Christians."[30] Shembe responded, "I do not say they are not Christians; but I say that they were not baptized by the baptism of John."[31] Shembe's statement implies that it is his belief that the baptism provided by the American Board of Commissioners for Foreign Missions (Congrega-tionalist), the mission society at Groutville, was no baptism at all because it was not by the full immersion described in John. Though they were Christian, their conversion was incomplete.

For Shembe and the theology of the Nazareth Baptist Church, baptism by the proper rites was more than simply following God's wishes and adhering to what was believed to be the biblical model. Within Shembe's teachings, baptism washed the sinner clean and provided the worshiper with spiritual strength, making it easier to avoid sin and unclean ways. The church's theology, then, conceived of baptism to be a rite of purity that assisted the worshiper in adhering to proper observance of God's laws, thereby also enhancing one's chances of salvation. Conversely, those who were unbaptized would find salvation difficult. Within these teachings, being unbaptized in itself will not keep one from gaining access to heaven, rather it is the steeliness of the hearts of the unbaptized that will do so. The "Catechism" describes the unbaptized as impure and hardened. They will be cast out (of heaven) because they refuse to confess their sins.[32] The unbaptized lack the wherewithal to adore God through proper observation of the Sabbath, adherence of God's laws, and the renunciation of impurity.

Multiple testimonies regarding Shembe and baptism were preserved in the *Acts* that are patently miraculous and prophetic. The testimonies discuss Shembe's own baptism as well as those he performed. The testimony of one prominent member, Khaya Ndelu, within the *Acts*, described how a miracle from an angel prevented Shembe from being baptized within the Methodist church. When a white Methodist missionary drew water and attempted to apply it to Shembe, an angel knocked his hand so that the water was spilt. The minister drew water three times, and each time the angel knocked his hand. According to this oral tradition, this is when Shembe parted ways with the Methodist church.[33] Which account of Shembe's parting from the Methodists should be seen as the ascendant one, Galilee's explanation of theological differences (see chapter 3) or Ndelu's miraculous tale of an angel's intervention? It is possible that both accounts derived from the mouth of Shembe and he attributed his departure from the Methodists to both ideological and divine impetuses. Yet if that is the case, the absence of the miraculous part from Galilee's testimony is a surprising omission. This suggests that Galilee's is likely the more factual account—that Shembe parted ways with the Methodists just as many theologians-in-the-making have left churches to found their own as their theologies matured. It seems probable that in this case, Ndelu's testimony was a later attribution to Shembe's prophetic biography. The tale does provide a powerful story to reinforce members' beliefs regarding the correctness of Shembe's baptismal rites and overall sacramental theology, and the erroneous nature of its practice among other Christian groups. When a story makes the assertion that an angel interfered in order that Shembe not be polluted by the "heretical" application of pouring on water, that is certainly a powerful illustration of the Methodists' "wrongness," your church's "correctness," and Shembe's distinctiveness, when the tale is retold and preserved as part of church lore.

Multiple tales from the *Acts* describe miracles that occurred during baptisms performed by Shembe. The retelling of such stories enhanced the faith of church members by demonstrating the supernatural power of Shembe, particularly while engaged in sacramental work. One such testimony involved Gaster Cele, as retold by Bheki Mkhize, about Shembe performing baptisms in the Indian Ocean. This testimony says that while Shembe was standing in the water, "There arose a mighty breaker. Shembe lifted two fingers up; then this wave abated."[34] All waves break, and any individual standing in the surf who raised their hand could likely time the raising of their hand and the breaking of a wave. But for the eyewitness, Cele, and Mkhize, who retold the tale, this was a miraculous display of Shembe's preternatural power, a power that allowed him to control nature so the wave did not interfere with his sacramental work, and did not reflect the natural process of ocean waves meeting the shore.

Relatedly, several other miraculous tales about baptisms from the *Acts* involve snakes. Because of Shembe's biblically grounded belief, later codified in Nazareth Baptist Church baptismal practice, that baptism must be performed in flowing natural water, church baptisms often took place in the same waters favored by snakes. One undated tale tells of a multi-racial crowd gathering at Mona, near the Tongati River, to witness baptisms. A snake was rumored to live in the deep end of the pool they were going to use that day, and a pastor, Pastor Ngcobo, was frightened to enter the water. This testimony describes how Shembe entered the pool, struck the water with his staff, and commanded the snake to come out. According to the two narrators of this testimony, Edmond Dladla and Petros Dhlomo, the snake came out and stood straight up while the water bubbled all over the pool. Shembe said to the snake, "I ask you to move out to the lower end of the reed and wait there, because I want to baptize here the people of our Father." The snake did so, according to the story, and remained there while Shembe performed baptisms. Upon conclusion Shembe said, "My child, return to your place, for I have done that work, for which our Father has sent me" and the snake returned to where it had originated.[35] This undated testimony is much like another from 1914 that tells of similar events at the Umvoti River. Like in the previous tale, this one says that Shembe commanded snakes to move to the shallow end, and they did so while the water furiously bubbled like boiling water.[36] On two other occasions, at Ginyezinye and at KwaMbonambi, testimonies from the *Acts* report of Shembe commanding all aquatic creatures, from crabs to tortoises to snakes, to move out of the way while baptisms were performed. As in the other tales, the narrators state that the animals obeyed, the baptisms were performed, and Shembe thanked them for their compliance upon conclusion.[37]

Recall too that Shembe believed, and church members continued to reinforce that belief by retelling the testimony, that he had received blessings and power from the Spirit upon conclusion of his own baptism. Shembe asserted that he exercised this power in all the baptisms he performed, a claim that was later recorded in the "Statute of Baptism." This statute cited Shembe as saying, "When I lay my hand on the head of someone, while he is still in the water, The Holy Spirit of God falls upon him and enters him, as a human being. Henceforth, he begins to do good and righteous things. Should the baptized person commit a sin, the Holy Spirit returns to me and informs me that this person, on whom I placed [the spirit], is troubling me and not treating me well."[38] As the baptismal statute indicates, Shembe believed that he received direct communication from the Holy Spirit if individuals he baptized were leading a sinful life. Shembe was therefore convinced there would forever be a prophetic linkage via the Holy Spirit between those he baptized and himself. This is a powerful claim as it asserts that Shembe was convinced he was the moral guardian of all those he baptized, whether they were part of his congregation or not, as the Holy Spirit would ensure he was notified when individuals were living sinfully. The inclusion of Shembe's claim in the statute demonstrates that this power was something church members believed was part of Shembe's supernatural might; those who compiled the statute would not have included it otherwise.

These miracles, whether an angel spilling water, Shembe breaking a wave with his hand, Shembe commanding animals, or the Holy Spirit reporting the wicked to Shembe, were recounted and preserved by members for a purpose. Their retelling strengthened the overall mystique of Shembe, bolstering members' faith in him and his theology. Such miracles, after all, were believed to derive from God, through the power he granted to Shembe. Though Shembe used scriptural references to justify the church's use of natural water and full immersion within their practice of baptism, the events surrounding his performance of baptisms, and the power assigned to Shembe, reinforced the prophetic aura of Shembe and strengthened the theological and intellectual bounds of the theology and worldview he articulated.

Not only could the tales about Shembe and baptism serve as a vehicle to enhance his aura and members' faith in him, but for individual members, their particular baptism, performed with the correct rites Shembe had taught, was an important personal step in their salvation for three reasons. First, their baptism was public acknowledgement that they embraced the teachings of Shembe and the Nazareth Baptist Church. Second, the rite formally brought them into the community of the chosen. Third, baptized members who subscribed to the church's teachings would quite likely endorse Shembe's belief that baptism assisted the maintenance of one's purity, providing assurance to the worshiper that they were indeed on the correct path of salvation. In this manner, baptism socially, spiritually, and ideologically integrated the individual worshiper within the community of the chosen.

Ukusina

Unlike the previous two sacraments, Shembe did not begin to formulate the theology of the sacrament of *ukusina* (dance worship) during his years with the Methodist and African Native Baptist churches. Rather, he implemented dance as a sacramental form of worship more than a decade after the church's founding, in the early-mid 1920s, through inspiration from Psalm 150.[39] This six-verse chapter refers to praising God's majesty and generosity through dance and with music from a variety of instruments, and Shembe created a new sacrament to do so.[40] The church's practice of dance worship integrated the music of drums and horns, accompanied by the singing of hymns. To maintain the moral purity and proper concentration of worshipers, Shembe declared that *ukusina* was to be performed in four regiments, divided by age and gender (men, women, boys, and maidens). Each group danced in its own distinctive attire, which members believed was sacred and fitting for the adoration of God by dance movements.[41] So that it would not interfere with the Saturday Sabbath, Shembe instituted performance of the *ukusina* on Sundays, entirely separate from the Sabbath service. The sacrament was entirely unique to the church, set it apart from other Zionist churches, and was the feature that most interested visitors.

Women's division performing *ukusina*, undated
Used by permission of the Campbell Collections of the University of KwaZulu-Natal

Ukusina, arguably the Nazareth Baptist Church's most distinctive sacrament, is nearly absent from the church's own record. This is likely due to three interrelated factors. First, the other three sacraments had their roots in the period prior to the church's emergence, while *ukusina* did not emerge until the early-mid 1920s, a decade or more after the church's founding. This left less time for the generation of relevant records between the time of *ukusina's* emergence and Shembe's death in 1935, when compared to the other sacraments. Second, because it was wholly original, Shembe did not need to challenge other Christian understandings of the rite, as he did with baptism and communion, and provide theological justification for his own. This may have played some role in his lack of comment, or at the least, lack of preservation of those comments, regarding the founding of *ukusina*. Third, and most significantly, there must not have been any miraculous moments in the founding and institutionalization of *ukusina*, as there generally were with the other sacraments. Had there been, it seems safe to assume that such tales would have entered into the church's own records, even infrequently, as was the case with the other three sacraments. What we know of the emergence and early practice of *ukusina* comes from the documentary and photographic record of non-members who observed *ukusina* performances, including police agents, reporters, and authors like Esther Roberts. The dance sacrament has also been relatively well-studied by scholars from an array of disciplines over the history of the church, producing some strong secondary sources.[42] There is, therefore, plenty of source material about *ukusina*. But frustratingly, unlike the other sacraments, none of it is primary in nature, containing direct remarks from Isaiah.

Galilee Shembe made clear in separate interviews with scholars Hans Jürgen Becken and James Fernandez that his father's inspiration for the dance sacrament was Psalm 150.[43] But in what manner was Shembe "inspired?" It is tantalizing to assume that this inspiration was identical to the process by which Isaiah came to learn to pray and how the name of Ekuphakameni simply "came to him." Given the thoroughly prophetic manner in which Shembe explained most of his biography and justified much of his theology, this does not seem a great leap of imagination.[44] Without specific recorded remarks from Shembe regarding the nature of this inspiration, though, the best one can offer is supposition based upon analogous circumstances. Yet even in the absence of such direct words from Isaiah, for members, Shembe's prophetic aura lent the sacrament all the authority it needed. While for the average human such spontaneous inspiration from some Bible verses may seem like nothing more than a momentary flash of genius, Shembe was not an ordinary human and his flares of insight were not mundane events to him or his followers. For Shembe and the Nazareth Baptist Church, his implementation of *ukusina* in the 1920s, based upon his reading of Psalm 150, was likely not understood as a spontaneous notion of a fun way to worship, even though it may have later appeared that way to non-members.[45] Rather, Shembe's supernatural power, as evidenced in his ability to prophesy, granted him the ability to read the verse in a special and directed manner, the way that he and his followers believed God wanted him to. Shembe's interpretation of the Bible then, including Psalm 150, in his mind and in that of his followers past and present, was no normal reading. It was the comprehension of a prophet, peering at the verses through prophetic glasses, whose very literacy was attributed to a prophetic gift.[46] *Ukusina*, then, was not a prophetically derived institution, at least not directly so, but for members it was a sacramental form of adoration generated by the most important person in millennia. Shembe and the members of the Nazareth Baptist Church were committed to their faith in the notion that *ukusina* was meant to be and was how God wanted to be worshiped.[47]

Practitioners of *ukusina* believed the dance they performed on earth was the same as the dance performed in heaven, thereby linking them to God, the angels, and the ancestors.[48] It is the recreation of these celestial movements, the worshiper's mirroring of the steps of the heavenly host, that makes *ukusina* a church sacrament and a sacred form of worship. While the members of the Nazareth Baptist Church may hold the belief that their *ukusina* simulates the movements of the celestial host, the actual form of dance used in *ukusina* was, in fact, based upon Zulu traditional dance (*ingoma*), albeit significantly modified. It should come as little surprise that in his actualization of Psalm 150, Shembe would have borrowed a form of dance known to him. It would be a mistake, however, to interpret Shembe's use of the *ingoma* as a statement of cultural and symbolic resistance.[49] Shembe never encountered cultures beyond those that were part of southern Africa during the late nineteenth and early twentieth centuries. There is nothing remarkable about him selecting and using a Zulu dance pattern in the creation of his own form of dance worship. Shembe needed a style of dance, and when he mined his cultural knowledge, that was what he found. It would be amazing indeed, supernatural even, if he had chosen a form of dance from another part of the world of which he had no knowledge whatsoever. Simply using an element of an indigenous culture within a colonial context is not necessarily a statement of resistance; it could just as easily reflect the plain fact that the individual is using that which is culturally known to them.[50] Given the number of changes to the dance style and dance uniforms by Shembe, as well as subsequent central leaders, the dance of the Nazareth Baptist Church has ceased to be indigenous, the Zulu *ingoma*, and has become something new, the Nazareth Baptist Church Christian *ukusina*. Tradition was embraced through the *ukusina*, but considerably redefined.[51]

Shembe's changes to the men's uniform and dance style were illustrative of the overall transformation of *ukusina* from its Zulu roots to a new Christian sacrament.[52] While the uniforms of the women, maidens, and boys were specially designed by Isaiah from the beginning of the dance sacrament, the men originally danced in their church gown, or *umnazaretha*, until a special dance uniform was designed in the mid-1920s.[53] The new men's uniform of the 1920s drew upon traditional Zulu attire, yet was redirected to new Christian and sacred purposes.

Shembe's alterations to the *ingoma* dance uniform demonstrated his interest in purity, modesty, and piety in the creation of *ukusina*. The church's version of the men's hide girdle (*injobo*) was longer and fuller than traditional ones, to better conceal the man's body. The more concealing version of the *injobo* was additionally accompanied by a change in dance behavior that further accentuated the interest in morality and worship. Traditional Zulu dancing utilized high kicks which allowed the individual to showcase his strength and dexterity. In the church's version, while individuals continued to break off from the regiment in moving from the front to the back, and perform their own short dance moves as they circulated, as was traditional practice, the kicks were far lower, thus reducing the chance that a man might reveal what his *injobo* was designed to conceal. Lower kicks, however, were not solely for body modesty. The lower kicks also revealed a shift in attitude and intent from the *ingoma* to *ukusina*. In traditional regimental dancing the individual was expected to behave as an exhibitionist and impress and amuse with his dance rhythms and high kicks. The Nazareth Baptist Church's *ukusina*, conversely, was not about entertainment for the crowd or public displays of skill by the dancer. Rather the *ukusina* Shembe designed was a dance of piety, concentration, and meditation, those attitudinal qualities appropriate to sacred worship.[54] During my own Sunday visits to *ukusina* ceremonies, I witnessed priests winding their way through the crowd admonishing church members about the worshipful purpose of the dance and warning them not to flaunt, lest they offend God with their selfish and irreverent dancing.

A bit surprisingly for an avowed pacifist, Shembe preserved the martial accessories of the *ingoma* uniform, but altered them significantly for the men's dance uniform. The shields were considerably reduced in size. Whereas traditional Zulu shields were nearly the height of a human and several feet wide, the church's were roughly one foot square. The reduction of the shields exemplified the fact that their usage was decorative and performative, not defensive. The dancing men may be soldiers of God, but they were not soldiers of battle.[55] Additionally, the *assegai* (short spears), the traditional Zulu weapon of the Shakan era, was replaced with wooden broom handles or fly whisks to symbolize peace and industriousness. Such modifications to shield and spear represent a denuding by Shembe of the martial connotations of the

Zulu original in the creation of a new church sacrament directed to peace and worship. This reinforced Shembe's political position that any change in the conditions for South Africa's non-whites would come through obedience, adoration, and faithful confidence in God's plan of atonement and salvation, and would never be actualized through physical resistance.

Men performing *ukusina* in their *umnazarethas*, undated
Used by permission of the Campbell Collections of the University of KwaZulu-Natal

The *ukusina* sacrament, while invented and without Christian precedent, was legitimated by Shembe's prophetic aura and the faith he had in himself, and his members had in him, to always know what was in accordance with God's will. Shembe's inspiration from Psalm 150 was no ordinary biblical exegesis, to him or the church's membership. The *ukusina* was special and holy to parishioners if for no other reason than who created and instituted it. While *ukusina* was an invention as a sacrament, part of the *ukusina* was not invented; the dance uniforms and the dance style were based upon a mode of Zulu dance from the precolonial era. As the discussion of the changes to the men's uniform revealed, the alterations Shembe made to the uniforms were considerable. When coupled with the modifications to the dance movements and a redirection of the purpose of the performance, the Nazareth Baptist Church's *ukusina* became something new, a hallowed Christian sacrament, and ceased to be the entertaining Zulu *ingoma*.

The *ukusina* provided opportunity for individual worship and reflection simultaneously with collective worship. As many observers have noted, the steady beat of the drums and the regular rise and fall of the horns, coupled with the lengthy dance sessions of repetitive dance steps, produced a space that lent itself well to meditation. The fact that one did so as part of a regiment, with other regiments arrayed nearby, additionally produced an atmosphere of collective worship and community. Performance of the *ukusina*, therefore, had the potential of enhancing, for both individuals and the overall congregation, their sense of community. It also had the potential of increasing their notion of chosenness, due to their belief that their ritual motions were identical to those of the heavenly host. Because he was the one who revealed it on earth, the holy dance, like the other sacraments, ritualistically underpinned Shembe's status as a prophet. This, in turn, bolstered the church's theology, and the place the congregation believed it had in advancing the atonement and salvation of Africa by spreading the perfect message of salvation Shembe had revealed.

Umnazaretha

The church's fourth sacrament, the *umnazaretha* (uniform), is the most directly prophetic sacrament in the Nazareth Baptist Church. Most obviously the uniform stands as a symbol of membership that is readily identifiable among South Africans. Zionist churches are well known for their uniforms, though the Nazareth Baptist Church is particularly distinctive for their all white uniforms, as white with complementary colors is far more common among Zionist churches. Yet more significant than the obvious social connotation of membership, the uniform was additionally a powerful symbol within church theology and lore that was prophetically tied to many stages of church history. The *umnazaretha* is so overtly prophetic within the Nazareth Baptist Church that even members, as opposed to solely Shembe as with most other prophetic activity, have even described prophetic experiences involving the uniform through their conversion stories. While Shembe's prophetic aura inspired the faith and confidence of church members concerning Shembe's institutionalization of the other sacraments, faith in the efficacy of the uniform requires nothing more than the belief that Shembe received prophecies. This efficacy is attested to by church lore from both Shembe and church members.

The prophetic nature of the *umnazaretha* is evident from member testimonies that narrate material even as far back as the period before Shembe's birth. Multiple testimonies from the *Acts* recount the prophecies Shembe's mother, Sitheya, claimed to experience during the time of her pregnancy with Isaiah. These accounts report that from her sixth month of pregnancy onward, Sitheya received a recurrent dream of people in white gowns. These people told her she was going to "give birth to the lord who will save the nations."[56] For members, retelling and preserving such a tradition serves a dual role. First, it affirms Shembe's extraordinary nature and prophetic status at all stages of his life, even prior to birth, as chapter three insisted. Second, it demonstrates that the *umnazaretha* is the attire of the heavenly host, affirming that the appearance and practice of the *umnazaretha* sacrament by God's new chosen people on earth, mirrors the uniform of those in heaven. As I argued in chapter three, testimonies of Sitheya's pregnancy quite likely contain retroactive elements, rather than a faithfully transmitted first-hand account from ca. 1865. The three narrators of this testimony assert that Sitheya told about her dreams at the time they occurred, but she was laughed at, as was Joseph when he relayed his dreams in Genesis 37:6-7. It seems difficult to imagine a Zulu being mocked for recounting a dream in the mid-nineteenth century given the huge significance dreams and dream interpretation had in Zulu culture, a culture that was only beginning to be challenged in the 1860s. Yet asserting that Sitheya was mocked does allow the narrators of such testimony to both draw biblical parallel to a similar story from Genesis, while also demonstrating the arduous path of the righteous faithful. The faithful individual who faces scorn, as does Sitheya in this testimony, yet perseveres in their faith despite social discrimination, is a common religious trope.[57] Despite the likely embellishment of Sitheya's words, to the faithful this is a trustworthy story from Isaiah's own mother that confirms Shembe's distinctive status, even before birth, and the heavenly nature of the church's uniform, communicated to Sitheya by prophecy.

Just as Sitheya's recurring dream prophecies were believed to have demonstrated the vestments of the heavenly host, so too did Shembe claim to have received prophecies of the *umnazaretha* from an early period of his life, before the church began. Chapter three recounted a series of prophecies that occurred around 1906, that ultimately convinced Shembe to take up his ministerial calling. In the third prophecy in this sequence, Shembe experienced astral travel and viewed his own maggot-ridden corpse that he was told would result if he did not heed his prophetic instructions. During the astral travel, but before viewing his own corpse, Shembe saw a host of heavenly individuals clad in white gowns and veiled with white nainsook cloth.[58] The very prophetic experience, then, that convinced Shembe to forsake his wives, assume his prophetic calling, and embark on a ministerial career, is the same prophecy that revealed the appearance of the *umnazaretha*. Given that Shembe described the vision of his own corpse as dreadful, it seems safe to assume that this supernatural experience left a profound imprint on him. So intense was this experience one might even say that his vision of the uniform was a mental image burned upon his brain like a sort of prophetic photostat.

Shembe described another glimpse of the heavenly host clad in the *umnazaretha* in 1915, while atop the church's holy mountain. During the prophetic experience of his anointing, Shembe described how God soared upon a white cloud, accompanied by the multitude of the saints of heaven wearing white robes.[59] Like the vision of his corpse, Shembe's description of the saints clad in the *umnazaretha* was again a hugely significant one for him, as it was part of his anointing. Shembe believed he had several prophecies, then, and powerful ones at that, that revealed the uniform to him.

The *umnazaretha* sacrament began somewhere between the founding of the church in 1910 and the mid-1910s. The earliest records available on the church demonstrate that the membership used uniforms, suggesting that the *umnazaretha* was practiced from the church's earliest years.[60] Whether the first converts wore the uniform immediately after the church's founding, however, or whether the 1915 anointing prophecy prompted the practice, cannot be known with certainty. It is possible that the 1915 prophecy reinforced an existing practice created between 1910 and 1915, or that this additional prophetic glimpse of the heavenly uniforms is what began the sacrament.

I suggest that the latter is more likely, that the second glimpse of the heavenly host in uniforms in 1915 generated the *umnazaretha* sacrament. Shembe had many visionary experiences, after all, full of an array of symbols and individuals, mundane and supernatural. While some singular glimpses, like Jehovah on a cloud, his rotten corpse, and the lightning-spewing aerial creature whose strike put him in a coma, affected Shembe for a lifetime, for the most part singular sightings were almost ordinary for Shembe, he had such a high frequency of prophetic activity. In recounting his first sighting of the gowns, Shembe gave scant attention to the apparel of the heavenly host, describing it in just a few words. The narrative emphasis in how he recounted this earlier prophetic experience was upon his impurity and how his spirit could not reach these pure beings.[61] In the 1915 prophecy, however, Shembe placed a strong emphasis upon the uniforms, telling of how he saw not just the saved and the angels wearing the robes, but also Jesus, who gave Shembe communion, and even Jehovah himself![62] This vision of 1915 left no doubt whatsoever, in Shembe's mind, about what all those in heaven wore, even including Jesus and God. The combination of this being Shembe's second viewing of the gowns, the narrative emphasis Shembe placed upon the gowns in his retelling of the prophetic experience, coupled with who was wearing it in the second prophecy, strongly suggests a 1915 origin for the *umnazaretha*.

For members of the Nazareth Baptist Church, who believed that Shembe's prophetic experiences were true and that these two prophetic experiences (those related to his calling and anointing) were among the most important Shembe received, it would logically follow for the faithful that the style and appearance of the *umnazaretha* one wore was an exact replica of the heavenly version. The belief in the exactness of the uniform on earth as it was in heaven united the Nazareth Baptist Church faithful with the heavenly host, including those who were already saved. Donning the same uniform as those who were already saved strengthened the faith of the wearer as it symbolized the promise of their own future salvation. Believed to be a symbol of one's purity gained through baptism, the *umnazaretha* protected one from the dangers of an impure world that could harm the worshiper's chances of salvation. During the time of Isaiah's central leadership, the robes were worn only by men, while women wore long shawls of white nansook. Even among the men, the practice began initially among the young men, those who labored within the white-controlled economy and needed the protection from impurity the most. Wearing the uniform came to be a requirement of men of all ages over the course of the late 1910s and early 1920s.[63] As Shembe began to ordain ministers, they too donned the uniform, of identical design, but colored blue, green, or black. The logic of the *umnazaretha*'s exclusionary use by men in the early church was that men, because they worked outside the community and could not maintain laws of prohibition as easily, needed an additional source of protection in maintaining their purity. For Isaiah then, the uniform combined the maintenance of a member's purity on earth through proper adherence to God's laws, and linked the worshiper to the promise of salvation by their donning of the attire of the saved.

The uniform became so powerful a symbol to the church's membership that it has become more than a sacrament but also a supernatural object itself that figures in prophetic events. A particularly famous story in the church, with six versions preserved in the *Acts*, concerns a Zulu equivalent of John the Baptist, named Johane Zandile Nkabinde. The stories of Nkabinde are put to the political purpose of illustrating how this minister, even though unaffiliated with Shembe, forecast Shembe's coming significance nonetheless, suggesting to the reader or listener that even ministers within Protestant denominations could not ignore Shembe's prophetic might and eschatological purpose for Africa. Prior to 1906, Nkabinde, a Lutheran minister at Nquthu, claimed he had a dream of a man with one foot in the sea and one on land. The man in the dream unfurled a roll of white cloth from east to west (from ocean inland), covering the entire country. In the dream Nkabinde heard a voice say, "Behold, the whole country will be dressed in a white gown."[64] Though the collection of tales on Nkabinde do not make overtly clear that he converted from Lutheranism to the Nazareth Baptist Church, it does seem this can be safely inferred. Nkabinde's conversion is the most likely reason why his prophetic experience would be known to the members of the Nazareth Baptist Church and preserved in the *Acts* in multiple versions. Moreover the tales are overall sympathetic in tone. Even accounting for some embellishing by the narrators, the tone does suggest the original author was a member and not part of another denomination. These testimonies imply that Nkabinde's conversion was inspired by his dreams of white cloth.

Nkabinde's narrative is not the only one in Nazareth Baptist Church lore where the *umnazaretha* is a core part of a prophecy. The uniform is so powerful a symbol within the church that more than one member attributed their conversion to prophetic dreams involving the *umnazaretha*. In her conversion story, Gertie Mbambo reported having an initial dream where white cloth appeared, crossed over her body until it enveloped her, before melting and turning to oil. A subsequent dream of Mbambo's contained a man she later identified as Shembe, who appeared to her and said he would come and pray for her. In a waking vision, she reported that the Holy Spirit came over her and she saw the mountains of the country wrapped in white cloth. She believed the Spirit told her to attend a Nazareth Baptist Church service. She later did, insisted she was healed by Shembe, and converted to the Nazareth Baptist Church as a result.[65] Another conversion narrative involving the uniform comes from Abednego Josiah Mthembu, and was recounted at the start of this chapter. Mthembu's frequent dreams of people in white gowns reminded him of his vow to convert, following the supposed healing of his friend's crippled mother.[66]

In all three of these narratives (Nkabinde, Mbambo, and Mthembu) the *umnazaretha* takes on an almost prophetic quality of its own, figuring centrally in dreams that converts attributed as a factor in their conversions. Given the significance of the uniform in the biography of Shembe, and its vital role in the belief that it maintained the purity of the faithful and helped insure their salvation, it is not surprising that it has additionally served as inspiration in the dreams of members. The uniform is an undeniably prophetically grounded sacrament and has become a sacred symbol, as evidenced from its very beginning in the visions of Shembe to the supernatural place it holds in the dreams members have described. The design of the robes has remained unchanged over the course of the Nazareth Baptist Church's history, though as noted, its usage did expand over time. Given that members believe that their uniform is the same as that worn by the saved, the angels, and even Jehovah, wearing the *umnazaretha* connects those who wished to be saved to those in heaven. The *umnazaretha*, then, serves as a physical symbol of one's chosenness, a soteriological uniform that displays that the individual is part of a community upon the only correct path of atonement and salvation.

Conclusion

All of the sacraments of the Nazareth Baptist Church had a powerful role in bolstering the faith of members, affirming the teachings and worldview of the church, and ritualistically enhancing the membership's sense of community and identity. Because of Shembe's indispensable role in instituting the sacraments, his prophetic aura and the faith members had in him as Jehovah's anointed, lent the sacraments the same credibility and believability that his mystique lent to the rest of the church's theology. The prophetic confidence Shembe had in himself, and church members had in him, meant that for the church's faithful, all of Shembe's theological conclusions were believed to be in accordance with God's will. This faith in the correctness of Shembe's teachings is what granted the sacraments their initial power in the minds and hearts of members. A sacramental theology, however, also gains efficacy for members, individually and collectively, through its performance. Whether donning the uniform in the belief that it aided the maintenance of one's purity, or dancing the *ukusina* on Sunday with one's fellow congregants, the Nazareth Baptist Church's sacraments, as sacraments generally do across Christendom, reinforced the community's sense of identity. For the Nazareth Baptist Church, that identity included the collective belief that they were God's new chosen people, who were commissioned with preaching the world's only proper message of salvation.

CHAPTER VII

Conclusion

Semper aliquid novi Africam adferre. [Africa always brings us something new.]
—Pliny, *Historia Naturalis*, bk. 8, sect. 42

Neither Resistant nor Acquiescent: Positioning the Nazareth Baptist Church Historiographically

This book has acquainted the reader with one of the greatest debates in the study of colonial Africa. That grand debate, across decades of scholarship, concerned the question of whether or not, and by what means, colonized peoples resisted imperialism. Scholarly consensus on the matter mirrored the same theoretical shifts in Africanist historiography more broadly in writing about how the colonized reacted to the colonizer. Zionist churches, including the Nazareth Baptist Church, were among the colonized populations analyzed in this debate. However, I contend that all these historiographic approaches generated misreadings of the Nazareth Baptist Church that did not accurately capture the church from its own point of view. It does not matter whether one employs Western/European or African/Zulu definitions of politics and resistance, which was one of the central critiques each school of thought launched at another. Members of the Nazareth Baptist Church were not interested in resistance, and therefore employed none of these notions. Ultimately it was not the use of Western or African categories of knowledge that was at issue in previous studies, but rather the very questions being posed of the leaderships and memberships of Zionist churches to begin with.[1]

Within many nationalist studies of the 1960s–1980s, Zionist churches were seen as heroic communities of resistors who defied missionaries and Western forms of Christianity.[2] This was the understanding of the Nazareth Baptist Church advanced by Absolom Vilakazi, with Bongani Mthethwa and Mthembeni Mpanza, in *Shembe: The Revitalization of African Society*.[3] They accused previous authors, namely Bengt Sundkler[4] and G. C. Oosthuizen,[5] of having weak grasps of Zulu culture that led them to misguided assumptions based upon Eurocentric notions. A nationalist reading of the Nazareth Baptist

Church, one informed by a proper knowledge of Zulu culture and language, would reveal, according to these authors, that the Nazareth Baptist Church should be seen as a religious vessel for the revitalization of Zulu religion and society and the redemption of Zulu ethnic identity. For Vilakazi, Mthethwa, and Mpanza then, the Nazareth Baptist Church was very much a political organization engaged in cultural, social, and economic resistance. However, according to these authors, because everything about the church was thoroughly Zulu, the resistance was not readily seen by non-Zulu eyes and required the rejection of Western categories to be appreciated.[6]

The key to understanding a church like the Nazareth Baptist Church, though, is not the total rejection of Western categories and the full embrace of Zulu ones. As I demonstrated in multiple parts of this book, it was not Shembe's goal to resist Western culture and establish a Zulu ethnic and cultural stronghold. Though he was unquestionably a product of Zulu culture, and sometimes used the culture he knew best in building his church, he had no problem with things Western and employed foreign models, particularly biblical, with even greater frequency than Zulu ones.

In addition, Shembe's interpretation of Zulu culture and identity was entirely colored by his prophetic ministry. His notion of Zuluness was built upon the belief in Zulus, Africans, and later all humanity as the church's theology spread, being God's new chosen people who needed to obey Jehovah's laws and strictly adhere to observance of a Saturday Sabbath. This notion of communal identity and morality transcended ethnicity and had little in common with that endorsed by Zulu nationalists. When Zulu nationalists courted Shembe, they were disappointed to find that Shembe's interest was in teaching the proper worship of God and illuminating the path to salvation, not in resisting whites or revitalizing Zulu identity in the face of Westernization. Shembe's precepts and interests were his own, and they were not in alignment with Zulu nationalists. The failure of avowed Zulu nationalists to ally with or co-opt Shembe and his membership is a clear indication that the Nazareth Baptist Church's particular interpretation of Zulu culture and identity was unordinary and outside a nationalist or ethnic revivalist paradigm.[7] Vilakazi, Mthethwa, and Mpanza's nationalist reading of the Nazareth Baptist Church served well as a historiographic counter to the earlier Protestant theological condemnations of the church from Sundkler and Oosthuizen. It falls short, however, in providing an accurate representation as it transforms Shembe and his membership into the resisting Zulu nationalists the authors wanted them, and all colonized peoples, to be, and not the historical actors they were: individuals who produced a distinctive interpretation of colonialism, African culture, and Western tradition, all from within a prophetic worldview and without a resistant posture.[8]

From the late 1970s into the 1990s, materialist works reversed the nationalist's image of Zionist churches as strongholds of ethnic resistance, and transformed them into politically acquiescent groups who purposefully avoided politics. Many of these works critiqued the leaderships of Zionist churches for not taking overt political stances against white supremacy, economic injustice, or human rights violations by the state. There is no significant study from this theoretical angle that singularly concerns the Nazareth Baptist Church. However, numerous Protestant and Catholic theologians in South Africa leveled an implicit criticism of Zionist institutions generally. Deeply informed by the materialist concerns of black theology and liberation theology, some Protestant and Catholic theologians offered calls for Christian unity and active resistance.[9] This perspective culminated with release of the Kairos Document in 1985.[10] Those who did not resist, like the members of most Zionist congregations, were seen as failing their Christian brethren who were.[11] For their disengagement from politics and their failure to advocate a pan-ethnic alliance against white supremacy, Zionist churches were viewed by such writers at best, as acquiescent, and at worst, as collaborationist for their failure to resist.[12] We must remember, though, that most people do not take part in resistance and their failure to do so does not make them collaborationist.[13]

While the need to resist the white supremacist conditions of colonial South Africa seemed an obvious choice for many individuals and organizations, it was by no means a universal one within any sector of the South African population.[14] From the point of view of the leaders and members of the Nazareth Baptist Church, asking why their church was not involved in resistance politics might have made as much sense as asking why they were not involved in international diplomacy or the department of energy. Simply put, within the worldview of the church, politics was not their affair; salvation was their domain. Politics was not allowed to enter church grounds, even amid the worst political violence in KwaZulu and Natal in the 1980s and early 1990s. When one passed through the holy gates of Ebuhleni, one left politics and all the world's troubles at the gate and did not bring them into the place of peace.[15] Though individual members, particularly the younger generation, were certainly split between the ANC and IFP, much like the rest of the region, such a political division was not allowed to enter the church or affect its affairs. The conversations that dominated the church grounds concerned internal matters such as upcoming church events, the schedule of the central leaders, and gossips about ministers and members, and not the wider political world of South Africa.[16] Members unquestionably lived in a violent and racially fraught world in their everyday lives. But within the hallowed boundaries of the church's whitewashed stones, only the agenda of the church was spoken about and allowed to flourish.

The political perspective espoused by Shembe and embraced by his church's membership was not acquiescent, as in the opposite of resistant. For members politics was not their affair because it was in the hands of Jehovah. Within their prophetic worldview, as shaped by Shembe's prophecies, colonialism and white supremacy were necessary in order to exact atonement for Africans and advance their salvation. To fight them meant that one did not trust God's plan and was endangering the opportunity for salvation that God was providing. Such a worldview is neither resistant nor acquiescent, but an alternative interpretation altogether, in this case grounded upon prophecy.

From the 1990s onward, scholars writing from a postcolonial angle insisted that materialists had employed Eurocentric notions of politics and resistance, and as a result, had entirely missed the resistance beneath the surface in calling Zionists acquiescent. These scholars contended that the colonized were politically and economically marginalized and as a result expressed their resistance in symbolic and internal ways.[17] This perspective can be found in scholarship on Shembe and the Nazareth Baptist Church as well. Brown, Muller, Gunner, and Papini have all cast Shembe in the role of resistor, who offered an alternative rendering of Christianity and a subversion of Westernization, as a form of passive resistance.[18] They contend that the resistance was not readily obvious, was expressed culturally and symbolically through an alternative rendering of Christianity and Western culture, and must be assiduously mined by the scholar with full cognizance of African categories of knowledge.

However, it does not matter whether one employs European or African notions of resistance and culture when examining the Nazareth Baptist Church. As chapters 5 and 6 revealed, Zulu elements can indeed be found in the church. Yet just as Isaiah Shembe's Zulu nationalist contemporaries were disappointed to discover, not every cultural expression of the colonized constituted an instance of resistance or nationalist revival. Shembe's worldview was unique—a bricolage of biblical, Christian, Western, African, and Zulu elements arranged by prophecy. The "resistance" of the Nazareth Baptist Church's leaders and members is not culturally coded and hidden, awaiting excavation with the correct Afrocentric toolkit; it is simply absent. Decades of nationalist and postcolonial writings may have made it seem normative to "discover" resistance in almost any action of an indigenous historical actor within a colonized milieu,[19] where even the color of one's boots can be viewed as a coded form of resistance against Westernization and industrialization and its accompanying mores.[20] Famed anthropologist Marshall Sahlins called this the new functionalism where the "hidden" resistive thoughts and actions of the subject are "translated" by the scholar, thereby transforming "the apparently trivial into the fatefully political."[21] Yet such "discoveries" of hidden forms of resistance say far more about scholarly fashion and the quest to find resistant heroes within every colonial milieu than they reveal about the Nazareth Baptist Church.[22] As I have argued throughout this book, the priority of Shembe and the membership of the Nazareth Baptist Church was to advance Shembe's theology and illuminate the path of salvation for Africans. Resisting Westernization and the state was never part of the agenda of Shembe, the church's leadership, or the membership as a collective (though some individual members surely thought in such terms beyond the bounds of the church).

Each of the intellectual and historiographic shifts above was rooted in accusations against the prior school of thought employing the wrong point of reference, thereby analyzing the Nazareth Baptist Church through an incorrect cultural lens. Yet a paradigm of politics and resistance will never entirely capture the worldview of Shembe and his membership, and it does not matter how carefully one uses African or European categories of knowledge. An emphasis upon resistance privileges politics and directs our interpretations outward, away from Shembe and the Nazareth Baptist Church, and toward colonialism and the state. Using these markers to understand his actions inherently marginalizes Shembe and the church's membership, as the scholar aligns himself or herself with modes of authority other than that of the historical actors.[23] To accurately capture the worldview of Shembe and the Nazareth Baptist Church, scholars must instead align themselves with the same modes of authority utilized by the church's founder and members.[24] As I have averred throughout this book, the worldview Shembe built and maintained, and the church's membership adopted, was a prophetic worldview with a spiritual and theological orientation. The goal of Shembe and the Nazareth Baptist Church's membership was to live in accordance with God's prophetically revealed wishes and divine plan of human history. Their collective priority in prophetic and spiritual matters gave the Nazareth Baptist Church an involutionist worldview.[25] Shembe and church members additionally believed that politics was in the hands of God and ultimately nothing could be done about the colonial world they lived in, as they believed God wanted it that way. Not only were the Nazareth Baptist Church's modes of authority, sources of power, and categories of understanding principally religious, they were also internally produced and privileged the church's narrative of itself. External matters, like politics, were folded into the church's grander narrative of human history that subsumed empire into a necessary ingredient of salvation.[26]

Comparative Dimensions

Though the precise details of the worldview held by Shembe and his congregants were unique, my overall argument has application beyond the Nazareth Baptist Church. Shembe and the members of the Nazareth Baptist

Church were not the only colonized community whose response to imperialism was neither resistant nor acquiescent. This suggests that scholars need to carefully explore the details of particular colonized communities in acknowledgement that the variety of responses was perhaps greater than we have yet appreciated and does not always fit notions of resistance or the absence of it. Spaces existed within the margins of empires that allowed some populations, at least at some moments in time, to view the impact of colonialism as secondary to other interests or as an obstacle that could be worked around.[27] I offer a number of comparative illustrations that suggest that many colonized communities understood imperialism in ways that fell outside of a resistance or acquiescence paradigm.

For example, a very similar explanation of imperialism developed among the membership of another Zionist church that emerged during Africa's colonial era, l'Église de Jésus Christ sur la Terre par le Prophète Simon Kimbangu (hereafter Église Kimbanguiste). The Église Kimbanguiste was founded by the prophet Simon Kimbangu, in the Bas-Congo province of the Belgian Congo, in 1921. His preaching and healing was met with such excitement by various peoples of the Belgian Congo, French Congo, and Angola it generated a fervent excitement for Christianity known as the Nkamba Pentecost. A host of other prophets, claiming inspiration from Kimbangu, also began to heal and preach throughout the region. Such prophets became known collectively as Ngunzists, although they exhibited a great deal of diversity in their beliefs. They operated without the blessing of Kimbangu, yet claimed to work in his name.

Within just months of the church's founding, Kimbangu was arrested by Belgian colonial agents, along with about one hundred others. Various Ngunzists and followers of Kimbangu were convicted of anti-colonial treason and received jail terms and/or hard labor. Kimbangu was initially sentenced to death, but following a commutation by King Albert was instead given a sentence of one hundred lashes and life imprisonment. Kimbangu was jailed in Elizabethville (now Lubumbashi) on the other side of the Belgian Congo, where he remained until his death in 1951. Kimbangu's family continued the church underground from 1921–1959, and believed that Kimbangu continued to guide them by supernatural means. Those the Belgians convicted of practicing the illegal religion of Kimbanguism during these years were arrested and deported to another part of the Belgian Congo. While deportation was intended to atomize the church, it did quite the opposite and spread Kimbanguism to all parts of the Belgian Congo.

In spite of the hugely intolerant response of the Belgians to Kimbangu and the Église Kimbanguiste, when compared to the relative tolerance the South African colonial state eventually showed to Shembe and the Nazareth Baptist Church, the parallels between Kimbangu and Shembe and the Église

Kimbanguiste and the Nazareth Baptist Church are many. The particulars between these prophets and churches certainly vary, but the historical actors in both cases possessed worldviews grounded upon a prophetic interpretation of the world that subsumed colonialism into an internal narrative that, they believed, required a religious response. In the words of Kimbangu's son, Diangienda Kuntima, who followed his father as central leader of the church, the Église Kimbanguiste did not involve itself in ideologies, doctrines, or theories with strictly temporal orientations. In the church's view, all earthly matters must account for heavenly ones; divine intervention is part of historical evolution.[28]

As Diangienda's statement suggests, within the worldview of the leaders and members of the Église Kimbanguiste, colonialism could not have been the result of random terrestrial events, but must have been divinely guided. It is this understanding of empire, then, that informed how Kimbangu and his followers interpreted the Congo's conquest and control by whites. Within their understanding of their place in colonial Africa, imperialism enabled the spread of the word of God, thereby setting the stage for Kimbangu's ministry.[29] Kimbangu, like Shembe, preached obedience to the state because the agents of the colonial state were believed to be advancing God's plans for Africa. Colonial rule was therefore something that must be endured without complaint, with a total devotion to God. A biographer of Kimbangu recorded Kimbangu as saying, "A wife cannot divorce because of the suffering she endures. Continue with your white men as your own husband. Give them anything rulers ask you, give your heart to God. I am the first to pay the tax, because people think of not paying tax."[30] Within the memory of the Église Kimbanguiste seemingly oppressive actions by colonial agents are remembered not as despotic acts that required resistance but as events steered by God because that is how he wanted history to unfold. The catechism of the Église Kimbanguiste, for instance, claims Kimbangu's arrest was the fulfillment of John 17:14, not tyranny from whites.[31] Similarly, the exile of some 100,000 Kimbanguists throughout the Belgian Congo was remembered as God's way of spreading their faith throughout the country. Because the followers of Kimbangu were poor and could not afford to send catechists into every region, exile was how God enabled evangelism, according to the church's catechism.[32] Within this worldview, much like that of the Nazareth Baptist Church, white colonial agents were not tools of foreign hegemonic oppression, even when engaged in such seemingly devastating actions as imprisoning the church's founder and deporting its members, but servants of God who were helping to fulfill his divine plans for Africa.

A parallel sentiment was expressed more recently by Zionist leaders in South Africa, amid the rampant violence of 1980s Apartheid South Africa. In 1985, Bishop N. H. Ngada was the lead author of a report titled *Speaking for*

Ourselves, that contained research findings from an eight-member committee of Zionist leaders (though they preferred the term Churches of the Spirit) representing as many Zionist institutions. Ngada summated their findings in this way,

> Our communities are sometimes accused of being too inward-looking and then people ask about *politics*. It is difficult for us to know how to answer this question. The members of our churches are the poorest of the poor.... Our people know what it means to be oppressed, exploited and crushed.... But we also know that God does not approve of this evil and that racial discrimination and oppression is rejected in the Bible.
> And so what do our people do about it? They join political organizations or trade unions and take part in the struggle for our liberation. But it is a matter of individual choice. Members of the same Church will join different political organizations or trade unions and some will choose not to join anything. Politics is not a Church matter. People meet together in our Churches to pray and to worship and to experience the healing of the Spirit. They go to political organizations in order to take action against our government.[33]

The thoughts expressed by Ngada and this panel of Zionist leaders suggest that the inward-looking focus upon worship and spiritual matters, and the philosophy of leaving political activity and resistance to personal choice was common among more Zionist congregations than just the Nazareth Baptist Church and Église Kimbanguiste. The Zionists Ngada and the others represented were free to choose a course of resistance, or not, as individuals outside the church, but none of the institutions saw resistance politics as their responsibility. While some Protestant and Catholic leaders in South Africa may have developed a political consciousness by the 1980s that mandated resistance, there is nothing inherent in Christianity that makes resistance by Christian congregations any more normative than a disinterest in politics and seeing political affairs as the unfolding of God's will. Across Christian history, one can find congregations with every range of possible relationship with, and interpretation of, political authorities. Criticisms against Zionist institutions for being politically acquiescent and lacking a proper materialist consciousness were judgments made by those who resisted, as though the primacy of politics and the need for direct engagement in politics should have been the obvious choice for any non-white individual or organization.

Such a posture toward colonialism could potentially even be found in some surprising places, at least at some moments in history. While one might first imagine that the concept of resistance, even revolution, would best describe every individual and epoch of the Communist Party of South Africa (hereafter CPSA), even it, at least for a time, had a stance toward colonialism that one could not truly typify as resistant or acquiescent.[34] Founded in 1921, the organization underwent a shift in leadership and ideology from 1929–1931, as did many communist parties. Chairman Sidney Bunting was expelled and replaced with Douglas Wolton, a signal of the ideological shift toward Stalinism within the CPSA and the growing influence of Comintern. From 1928–1935, Comintern supported the ideological concept of the "Third Period," a notion that the world was on the brink of widespread economic collapse and working class radicalization. Once discord took hold, the time would be right for widespread global proletarian revolution. In the meantime, while waiting for the "Third Period" to come to fruition, many Communist parties took the greatest interest in targeting rivals on the left in preparation for the need to have a "properly" radical vanguard readied, not in targeting capitalism, which they believed would soon collapse under its own weight. The ideology of the "Third Period" lent itself to a worldview for CPSA members that was focused upon the party's internal affairs and its links to international communism, with almost no regard for the actions of colonial agents, who were interpreted as relics whose power was about to be eradicated.[35]

So for a stretch of roughly seven years it would not be proper to describe the CPSA as resistant. The CPSA was not engaged in active resistance as it waited for worldwide discord to emerge. But neither would it be accurate to describe the CPSA as acquiescent, as the members of the organization did espouse a long-term interest in destroying the colonial state and replacing it with a black workers' republic. While the leadership and membership of the 1920s–1930s CPSA derived its worldview from international communist ideology of the era, not from prophecy and religion as did those who belonged to the Nazareth Baptist Church, Église Kimbanguiste, or the various Zionist churches described by Bishop Ngada, they all nonetheless shared the fact that they viewed something other than colonialism as the principal determinant of their present and future. For all of them, the machinations of the colonial state and its officials were secondary to their own concerns, whether those interests were preparing for global proletarian revolution or the atonement and salvation of humankind. If even a communist party could have an involutionist position somewhere between resistance and acquiescence, if only for a time, surely other communities in colonized places were capable of generating such worldviews that subsumed colonialism within another explanatory framework.

After Apartheid

Andreas Heuser has demonstrated how the public image of Zionist churches has undergone a redemptive reassessment in the new post-Apartheid South Africa. Just a generation before, significant numbers of South Africans had critiqued Zionist institutions and their memberships for their lack of a resistant posture against white supremacy. But in the new South Africa, many Zionist leaders and members were hailed for the wisdom of their "third path" between total acculturation, now deemed a cultural failure, and physical resistance, now deemed a political failure.[36] This third path was now praised as the crafty choice as it allowed for the preservation of black culture(s) while escaping the repressive hands of the state by creating an alternative space for black Christians. The Nazareth Baptist Church was part of this redemptive exercise of the post-Apartheid African Renaissance, as exemplified by the awarding of the King Cetshwayo African Image Award to Vimbeni Shembe in 2001, on behalf of his grandfather, Isaiah Shembe.[37]

Though the South African public image of Zionist churches shifted after the demise of Apartheid, the memories and narratives the memberships of many Zionist churches told about the period prior to Apartheid's collapse did not. The testimonies from representatives of South Africa's two largest Zionist churches, the Zion Christian Church and Nazareth Baptist Church, to the Truth and Reconciliation Commission, describe how their respective churches did not engage in resistance but generated a response to the Apartheid state principally informed by religion that was neither resistant nor acquiescent. This would have been the perfect opportunity, given that it was going on a very public record, to spin a glorified version of history that celebrated the ways in which their churches had supported the anti-Apartheid struggle. Yet the text of both testimonies refrained from doing so and instead presented, rather unapologetically, their church's political positions on Apartheid, to the occasional frustration of the panel administering the hearings.

Rev. Emmanuel Motolla, spokesperson for the Zion Christian Church, described how the leaders and members of his church engaged in a "spiritual war against hatred" that taught its members proper morality, pride, and pacifism.[38] Motolla explained how this position could be traced back to their central leader in 1948, Bishop Edward Lekganyane. When young church members asked the bishop if they were free to join African political movements he "advised them that as long as their extra-church activities were not in conflict with the practices of the church, they were free to participate." Like the Nazareth Baptist Church, the leadership of the Zion Christian Church allowed their members to engage in politics beyond the church, but the institution itself did not take a resistant stance nor directly engage in politics beyond teaching their membership to not resort to hate.

Two decisions by the leadership of the Zion Christian Church were deemed collaborationist by outsiders, but were considered otherwise by those within the Zion Christian Church. First, while many people in and out of South Africa had advocated disinvestment as a tool to combat Apartheid, Motolla explained that, "We place on record that we were and are opposed to disinvestment as a means to an end. During the time when companies were disinvesting, the church encouraged its members to enter the business arena to create jobs." In his testimony, Motolla explained how his church ran a mill and a transportation company to generate jobs and improve the lives of their congregants. Their interest in development for their membership was more significant than whether or not that fit with international sanctions policy or outsiders' notions of what they ought to be doing.

The second incident, and a famous one at that, was one Motolla chose not to address, despite Archbishop Desmond Tutu's probing query on the matter and his invitation, bordering on pleading, for Bishop Barnabas Lekganyane to address the commission about it. In 1985, President P. W. Botha visited the Zion Christian Church's 75th anniversary celebration at their headquarters in Moria. Many individuals saw the event as an endorsement of the Apartheid government and racial treason of the highest order by the leaders and members of the Zion Christian Church. Given that Motolla purposefully avoided addressing the topic, one can only surmise at the leadership's logic in 1985. However, it would not be unreasonable to suggest that Botha's 1985 visit was a symbolic extension of the church's position not to engage in hate, even against those who oppress. When Barnabas Lekganyane spoke at the 1985 celebration, he did not address Botha or politics but preached about love and peace, and concluded his sermon with a prayer saying, "keep our State President and Mrs. Botha and us safe from harm."[39]

During the follow-up questions to Motolla's testimony, one of the Truth and Reconciliation Commission panel members (Rev. K. Mgojo) stated, "I would have liked to have heard about what programmes were those which your church was involved in, in fighting against apartheid." Motolla responded by saying,

> As a church, the Zion Christian Church did not lead people into a mode of resistance against apartheid.... We thought genuinely we needed to teach our people to be able to stand upright and not to hurt others, but to refuse to be hurt by others ... And if by non-participation, it is meant that Bishop Lekganyane did not go and stand up in the street and say, let us fight, let us go to wa[r], then as far as that is concerned, if that is the omission you are referring to, we plead guilty, Chairperson.... But we taught our people, all these people who are members of this church, listen to his Grace's sermons regularly and they are taught nothing less than rejecting that which is evil and unjust.

While seen as acquiescent and collaborationist by many, particularly after Botha's 1985 visit, it appears the leadership of the Zion Christian Church may have acted based upon the premises of their own worldview, grounded in religion and morality. Those premises were not in alignment with the anti-Apartheid movement, but the leadership of the Zion Christian Church did not care about that, either during Apartheid or after it.

The testimony provided to the Truth and Reconciliation Commission by the Nazareth Baptist Church similarly provides evidence of the church's prophetic position on politics. In his testimony of 18 November 1997, senior minister and spokesperson Rev. Mthembeni Mpanza provided a lengthy history of Shembe and the early church, with interspersed remarks about how their congregation suffered during the era of white supremacy. Yet only about ten-fifteen percent of Mpanza's testimony concerned the collective memory of persecution the members of the Nazareth Baptist Church feel they suffered in their early history. Equally interesting is the fact that Mpanza targeted missionaries for most of the troubles the Nazareth Baptist Church suffered at the hands of the white world. He stated, "This warfare against SHEMBE by the Missionaries had a very negative impact on the growth of this church. Because of the short time given to me to prepare this hearing I am unable to give all the specific incidents [that] led to the sufferings, scorn, persecution and false representation against the church from the time of the Prophet to this day." Mpanza attributed the government's early surveillance and harassment of Shembe and the membership of the Nazareth Baptist Church to incitement by missionaries when he explained, "The Missionaries had vowed to wipe it off from its existence and in so doing, they agitated the government of the day to thwart its activities."[40] As Mpanza's testimony reveals, the Nazareth Baptist Church does possess some collective memory of harassment from its early decades. Nonetheless, ruthless oppression and the need for resistance does not dominate the congregation's history of itself, even in testimony delivered at the Truth and Reconciliation Commission, whose entire purpose was the airing of past injustices.

Rev. Mpanza continued his testimony by explaining the church members' attitude to politics, as he said Shembe had taught them. Mpanza reported to the commission,

> Isaiah Shembe, as a Prophet, taught his people to respect the authorities, but promised that through our constant prayer and supplication to God, one day God will answer our prayers.... So, for AmaNazaretha, whenever they were confronted by the Government or other Missionary churches, all they had to do was to ask the congregation to kneel down and have "Isiguqo," which is a special prayer to God.[41]

As Mpanza made clear, when a member of the church experienced adversity in everyday life, whether that adversity was political (coming from the government) or social (coming from Protestants and Catholics), the response was the same. Shembe's instructions were to pray, an approach to the world beyond the church that parishioners continued to follow throughout the years of white supremacy. As Shembe and the church's membership saw it, relief from the conditions of colonial Africa would only come through the mercy of Jehovah in accordance with his divine plans. Prayer helped the worshiper endure the period of atonement they felt was necessary for African salvation. Moreover, enduring such adversity imposed by the world outside the church was an expression of faith and love to God, by the adoring worshiper, as it demonstrated that they embraced God's divine plan and omnipotent wisdom in knowing what was best in bringing about African salvation.

Later in his testimony, Rev. Mpanza suggested that the black community needed to reflexively consider how it contributed to its own problems through immoral living, and not blame others for all their troubles. Mpanza noted that "there is a culture of indolence, lack of work ethics and general irresponsibility which we have to address without fail.... The greatest enemy of the Black man is liquor.... Drunkenness goes hand in hand with laziness, irresponsibility and uncouthness." Apartheid provided a convenient scapegoat, a cover for what Mpanza, and the church's leaders who helped him prepare his statement, saw as inexcusable immoral excesses. As Mpanza explained it, "It is quite interesting to listen to other people confessing their sins, and we tend to regard ourselves as holier than thou. But time will tell, and is already telling that there is a lot which is lacking in Black society. The greatest mistake we can make is to fail to appreciate our weaknesses and keep blaming others for our iniquities."[42] Suggesting that blacks need to be accountable for their own moral shortcomings, and not blame the country's lengthy history of white supremacy for the current state of affairs, is hardly what one could describe as resistant language or anger over past injustices. Like the testimony from the Zion Christian Church, that from the Nazareth Baptist Church is clearly employing an internal logic, one that scarcely even fulfills the central purpose of the Truth and Reconciliation Commission of airing past injustices to build a new South Africa.

In his analysis of the testimonies from these two churches, Robin Petersen considers these scripts and their silences to be evidence of "resistance in a different key."[43] I would agree that the testimonies of both Motolla and Mpanza are in a "different key" and rarely aligned with the goals of the Truth and Reconciliation Commission as its designers envisioned. However, I think it a mistake to consider the lack of a discussion of resistance as a form of resistance. The reason these testimonies are in a "different key" is because the histories and political positions of both churches were grounded in an involutionist religious logic of their own, a logic which did not embrace notions of resistance or acquiescence in determining their historical relationship to the South African state. The reason Motolla and Mpanza addressed resistance only when prompted was not to subvert the Truth and Reconciliation Commission and redirect its mission, as Petersen suggests, but because the very concept was not at the heart of how these congregations had behaved historically. The religious and moral concerns that shaped the worldview and guided the actions of both congregations comes through clearly. It does not appear that either Motolla or Mpanza were "playing politics" and attempting to use the forum of the Truth and Reconciliation Commission to whitewash their churches' histories or showcase how their institutions were strongholds of black resistance amid white supremacy, though they surely could have. The fact that they did not engage in a rhetoric of resistance, and did not say that which might have been fashionable, even desirable, to the Truth and Reconciliation Commission's faith communities panel, strongly suggests that their testimonies reveal the genuine philosophies their churches had—living according to the prophetically revealed plans of their central leaders, as they believed God was instructing them.

As these Truth and Reconciliation Commission testimonies reveal, as have the previous chapters of this book, for the founder and members of the Nazareth Baptist Church the dominant story of its early history was, and continues to be, the story of Shembe and his prophetic role in providing salvation to Africans as they believed God instructed. Shembe's understanding of politics, therefore, was neither Western nor African, but prophetic. Shembe and the Nazareth Baptist Church faithful were never engaged in political resistance or acquiescence because both concepts were meaningless from their point of view. For them, the ultimate authority was God, not an official of the state or a traditional chief. Within the worldview of Shembe and the church's membership, politics was an element in God's cosmic plan that unfolded as he saw fit. Political officers and indigenous leaders were but pawns on God's cosmic chess board as they served their role in the unfolding of Africa's salvation. For this community, colonial South Africa was not an extension of Western empire and white supremacy in need of resistance, but agents of God helping to pave the path of salvation for the new chosen people. Seemingly oppressive actions of the state, in the minds of Shembe and his followers, were sins against God and derailments of their salvific plans, not politically oppressive actions from a white supremacist state that needed to be actively or symbolically resisted or acquiescently ignored. Therefore, within the worldview of the worshipers of the Nazareth Baptist Church, there was no point in being involved, or not involved, in politics. God had the situation well in hand, and was providing prophetic updates to Shembe on how his new chosen people should worship him and achieve salvation. Politics and colonialism, then, to the church, were entirely subsumed by religion.

Throughout this book I have advanced the argument that the founder and members of the Nazareth Baptist Church possessed a prophetically informed worldview that was constructed through the prophetic experiences of Isaiah Shembe and institutionalized in the church he founded and led. Prophecy was Shembe's *uhlanga*, the source from which his theology and worldview had sprung. The history, theology, and identity of the Nazareth Baptist Church all served to maintain this worldview for Shembe and church members. Shembe and the members of the Nazareth Baptist Church were firmly committed, with the kind of confidence fueled by faith, to the worldview Shembe built and the church propagated. Because it was grounded in prophecy, this was no ordinary explanation of the world for members, but a divinely revealed plan that placed them and their church at the epicenter of their own salvific history. Their worldview was an involutionist, inward-looking one that subsumed every other matter, even empire, into the church's own explanation for the conditions of colonial South Africa.

In this manner, Shembe and the Nazareth Baptist Church reveal a new way of thinking about colonial Africa, the range of responses produced by colonized populations, and the ways in which the colonized explained imperialism within their own epistemologies. The cases of the Église Kimbanguiste, Zion Christian Church, the Zionist churches in *Speaking for Ourselves*, and even the Communist Party of South Africa all suggest that the Nazareth Baptist Church was not anomalous in this regard. A variety of colonized populations, at least at some moments in time, understood and explained colonialism in involutionist manners that rejected notions of political primacy and imperial oppression in need of resistance. Accessing those worldviews is perfectly possible, provided the scholar is willing to put aside the nationalist and post-colonial quests to excavate "hidden" resistance within the speaking of every word and the lifting of every finger of every colonized individual. Resistors and resistance are unquestionably a vital part of the story of colonialism and those narratives do indeed need telling. But to truly understand the history of empires and the colonized, we must be cognizant of how textured and complicated the story can be. Within the margins of all empires lived those who understood their imperial experiences on their own terms, and outside of a resistance paradigm. Their histories are equally vital parts of the histories of empires and provide us a fuller and richer appreciation for the array of experiences individuals and communities had within colonial worlds.

Notes

Chapter I

1. Mthembeni P. Mpanza, "The Biography of Isaiah Shembe," 46. Durban Local History Museums, accession number 98/653.

2. Irving Hexham and G. C. Oosthuizen, eds., trans. Hans-Jürgen Becken, *The Story of Isaiah Shembe, Volume One: History and Traditions Centered on Ekuphakameni and Mount Nhlangakazi* (Lewiston, NY: Edwin Mellen Press, 1996), 79-84. Testimonies of Petros M. Dhlomo, Muntuwezizwe Buthelezi, Johannes Duma, and Solomon Mdluli; Mpanza, "The Biography of Isaiah Shembe," 46; and Evangelist Khaya Ndelu in Robert Papini, *Rise Up and Dance and Praise God*, Education Pamphlet No. 3 (Durban: Local History Museums, 1992), 26.

3. Hexham and Oosthuizen, *The Story of Isaiah Shembe, Vol. One*, 81. Testimony of Petros M. Dhlomo.

4. In the early years of the church, Shembe and his congregation used the Zulu term *nsundu*, or brown, to refer to Africans more often than *omnyama*, or black. Both terms can be used to mean dark-skinned person.

5. Adam Ashforth, *Witchcraft, Violence, and Democracy in South Africa* (Chicago: University of Chicago Press, 2005), xiv; Robert J. Houle, *Making African Christianity: Africans Reimagining Their Faith in Colonial South Africa* (Bethlehem, PA: Lehigh University Press, 2011), xxiii.

6. Gregory makes the same point regarding martyrdom narratives. Brad S. Gregory, *Salvation at Stake: Christian Martyrdom in Early Modern Europe* (Cambridge, MA: Harvard University Press, 1999), 9-10, 12-15.

7. In the mythology of Nguni-speaking peoples, including the Zulu, *uhlanga* (and related spellings of the word), refers to the source, the original bed of reeds, whose maturation produced creation. Henry Callaway, *The Religious System of the Amazulu in the Zulu Language with Translation into English and notes in four parts* (Facsimile reprint of 1885 ed., Cape Town: C. Struik Ltd., 1970), 2.

8. A worldview is a multidimensional network of theoretical, practical, and social strategies for establishing human identity through a negotiation of person and place. David Chidester, "Worldview Analysis of African Indigenous Churches," *Journal for the Study of Religion* 2, no. 1 (1989): 16. See also Robert Doran, *Birth of a Worldview: Early Christianity in Its Jewish and Pagan Context* (Boulder, CO: Westview Press, 1995), 1-2, 6-7.

9. Terence Ranger, "Religious Movements and Politics in Sub-Saharan Africa," *African Studies Review* 29, no. 2 (1986): 51.

10. See Shula Marks, "Patriotism, Patriarchy and Purity: Natal and the Politics of Zulu Ethnic Consciousness," in *The Creation of Tribalism in Southern Africa*, ed. Leroy Vail (Berkeley:

University of California Press, 1989), 215-240, for a discussion of the roots of Zulu ethnic consciousness. For a variety of debates and perspectives on Zulu identity see Benedict Carton, John Laband, and Jabulani Sithole, eds., *Zulu Identities: Being Zulu, Past and Present* (New York: Columbia University Press, 2009).

11. Norman Etherington, "Kingdoms of This World and the Next: Christian Beginnings among Zulu and Swazi," in *Christianity in South Africa: A Political, Social, and Cultural History*, eds. Richard Elphick and Rodney Davenport (Berkeley: University of California Press, 1997), 97-98.

12. For more on the British conquest of the Zulu see Jeff Guy, *The Destruction of the Zulu Kingdom: The Civil War in Zululand, 1879-1884* (London: Longman, 1979).

13. Princes shall come out of Egypt; Ethiopia shall soon stretch out her hands unto God. KJV

14. The term is metaphorical and should not be confused with the historic Ethiopian Orthodox Tewahedo Church, which remains part of the Oriental Orthodox communion and has no relationship to these sorts of churches.

15. Mthembeni P. Mpanza, "Submission to the Truth and Reconciliation Commission by Ibandla lamaNazaretha on the 18th November 1997: East London" (n.p., n.d.).

16. Mahmood Mamdani, *Citizen and Subject: Contemporary Africa and the Legacy of Late Colonialism* (Princeton, NJ: Princeton University Press, 1996), 7, 27-28, 30, 89. Frederick Cooper makes the same assertion in *Africa since 1940* (Cambridge: Cambridge University Press, 2002), 10, 55.

17. Mamdani, *Citizen and Subject*, 7.

18. Cooper, *Africa since 1940*, 55.

19. The basic biography of Shembe and the early history of the church in the forthcoming pages was recounted by Shembe and church members on numerous occasions and can be considered widespread, common knowledge. See Robert Papini, "Carl Faye's Transcript of Isaiah Shembe's Testimony on his Early Life and Calling," *Journal of Religion in Africa* 29, no.3 (1999): 243-284, for a narrative of Shembe's early life in his own words.

20. See Hexham and Oosthuizen, *The Story of Isaiah Shembe, Vol. One*, 59–62, 67–69, 92–93.

21. The American Board of Commissioners for Foreign Missions was a United States-based Congregationalist mission body, headquartered in Boston, that maintained African missions in Gabon and South Africa.

22. Papini, "Carl Faye's Transcript," 279.

23. For a more detailed examination of the succession dispute see Joel E. Tishken, "Whose Nazareth Baptist Church? Prophecy, Power, and Schism in South Africa," *Nova Religio* 9, no. 4 (May 2006): 79-97.

24. The strongest dissent formed around Galilee's son, Mini Shembe, who some followers considered to be the ideal successor, given his training as a priest and his experience on the South African Council of Churches. He formed his own branch of the church at Gauteng, now led by his son Phakama Shembe.

25. Richard N. Price, review of Richard Gott, *Britain's Empire: Resistance, Repression and Revolt* and Kwasi Kwarteng, *Ghosts of Empire: Britain's Legacies in the Modern World* (H-Empire, H-Net Reviews. April, 2012).
    URL: <https://www.h-net.org/reviews/showrev.php?id=3D35775>.

26. Eric Allina-Pisano, "Resistance and the Social History of Africa," *Journal of Social History* 37, no. 1 (Fall 2003): 188-189. See also Terence Ranger, "Connections Between 'Primary Resistance' Movements and Modern Mass Nationalism in East and Central Africa," *Journal of African History* 10, nos. 3-4 (1968): 437-453 and 631-641.

27. Some of the best known examples from this period include: Terence Ranger, *Revolt in Southern Rhodesia, 1896-97: A Study in African Resistance* (London: Heinemann, 1967); Allen Isaacman and Barbara Isaacman, *The Tradition of Resistance in Mozambique: Anti-Colonial Activity in the Zambesi Valley, 1850-1921* (London: Heinemann, 1976); and Cynthia Brantley, *The Giriama and Colonial Resistance in Kenya, 1880-1920* (Berkeley: University of California Press, 1981).

28. Matthew Schoffeleers and Ian Linden, "The Resistance of the Nyau Societies to the Roman Catholic Missions in Colonial Malawi," in *Historical Study of African Religion*, eds. T. O. Ranger and I. N. Kimambo (London: Heineman, 1972), 252, offer this critique in their study of religious resistance.

29. The collection of articles in the 1300-page tome, Robert I. Rotberg and Ali A. Mazrui, eds., *Protest and Power in Black Africa* (New York: Oxford University Press, 1970) provides illustration of the nationalist emphasis upon resistance and the neglect of other sorts of responses.

30. Ranger, "Religious Movements and Politics," 2. For examples of works contending that religious movements were nascent forms of the independence struggle see Effraim Andersson, *Messianic Popular Movements in the Lower Congo* (Uppsala: Almquist and Wiksells, 1958); J. Van Wing, "Le Kimbanguisme vu par un temoin." *Zaire* 12, no. 6 (1958): 563-618; and George Shepperson, "The Politics of African Church Separatist Movements in British Central Africa, 1892-1914," *Africa* 24, no. 3 (1954): 233-246. For historiographic surveys of religion as resistance see Terence Ranger, "Religious Movements and Politics in Sub-Saharan Africa," *African Studies Review* 29, no. 2 (1986): 1-69, and Caroline Neale, *Writing "Independent" History: African Historiography 1960-1980* (Westport: CN; Greenwood Press, 1985), 59-101.

31. For some examples see Frederick Burkewood Welbourn, *East African Rebels: A Study of some Independent Churches* (London: SCM Press, 1961), and Robert Cameron Mitchell, "Religious Protest and Social Change: The Origins of the Aladura Movement in Western Nigeria," in *Protest and Power in Black Africa*, ed. Robert I. Rotberg and Ali A. Mazrui (New York: Oxford University Press, 1970), 458-496.

32. See James Fernandez, *Bwiti: An Ethnography of the Religious Imagination* (Princeton, NJ: Princeton University Press, 1982), and Absolom Vilakazi, with Bongani Mthethwa and Mthembeni Mpanza, *Shembe: The Revitalization of African Society* (Johannesburg: Skotaville, 1986).

33. K. Asare Opoku, "Religion in Africa during the colonial era," in *UNESCO General History of Africa, Vol. VII: Africa under Colonial Domination 1880-1935*, ed. A. Adu Boahen (Paris: UNESCO; London: Heinemann; Berkeley: University of California Press, 1985), 533.

34. See Ian Linden, *Catholics, Peasants, and Chewa Resistance in Nyasaland, 1889-1939* (London: Heinemann Educational, 1974); Cherryl Walker, *Women and Resistance in South Africa* (London: Onyx Press, 1982); and Donald Crummey, ed., *Banditry, Rebellion and Social Protest in Africa* (London: J. Currey, 1986).

35. Allina-Pisano, "Resistance and the Social History of Africa," 189-190. For examples see Edward I. Steinhart, *Conflict and Collaboration: The Kingdoms of Western Uganda, 1890-1907* (Princeton, NJ: Princeton University Press, 1977); and Allen Isaacman and Barbara Isaacman, "Resistance and Collaboration in Southern and Central Africa, c. 1850-1920," *International Journal of African Historical Studies* 10, no. 1 (1977): 31-62.

36. For examples of such scholarship see Nicholas Petryszak, "The Dynamics of Acquiescence in South Africa," *African Affairs* 75, no. 301 (October 1976): 459; and Matthew Schoffeleers, "Ritual Healing and Political Acquiescence: The Case of the Zionist Churches in Southern Africa," *Africa* 60, no. 1 (1991): 1-25.

37. See Vittorio Lanternari, trans. Lisa Sergio, *The Religions of the Oppressed: A Study of Modern Messianic Cults* (New York: Alfred A. Knopf, 1963), 3-62; Georges Balandier, "Messianism and Nationalism in Black Africa" in *Africa: Social Problems of Change and Conflict*, ed. Pierre L. Van Berghe (San Francisco, Chandler Pub. Co., 1965), 443-460; B. I. Sharevskaia, "Toward a Typology of Anticolonial Religious-Political Movements in Tropical Africa," *Anthropology & Archeology of Eurasia* 15, no. 1 (1974): 84-102; and Audrey Wipper, *Rural Rebels: A Study of Two Protest Movements in Kenya* (Nairobi: Oxford University Press, 1977).

38. Norman Etherington, "Recent Trends in the Historiography of Christianity in Southern Africa," *Journal of Southern African Studies* 22, no. 2 (1996): 215. See also Lyn S. Graybill, *Religion and Resistance Politics in South Africa* (Westport, CT: Praeger, 1995), 55-56.

39. See John W. De Gruchy, *The Church Struggle in South Africa* (Grand Rapids, MI: W. B. Eerdmans Pub. Co., 1979), 47; Bonganjalo Goba, *An Agenda for Black Theology: Hermeneutics for Social Change* (Johannesburg: Skotaville, 1988), 64; Allister Sparks, *The Mind of South Africa* (New York: Alfred A. Knopf, 1990), 293-297; and Peter Walshe, *Prophetic Christianity and the Liberation Movement in South Africa* (Pietermaritzburg: Cluster Publications, 1995), 110. Most individuals who wrote about Christian resistance did so in broad categories, referring to black theology, African Christians, or simply Christianity as a whole, in order to rhetorically present a broad front. In these cases Zionists were not referred to directly, but simply subsumed into depictions of a presumed giant black theological resistance. For examples of this kind see Desmond Tutu and John Webster, *Crying in the Wilderness: The Struggle for Justice in South Africa* (Grand Rapids, MI: W. B. Eerdmans Pub. Co., 1982); and Jim Wallis and Joyce Hollyday, *Crucible of Fire: The Church Confronts Apartheid* (Maryknoll, NY: Orbis Books, 1989).

40. Andreas Heuser, "Memory Tales: Representations of Shembe in the Cultural Discourse of African Renaissance," *Journal of Religion in Africa* 35, no. 3 (2005): 365, and Joel Marie Cabrita, "A Theological Biography of Isaiah Shembe, c. 1870-1935," (Ph.D. diss., University of Cambridge, 2008), 32.

41. Michael F. Brown, "On Resisting Resistance," *American Anthropologist* 98, no. 4 (1996): 729. For a similar critique against a legendary postcolonialist work see Paul S. Landau, "Hegemony and History in Jean and John L. Comaroff's *Of Revelation and Revolution*," *Africa* 70, no. 3 (2000): 515.

42. Tony Chafer, *The End of Empire in French West Africa: France's Successful Decolonization?* (New York: Berg, 2002), 117-118.

43. Sherry B. Ortner, *Anthropology and Social Theory: Culture, Power, and the Acting Subject* (Durham, NC: Duke University Press, 2006), 48-49; Brown, "On Resisting Resistance," 729; Allen Isaacman, "Peasants and Rural Social Protest in Africa," *African Studies Review* 33, no. 2 (September 1990), 11-12. McGrath makes a parallel argument about the modern allure of "heresies" as resistors to "orthodoxy." See Alister McGrath, *Heresy: A History of Defending the Truth* (New York: HarperCollins, 2009), 1-2.

44. David Robinson, "Beyond Resistance and Collaboration: Amadu Bamba and the Murids of Senegal," *Journal of Religion in Africa* 21, no. 2 (1991): 150, 168; Paul Stuart Landau, *The Realm of the Word: Language, Gender, and Christianity in a Southern African Kingdom* (Portsmouth, NH: Heinemann; Cape Town: David Philip; London: James Currey, 1995), 133; Sandra E. Greene, *Sacred Sites and the Colonial Encounter: A History of Meaning and Memory in Ghana* (Bloomington: Indiana University Press, 2002), 4.

45. For examples see Cynthia Hoehler-Fatton, *Women of Fire and Spirit: History, Faith, and Gender in Roho Religion in Western Kenya* (Oxford: Oxford University Press, 1996); and Robert R. Edgar and Hilary Sapire, *African Apocalypse: The Story of Nontetha Nkwenkwe, a*

Twentieth-Century South African Prophet (Athens: Ohio University Press; Johannesburg: Witwatersrand University Press, 2000).

46. See Jean Comaroff, *Body of Power, Spirit of Resistance: The Culture and History of a South African People* (Chicago: University of Chicago Press, 1985); James C. Scott, *Domination and the Arts of Resistance: Hidden Transcripts* (New Haven, CT: Yale University Press, 1990); Carol Ann Muller, *Rituals of Fertility and the Sacrifice of Desire* (Chicago: University of Chicago Press, 1999), 18-20, 65; Elizabeth Gunner, *The Man of Heaven and the Beautiful Ones of God* (Leiden: E. J. Brill, 2002), 7-9. For a parallel argument about Afro-Islam see Paul Stoller, *Embodying Colonial Memories: Spirit Possession, Power, and the Hauka in West Africa* (London: Routledge, 1995).

47. Jane Burbank and Frederick Cooper, *Empires in World History: Power and the Politics of Difference* (Princeton, NJ: Princeton University Press, 2010), 5, 11-13; Muhammad S. Umar, *Islam and Colonialism: Intellectual Responses of Muslims of Northern Nigeria to British Colonial Rule* (Leiden: E. J. Brill, 2006), 63, 254; Mrinalini Sinha, *Specters of Mother India: The Global Restructuring of an Empire* (Durham, NC: Duke University Press, 2006), 7-12; Donald Denoon, *A Trial Separation: Australia and the Decolonisation of Papua New Guinea* (Canberra: Pandanus Books, 2005), 16; Frederick Cooper, *Colonialism in Question: Theory, Knowledge, History* (Berkeley: University of California Press, 2005), 183-184; Jacob Olupona, "Introduction," in *Beyond Primitivism: Indigenous Religious Traditions and Modernity*, ed. Jacob Olupona (London: Routledge, 2004), 1, 18; Antoinette Burton, "Introduction: On the Inadequacy and the Indispensability of the Nation," in *After the Imperial Turn: Thinking with and through the Nation*, ed. Antoinette Burton (Durham, NC: Duke University Press, 2003), 4-5; Frederick Cooper, "Conflict and Connection: Rethinking Colonial African History," *The American Historical Review* 99, no. 5 (1994): 1519, 1529, 1530; A. Adu Boahen, *African Perspectives on Colonialism* (Baltimore: The John Hopkins University Press, 1987), 94, 110.

48. Price, review of Gott and Kwarteng, H-Empire, April 2012.

49. Umar, *Islam and Colonialism*, 208.

50. John Springhall, *Decolonization since 1945: The Collapse of European Overseas Empires* (New York: Palgrave, 2001), 204-205.

51. See Heuser, "Memory Tales," 362-387.

52. Heuser, "Memory Tales," 367.

53. Carol Ann Muller, *Rituals of Fertility and the Sacrifice of Desire* (Chicago: University of Chicago Press, 1999), 18-20, 65; Elizabeth Gunner, *The Man of Heaven and the Beautiful Ones of God* (Leiden: E. J. Brill, 2002), 7-9; and Robert Papini, "The Nazareth Scotch: Dance Uniform as Admonitory Infrapolitics for an Eikonic Zion City in Early Union Natal," *Southern African Humanities* 14 (December 2002): 79-80, 82-83.

54. Susan Seymour, "Resistance," *Anthropological Theory* 6, no. 3 (2006): 304-305; Sherry B. Ortner, "Resistance and the Problem of Ethnographic Refusal," *Comparative Studies in Society and History* 37, no. 1 (January 1995): 179, 186; Brown, "On Resisting Resistance," 733.

55. Robertson argues that scholars have tended to polarize the global and local, using the latter as a glorifying symbol of resistance against the hegemonic power of the former, when in reality the global and local are intertwined in far more complex and symbiotic ways. See Roland Robertson, "Globalisation or glocalisation?" *The Journal of International Communication* 1, no. 1 (1994): 37.

56. Taiwo poses similar questions for famous African clergymen like Samuel Ajayi Crowther, James Africanus Beale Horton, and S. R. B. Attoh-Ahuma and contends that they

presented their own complicated engagements with modernity. It is therefore unfair, according to Taiwo, to characterize them as aligned with colonialism simply because they were Christian. See Olufemi Taiwo, *How Colonialism Preempted Modernity in Africa* (Bloomington: Indiana University Press, 2010), 109, 126-127.

57. Bible scholars call this aspect of Shembe's worldview deuteronimistic, where the worshiper believes they are being punished for violating or failing to uphold God's laws. See Deuteronomy 28:15, "But if you will not obey the Lord your God by diligently observing all his commandments and decrees, which I am commanding you today, then all these curses shall come upon you and overtake you." NRSV Deuteronomy 28:16-68 outlines the variety of tragedies, including dominance by foreigners, that will result from failure to uphold God's laws.

58. Behrend makes a similar case for the Holy Spirit Movement's understanding of their place within modern Uganda. See Heike Behrend, *Alice Lakwena & the Holy Spirits: War in Northern Uganda 1986-97* (Oxford: J. Currey; Kampala: Fountain Publishers; Nairobi: EAEP; Athens: Ohio University Press, 1999), 139.

59. "Shembe's Prayer in Remembrance of His Nation," [Y16] *Catechism of the Nazarites*, uncatalogued, Durban Local History Museums, Durban, South Africa.

60. Rev. N. H. Ngada, with input from an eight-member panel of Zionist ministers, asserted that the history of Africa's independent churches must be written, "from the point of view of the Holy Spirit," thereby calling for the scholarly use of internal histories that account for divine and prophetic actions. N. H. Ngada, *Speaking for Ourselves: Members of African Independent Churches report on their pilot study of the History and Theology of their Churches* (Braamfontein: Institute for Contextual Theology, 1985), 16-20.

61. Those of us who study the Nazareth Baptist Church are especially indebted to Robert Papini for the material he compiled and contributed to the Durban Local History Museum, and to Hans-Jürgen Becken, Irving Hexham, G. C. Oosthuizen, Robert Papini, and Andreas Heuser, for the traditions they compiled and edited, now published in a five-volume series by Edwin Mellen Press titled "Sacred History and Traditions of the AmaNazaretha."

62. B. E. Ngobese, "The Concept of the Trinity among the Amanazaretha," in *Empirical Studies of African Independent/Indigenous Churches*, eds. G. C. Oosthuizen and Irving Hexham (Lewiston, NY: Edwin Mellen Press, 1992), 94.

Chapter II

1. Bengt Sundkler, *Bantu Prophets in South Africa*, (1948, repr., London: Oxford University Press, 1961), 329.

2. "A Letter of Shembe written at Zibone on the Sabbath, 22 August 1931," [Y76], *Catechism*, uncatalogued, Durban Local History Museums, Durban, South Africa.

3. Ann Laura Stoler, *Along the Archival Grain: Epistemic Anxieties and Colonial Common Sense* (Princeton, NJ: Princeton University Press, 2009), 9-14.

4. After he received a B. A. from the University of Fort Hare, Galilee worked as senior-master at Adams College (formerly Amanzimtoti Institute) in Amanzimtoti, until he became his father's successor to the church's central leadership in 1935.

5. In a famous article, one foundational to the development of postcolonialism, Homi K. Bhabha argued that the supposed fascination with literacy by the colonized is a fanciful legend colonizers told to justify the civilizing mission. Homi K. Bhabha, "Signs Taken for

Wonders: Questions of Ambivalence and Authority under a Tree outside Delhi, May 1817," *Critical Inquiry* 12, no. 1 (Autumn 1985): 144, 147, 159. While it may indeed be true that such a belief helped to prop up the notion of the white man's burden, that does not detract from the fact that there were individuals from colonial milieus, like Shembe, for whom literacy did possess such an awe. This is affirmed by Isabel Hofmeyr in her transnational history of *The Pilgrim's Progress*. See Isabel Hofmeyr, *The Portable Bunyan: A Transnational History of* The Pilgrim's Progress (Princeton, NJ: Princeton University Press, 2004), 145.

6. Nellie Wells, "Notes for film" (Film: *Dancin' up dem golden stairs*, c1930-34), 5 mins., video copy accession number 65/392, Durban Local History Museums, Durban, South Africa.

7. Native Economic Commission, 1931, pg. 6544. CNC 22/635.

8. Adam Payne, "A Prophet among the Zulus: Shembe a Power for Peace and a Restraining Influence," *Illustrated London News*, 8 February 1930, 204.

9. In 1883, the American Zulu Mission of the Congregationalists published the first complete Zulu translation of the Bible through the American Bible Society. It is very likely Shembe used this version because until 1924 it was the only Zulu-language Bible in existence. Eric Hermanson, "A Brief Overview of Bible Translation in South Africa," *Acta Theologica Supplementum* 2 (2002): 15.

10. E. Gunner, "The Word, the Book and the Zulu Church of Nazareth," in *Oral Tradition and Literacy: Changing Visions of the World*, eds. R. A. Whitaker and E. R. Sienaert (Durban: Natal University Documentation and Research Centre, 1986), 179; and Liz Gunner, "Hidden Stories and the Light of New Day: A Zulu Manuscript and Its Place in South African Writing," *Research in African Literatures* 31, no. 2 (Summer 2000): 1, 10. For parallels in other parts of colonial Africa see Karin Barber, "Introduction: Hidden Innovators in Africa," in *Africa's Hidden Histories: Everyday Literacy and the Making of the Self*, ed. Karin Barber (Bloomington: Indiana University Press, 2006), 1-24; and chapter one of Derek R. Peterson, *Creative Writing: Translation, Bookkeeping, and the Work of the Imagination in Colonial Kenya* (Portsmouth, NH: Heinemann, 2004), 1-31.

11. Carol Muller, "'Written' into the Book of Life: Nazarite Women's Performance Inscribed as Spiritual Text in 'Ibandla lamaNazaretha," *Research in African Literatures* 28, no. 1 (1997): 4, 12; and Gerald O. West, "Reading Shembe 'Re-membering' the Bible: Isaiah Shembe's Instructions on Adultery," *Neotestamenica* 40, no. 1 (2006): 160.

12. Andreas Heuser, "Strolling Bards of the Gospel in the War-zone of Cultural Memory: The Hymnbook of the Nazareth Baptist Church as the subtext of itinerant prophecy," in *The Hymns and Sabbath Liturgy for Morning and Evening Prayer of Isaiah Shembe's amaNazarites, Volume Five*, eds. Andreas Heuser and Irving Hexham, trans. Hans-Jürgen Becken (Lewiston, NY: Edwin Mellen Press, 2005), xxi.

13. Hans-Jürgen Becken, *Wo der Glaube noch jung ist: Afrikanische Unabhängige Kirchen im Südlichen Afrika* (Erlangen: Verlag der Ev.-Luth. Mission, 1985), 122-123.

14. Joel Cabrita, "Texts, Authority, and Community in the South African 'Ibandla lamaNazaretha' (Church of the Nazaretha), 1910-1976)," *Journal of Religion in Africa* 40 (2010): 65; Bengt Sundkler, *Zulu Zion and some Swazi Zionists* (Oxford: Oxford University Press, 1976), 186; Bengt Sundkler, *Bantu Prophets in South Africa*, (1948, repr., London: Oxford University Press, 1961), 194; Absolom Vilakazi, with Bongani Mthethwa and Mthembeni Mpanza, *Shembe: The Revitalization of African Society* (Johannesburg: Skotaville, 1986), 140.

15. John L. Dube, "The Book of Shembe" in chapter 23 of *Ushembe* (Pietermaritzburg: Shuter and Shooter, 1936), translated into English by Hans-Jürgen Becken, n. p., 1993. Irving

Hexham and Robert Papini were kind enough to share a pre-paginated version of Hans Jürgen Becken's translation of John Dube's biography of Shembe, *Ushembe*, with me. There were plans to include the translation in the "Sacred History and Traditions of the AmaNazaretha" series with Edwin Mellen Press. Ultimately those volumes took another direction and Becken's translation of *Ushembe* was not included. All my references to Dube's *Ushembe* refer to this unpublished and pre-paginated translation.

16. Liz Gunner, based on a conversation she had with Bengt Sundkler, once wrote that there was never an original "Grave Book" at all. Personal communication, Bengt Sundkler to Liz Gunner, June 1985, as cited in E. Gunner, "The Word, the Book and the Zulu Church of Nazareth," 186, n. 35. Gunner did not explain Sundkler's evidence for such a claim, and the conclusion strikes me as doubtful.

17. Dube, "The Book of Shembe," in chapter 23.

18. Robert Papini, "Introduction," in *The Catechism of the Nazarites and Related Writings, Volume Four*, eds. Robert Papini and Irving Hexham (Lewiston, NY: Edwin Mellen Press, 2002), xxi.

19. William A. Graham, *Beyond the Written Word: Oral Aspects of Scripture in the History of Religion* (Cambridge: Cambridge University Press, 1987), 16.

20. Gunner, "The Word, the Book and the Zulu Church of Nazareth," 186.

21. Gunner, "The Word, the Book and the Zulu Church of Nazareth," 186.

22. H. J. Becken, "The Nazareth Baptist Church of Shembe," in *Our Approach to the Independent Church Movement in South Africa*, ed. Lutheran Theological College, Missiological Institute; Christian Institute of Southern Africa (Mapumulo: Missiological Institute, Lutheran Theological College, 1965), 107; James Fernandez, "Precincts of the Prophet: A Day with Johannes Galilee Shembe," *Journal of Religion in Africa* 5, no. 1 (1973): 52-53.

23. Esther L. Roberts, "Shembe: The Man and his Work," ed. Robert Papini, 1999 (Master's thesis, University of South Africa, 1936), 53.

24. Robert Papini, "Introduction," in *The Catechism of the Nazarites*, xxv; Liz Gunner, "Keeping a Diary of Visions: Lazarus Phelalasekhaya Maphumulo and the Edendale Congregation of AmaNazaretha," in *Africa's Hidden Histories: Everyday Literacy and Making the Self*, ed. Karin Barber (Bloomington: Indiana University Press, 2006), 159.

25. Elizabeth Gunner, *The Man of Heaven and the Beautiful Ones of God* (Leiden: E. J. Brill, 2002), 41.

26. Elizabeth Gunner, "Power House, Prison House–An Oral Genre and Its Use in Isaiah Shembe's Nazareth Baptist Church," *Journal of Southern African Studies* 14, no. 2 (January 1988): 207.

27. Papini, "Introduction," in *The Catechism of the Nazarites*, xxv.

28. See Chapter 1 of "Meshack Hadebe's Testimony" in Gunner, *The Man of Heaven*, 141-143.

29. "Judiah, kwaZulu, 22 October 1933, Lord Shembe gives advice with these words" in "Memela," Durban Local History Museums, accession number 98/655.

30. "Words of Shembe and the Men's Assembly concerning the Restoration of Rev. P. J. D. Mnqayi 16 August, 1932," [Y80] *Catechism*, uncatalogued, Durban Local History Museums, Durban, South Africa.

31. Heuser, "Strolling Bards of the Gospel," xii.

32. Irving Hexham and G. C. Oosthuizen, eds., trans. Hans-Jürgen Becken, *The Story of Isaiah Shembe, Volume Two: Early Regional Traditions of the Acts of the Nazarites* (Lewiston, NY: Edwin Mellen Press, 1999), 285. Testimony of Petros Musawenkosi Dhlomo.

33. Hexham and Oosthuizen, *The Story of Isaiah Shembe, Volume Two*, 285. Testimony of Petros Musawenkosi Dhlomo.

34. Papini, "Introduction," in *The Catechism of the Nazarites*, xxxi.

35. Sundkler, *Bantu Prophets*, 328-329.

36. Papini, "Introduction," in *The Catechism of the Nazarites*, xvii-xviii.

37. As Papini amassed materials for the Durban Local History Museum and *The Catechism of the Nazarites* volume, he discovered some surviving written traditions that had not been included in the *Catechism*. Papini, "Introduction," in *The Catechism of the Nazarites*, xxviii-xxix.

38. Papini, "Introduction," in *The Catechism of the Nazarites*, xxviii.

39. See "Concerning Work" [Y35] and "Shembe's Counsel at Judia Home in Zululand" [Y36] *Catechism*.

40. Roberts, "Shembe: The Man and his Work," 35; Dube, "Shembe and Work," chapter 19.

41. Chapter fifteen of *Ushembe* is titled "The Advice of Shembe" and contains two traditions: "The Advice of the Suffering Servant Shembe at the Temple of Gospel, 12 September 1932" and "The Advice of Shembe, the Servant of Suffering at Zibindela, 12 December 1931.

42. Becken, "I Love to Tell the Story," 34-35; Hans-Jürgen Becken, "The Oral History of the Ibandla lamaNazaretha," in *The Story of Isaiah Shembe, Volume One: History and Traditions Centered on Ekuphakameni and Mount Nhlangakazi*, eds. Irving Hexham and G. C. Oosthuizen, trans. Hans-Jürgen Becken (Lewiston, N. Y.: Edwin Mellen Press, 1996), xv; Irving Hexham, "About the Texts and Translation," in *The Story of Isaiah Shembe, Volume Three: The Continuing Story of the Sun and the Moon. Oral Testimony and the Sacred History of the AMA-Nazarites Under the Leadership of Bishops Johannes Galilee Shembe and Amos Shembe*, eds. Irving Hexham and G. C. Oosthuizen, trans. Hans-Jürgen Becken (Lewiston, NY: Edwin Mellen Press, 2001), xiv-xv.

43. Papini, "Introduction," in *The Catechism of the Nazarites*, xiv. My subsequent discussion of the *Catechism* applies equally to the "red" and "yellow" versions, though it was a "yellow" version housed at the Durban Local History Museums that I utilized extensively in writing this book.

44. This twenty-one page document is not to be confused with the overall *Catechism*, and is a chapter within this larger volume. To distinguish, I used quotations marks around the name of the chapter-length catechism, while the title of the broader catechism is noted in italics.

45. Papini, "Introduction," in *The Catechism of the Nazarites*, xv.

46. For such an example in Lutheranism see "Church Discipline in the Christian Congregation: A Report of the Commission on Theology and Church Relations of the Lutheran Church-Missouri Synod, November 1985" at <http://www.iclnet.org/pub/resources/text/wittenberg/mosynod/web/cdis.html>. Accessed 3 March 2012.

47. Papini, "Introduction," in *The Catechism of the Nazarites*, xv.

48. Bengt Sundkler was permitted to view many of these testimonies, and wrote about those of prominent members such as Rev. Simon Mngoma and Denis Ngcobo. See Sundkler, *Bantu Prophets*, 329.

49. Bart D. Ehrman, *A Brief Introduction to the New Testament* (New York: Oxford University Press, 2004), 61, 117; D. A. Carson, Douglas J. Moo, and Leon Morris, *An Introduction to the New Testament* (Grand Rapids, MI: Zondervan, 1992), 181.

50. Bart D. Ehrman, *Lost Scriptures: Books that did not make it into the New Testament* (New York: Oxford University Press, 2003), 92.

51. Ehrman, *A Brief Introduction*, 130-132; Eugene V. Gallagher, "Conversion and Salvation in the Apocryphal Acts of the Apostles," *Second Century* 8, no. 1 (Spring 1991): 29.

52. Albertus Frederik Johannes Klijn, *An Introduction to the New Testament* (Leiden: E. J. Brill, 1967), 61-63; Francis Bayard Rhein, *Understanding the New Testament* (Woodbury, NY: Barron's Educational Series, 1974), 146-148.

53. James McConkey Robinson, ed., *The Nag Hammadi Library in English*, 3rd ed. (San Francisco: HarperCollins, 1990), 530.

54. Hexham and Oosthuizen, *The Story of Isaiah Shembe, Vol. One*, 145. Testimony of Phasika Mhlongo.

55. Hexham and Oosthuizen, *The Story of Isaiah Shembe, Vol. One*, 125-129. Testimonies of Edmond Dladla, Petros Dhlomo, Thomas Makhathini, and Azariah Mthiyane.

56. *The Acts of John*, verses 60-61, from J. K. Elliott, *The Apocryphal New Testament: A Collection of Apocryphal Christian Literature in an English Translation* (Oxford: Clarendon Press, 1993), 328.

57. Eugene V. Gallagher, "Extraterrestrial Exegesis: The Raëlian Movement as a Biblical Religion," *Nova Religio* 14, no. 2 (2010): 15-16; Jan Shipps, *Mormonism: The Story of a New Religious Tradition* (Urbana: University of Illinois Press, 1985), 53.

58. Ehrman, *A Brief Introduction*, 131-132.

59. Gallagher, "Conversion and Salvation," 15, 29.

60. See Shembe's encounter with some Protestant ministers where he mocked their sacramental theology in Hexham and Oosthuizen, *The Story of Isaiah Shembe, Vol. One*, 130-131. Testimony of Solomon Mdluli and Muntuwezizwe Buthelezi. This episode is not unlike that of John challenging a priest of Artemis to kill him in the name of their goddess. See verses 39-41 in *The Acts of John*, from Elliott, *The Apocryphal New Testament*, 322-323.

61. Sundkler, *Bantu Prophets*, 329.

62. Becken, "The Oral History of the Ibandla lamaNazaretha," xiv-xv.

63. "Appendix One," in *The Catechism of the Nazarites and Related Writings, Volume Four*, eds. Robert Papini and Irving Hexham (Lewiston, NY: Edwin Mellen Press, 2002), 222.

64. "Appendix One," in *The Catechism of the Nazarites*, 223.

65. Hexham says it is wrong to speak of Londa's work as translation in the conventional sense. To Londa and church members, his engagement with these texts is also revelation, a prophetically guided process. Irving Hexham, "Introduction," in *The Scriptures of the amaNazaretha of EKuphaKameni: Selected Writings of the Zulu Prophets Isaiah and Londa Shembe*, ed. Irving Hexham, trans. Londa Shembe and Hans-Jürgen Becken (Calgary: University of Calgary Press, 1994), xxi-xxii.

66. Hexham, "Introduction," *The Scriptures of the amaNazaretha*, xix-xx.

67. Becken, "I Love to Tell the Story," 33.

68. Becken, "The Oral History of the Ibandla lamaNazaretha," xv.

69. Becken, "I Love to Tell the Story," 33.

70. Becken, "The Oral History of the Ibandla lamaNazaretha," xvi-xvii.

71. Nombili Joe Mhlongo to Joel E. Tishken, personal communication, 8 January 2000.

72. Hexham, "About the Texts and Translation," xiv-xv.

73. Friedrich Schleiermacher, "On the Different Methods of Translation," in *German Romantic Criticism*, ed. A. Leslie Willson (New York: Continuum, 1982), 3, 9. For a critical

perspective on the role of translation in Anglophone history that favors preserving the "foreignness" of translated texts see Lawrence Venuti, *The Translator's Invisibility: A History of Translation*, 2nd ed. (London: Routledge, 2008), 1-34.

74. Irving Hexham, "Introduction," in *The Story of Isaiah Shembe, Volume Two: Early Regional Traditions of the Acts of the Nazarites*, eds. Irving Hexham and G. C. Oosthuizen, trans. Hans-Jürgen Becken (Lewiston, NY: Edwin Mellen Press, 1999), ix; Hexham, "About the Texts and Translation," xiv-xv.

75. Hexham, "Introduction," in *The Story of Isaiah Shembe, Volume One*, vii-viii.

76. *The Story of Isaiah Shembe, Volume One: History and Traditions Centered on Ekuphakameni and Mount Nhlangakazi* (1996); *The Story of Isaiah Shembe, Volume Two: Early Regional Traditions of the Acts of the Nazarites* (1999); and *The Story of Isaiah Shembe, Volume Three: The Continuing Story of the Sun and the Moon. Oral Testimony and the Sacred History of the AMA-Nazarites Under the Leadership of Bishops Johannes Galilee Shembe and Amos Shembe* (2001). Nine total volumes were originally planned, but ultimately there were only five published: the three above, a fourth volume containing a translation of the catechism, and a fifth with a translation of the hymnal: Robert Papini and Irving Hexham, eds., *The Catechism of the Nazarites and Related Writings, Volume Four* (Lewiston, NY: Edwin Mellen Press, 2002); Andreas Heuser and Irving Hexham, eds., Hans-Jürgen Becken, trans., *The Hymns and Sabbath Liturgy for Morning and Evening Prayer of Isaiah Shembe's amaNazarites, Volume Five* (Lewiston, NY: Edwin Mellen Press, 2005).

77. Personal communication from C. L. Sibisi to Karen Brown, in Karen Brown, "The Function of Dress and Ritual in the Nazareth Baptist Church of Isaiah Shembe (South Africa)" (Ph.D. Dissertation, Indiana University, 1995), 63, n. 18.

78. Gunner, "The Word, the Book and the Zulu Church of Nazareth," 186.

79. Hexham and Oosthuizen, *The Story of Isaiah Shembe, Volume One*, 79-84. Testimonies of Petros M. Dhlomo, Muntuwezizwe Buthelezi, Johannes Duma, and Solomon Mdluli.

80. Scholars agree that the authors and books of the New Testament possess remarkably diverse points of view, yet such disparity has not, in the main, undermined the faith of Christians over many generations. Ehrman, *A Brief Introduction*, 7-9.

81. This is merely a rough estimation of my own and does not represent any firm statistical analysis.

82. The details regarding the vaccination controversy can be found in Hexham, *The Story of Isaiah Shembe, Vol. 1*, 145-151. Testimony of John Mabuyakhulu.

83. "A Letter of Shembe written at Zibone on the Sabbath, 22 August 1931," [Y76] *Catechism*, and "Sabbath Maxims on the Morning of 22nd day of August 1931," in Gunner, *The Man of Heaven*, 121.

84. This too is a parallel to early Christianity as the Christian Gospels were written to convey theological truths, not accurate and verifiable historical facts. Ehrman, *A Brief Introduction to the New Testament*, 59-60.

85. "Concerning Domestic Animals and Dogs," [Y41] *Catechism*.

86. In a similar situation, Peterson notes that the records Gikuyu clerks produced contain invaluable information, even if they served internal political purposes. Peterson, *Creative Writing*, 22.

87. "The Words of Shembe at Khethokuhle, 13 March 1916," [Y72] *Catechism*.

88. Hexham and Oosthuizen, *The Story of Isaiah Shembe, Volume Two*, 28. Testimony of Khaya S. Ndelu.

89. Becken noted that the authenticity of the traditions was partially safeguarded by the fact that they were written, memorized, preserved, and even typed by members of the Nazareth Baptist Church for internal usage. They were not recorded or preserved with outsiders in mind, and therefore none of the documents was crafted to convey a certain image of the church which might please the researcher. See Becken, "I Love to Tell the Story," 34-35, and Becken, "The Oral History of the Ibandla lamaNazaretha," xvii.

90. The bulk of my data on KaGcwensa derives from an unpublished paper by G. C. Oosthuizen, "iBandla lamaNazaretha uNkuluknulu KaGcwesna," n. p., n. d. KaGcwensa also used the name Ma Mpungose, particularly prior to founding her own church, but largely utilized KaGcwensa after forming the Nazareth Baptist Church of God KaGcwensa, as suggested by Oosthuizen's exclusive usage of KaGcwensa in the unpublished paper on the movement. I employ KaGcwensa throughout for the sake of clarity.

91. Oosthuizen, "iBandla lamaNazaretha uNkuluknulu KaGcwesna," 24.

92. Joel Cabrita, "Isaiah Shembe's Theological Nationalism, 1920s-1935," *Journal of Southern African Studies* 35, no. 3 (September 2009): 610-611, 617-619.

93. Details of this vision are in Hexham and Oosthuizen, *The Story of Isaiah Shembe, Vol. Three*, 4-8. Testimony of Mama Dainah Zama and Petros Dhlomo.

Chapter III

1. Irving Hexham and G. C. Oosthuizen, eds., trans. Hans-Jürgen Becken, *The Story of Isaiah Shembe, Volume One: History and Traditions Centered on Ekuphakameni and Mount Nhlangakazi* (Lewiston, NY: Edwin Mellen Press, 1996), 101. Testimony of Khulumani Jinios Mzimela.

2. Bushman makes an identical argument when commenting upon Joseph Smith, Jr. and the Latter-day Saints. See Richard Lyman Bushman, *Joseph Smith: Rough Stone Rolling* (New York: Alfred A. Knopf, 2005), xxi.

3. For an example of how a supernatural aura amplified a leader's legitimacy within early medieval European Christianity, see the case of St. Eugendus in Isabel Moreira, *Dreams, Visions, and Spiritual Authority in Merovingian Gaul* (Ithaca, NY: Cornell University Press, 2000), 70-73.

4. Eugene V. Gallagher, "Extraterrestrial Exegesis: The Raëlian Movement as a Biblical Religion," *Nova Religio* 14, no. 2 (2010): 15-16; Jan Shipps, *Mormonism: The Story of a New Religious Tradition* (Urbana: University of Illinois Press, 1985), 53. In reference to cultural genres, Susan Stewart referred to this process as the generation of a "new antique," or an "attempt to bypass the contingencies of time," thereby producing a cultural object that is both in and out of time. See Susan Stewart, *Crimes of Writing: Problems in the Containment of Representation* (New York: Oxford University Press, 1991), 67.

5. Gallagher shows how accounts of miracles within the apocryphal Acts of the Apostles inspired conversions and portrayed what the religion already meant to those who had joined it and what it could mean to those considering it. See Eugene V. Gallagher, "Conversion and Salvation in the Apocryphal Acts of the Apostles," *Second Century* 8, no. 1 (Spring 1991): 29.

6. In a parallel example about the power of miraculous tales, MacMullen noted how public displays and reports of miracles inspired conversions to early Christianity. Ramsey MacMullen, "Two Types of Conversion to Early Christianity," *Vigiliae Christianae* 37, no. 2 (1983): 174, 187.

7. This is true of the case of Hildegard of Bingen, to take but one example. Astral travel, atmospheric and celestial phenomena, mountains, dialogues with God, admonishments to live properly, and instructions on how to correct Christianity were among the dominant elements within her prophecies. Barbara Newman, "'Sibyl of the Rhine': Hildegard's Life and Times," in *Voice of the Living Light: Hildegard of Bingen and her World*, ed. Barbara Newman (Berkeley: University of California Press, 1998), 9, 23-25.

8. Barbara Newman, *God and the Goddesses: Vision, Poetry, and Belief in the Middle Ages* (Philadelphia: University of Pennsylvania Press, 2003), 29-30; Steven F. Kruger, *Dreaming in the Middle Ages* (Cambridge: Cambridge University Press, 1992), 119-121; Keith Thomas, *Religion and the Decline of Magic*, (1971, repr., New York: Oxford University Press, 1997), 25-50, 78-96.

9. John M. Janzen, "The Consequences of Literacy in African Religion: The Kongo Case," in *Theoretical Explorations in African Religion*, eds. Wim Van Binsbergen and Matthew Schoffeleers (London: KPI Ltd., 1985), 231-233; Terence Ranger, "The Local and the Global in Southern African Religious History," in *Conversion to Christianity: Historical and Anthropological Perspectives on a Great Transformation*, ed. Robert W. Hefner (Berkeley: University of California Press, 1993), 86.

10. Many of Africa's largest Zionist churches, such as the Zion Christian Church, Église Kimbangusite, Église Harriste, Cherubim and Seraphim, Celestial Church of Christ, Legio Maria, as well as the Nazareth Baptist Church, were inspired and molded by prophetic experiences.

11. Colum Hourihane, "Introduction," in *Looking Beyond: Visions, Dreams, and Insights in Medieval Art & History*, ed. Colum Hourihane (Princeton, NJ: Index of Christian Art, Dept. of Art & Archaeology, Princeton University, 2010), xv.

12. Vilakazi and his coauthors insisted that the Nazareth Baptist Church was so Zulu it was a reconstituted form of Zulu indigenous religion that owed nothing to Christianity. See Absolom Vilakazi, with Bongani Mthethwa and Mthembeni Mpanza, *Shembe: The Revitalization of African Society*, (Johannesburg: Skotaville, 1986), 155-156. Oosthuizen also viewed the Nazareth Baptist Church as principally Zulu, but for him the Zuluness did not suggest a modern form of Zulu indigenous religion but a syncretized form of "bad" Christianity. See G. C. Oosthuizen, *Theology of a South African Messiah: An Analysis of the Hymnal of the Church of the Nazarites* (Leiden: E. J. Brill, 1967), 19, 25, 32, 56. Joel Cabrita argues that Shembe's theology represents a restoration of, and fidelity to, Zulu culture. See Joel Cabrita, "A Theological Biography of Isaiah Shembe, c. 1870-1935" (Ph.D. diss., University of Cambridge, 2008), 7, 21, 55, 66, 74, 77.

13. Terence Ranger made the same point regarding Mwana Lesa. See Terence Ranger, "The Mwana Lesa Movement of 1925," in *Themes in the Christian History of Central Africa*, eds. T. O. Ranger and John C. Weller (Berkeley: University of California Press, 1975), 45, 67. Kiernan asserts the same argument regarding Zionist churches as a whole. See Jim Kiernan, "Variations on a Christian Theme: The Healing Synthesis of Zulu Zionism," in *Syncretism/Anti-Syncretism: The Politics of Religious Synthesis*, eds. Charles Stewart and Rosalind Shaw (London: Routledge, 1994), 74-75.

14. Hans-Jürgen Becken, "The Oral History of the Ibandla lamaNazaretha," in *The Story of Isaiah Shembe, Volume One: History and Traditions Centered on Ekuphakameni and Mount Nhlangakazi*, eds. Irving Hexham and G. C. Oosthuizen, trans. Hans-Jürgen Becken (Lewiston, NY: Edwin Mellen Press, 1996), xvi-xvii; Samuel S. Simbandumwe, *A Socio-Religious and Political Analysis of the Judeo-Christian Concept of Prophetism and the Modern BaKongo and Zulu Prophet Movements* (Lewiston, NY: Edwin Mellen Press, 1993), 243.

15. The story of Sitheya is from Hexham and Oosthuizen, *The Story of Isaiah Shembe*, Vol. One, 5-7. Testimony of Petros M. Dhlomo, Muntuwezizwe Buthelezi, and Khaya S. Ndelu.

16. See Luke 1:26-38, and Matthew 1:18-21.

17. Hexham and Oosthuizen, *The Story of Isaiah Shembe*, Vol. One, 7-8. Testimony of Petros M. Dhlomo and Muntuwezizwe Buthelezi; John L. Dube, "He Recovered from Death, When He Was Still a Child," in chapter 2 of *Ushembe* (Pietermaritzburg: Shuter and Shooter, 1936), translated into English by Hans-Jürgen Becken, n. p., 1993.

18. Moreira, *Dreams, Visions, and Spiritual Authority*, 70; David G. Bromley, "Making Sense of Scientology: Prophetic, Contractual Religion," in *Scientology*, ed. James R. Lewis (Oxford: Oxford University Press, 2009), 87, 88; Muhammad Ibrahim Abu Salim and Knut S. Vikør, "The Man who Believed in the Mahdi," *Sudanic Africa* 2 (1991): 48-49; Bart D. Ehrman, *A Brief Introduction to the New Testament* (New York: Oxford University Press, 2004), 61.

19. An alternative wording of the account can also be found in the Acts. See Hexham and Oosthuizen, *The Story of Isaiah Shembe*, Vol. One, 8-9. Testimony of Petros M. Dhlomo. The two accounts agree on the overall substance of the story and prophecy, even though some of the wording differs in each.

20. Killie Campbell Africana Library, Album: African Religions: Shembe, Londa, "The thing that was my first Vision concerning Nkulunkulu."

21. Killie Campbell Africana Library, Album: African Religions: Shembe, Londa, "The thing that was my first Vision concerning Nkulunkulu."

22. Robert Papini, "Carl Faye's Transcript of Isaiah Shembe's Testimony on his Early Life and Calling," *Journal of Religion in Africa* 29, no. 3 (1999): 265.

23. Known also as *ukusoma*, *ukuhlobonga* was the Zulu custom of premarital nonpenetrative sex.

24. Papini, "Carl Faye's Transcript," 265, 267; Hexham and Oosthuizen, *The Story of Isaiah Shembe*, Vol. One, 12. Testimony of Petros M. Dhlomo; Dube, "A voice said: Shun Immorality," chapter 2.

25. Robert Papini, *Rise Up and Dance and Praise God.* (Durban: The Local History Museum, 1992), 26-27; Papini, "Carl Faye's Transcript," 267, 269; Hexham and Oosthuizen, *The Story of Isaiah Shembe*, Vol. One, 11-12. Testimony of Jeslinah Mchunu, Khaya S. Ndelu, Muntuwezizwe Buthelezi, and Petros M. Dhlomo; Dube, "The Story of the Peaches," in chapter 2. Interestingly, in none of these accounts does Shembe explain the symbolism of the spewing mountain.

26. Papini, "Carl Faye's Transcript," 269.

27. Hexham and Oosthuizen, *The Story of Isaiah Shembe*, Vol. One, 14-16. Testimony of Petros M. Dhlomo.

28. "Shembe's Discourse at Mqeku 20 May 1932," [Y71] *Catechism of the Nazarites*, uncatalogued, Durban Local History Museums, Durban, South Africa.

29. Norman Etherington, "Recent Trends in the Historiography of Christianity in Southern Africa," *Journal of Southern African Studies* 22, no. 2 (June 1996): 206, argues that Christianity and indigenous religions should not be seen as two distinct worlds but "as poles on a continuum between which individual Africans slid rather than jumped—a cause of frustration for...European missionaries who drew sharp mental boundaries between believers and pagans."

30. Shembe's later theological dissatisfaction with the African Native Baptist Church suggests it was an Ethiopian-style church that remained theologically close to Baptists. But this is

admittedly a supposition as little is known of the African Native Baptist Church beyond its connection to Shembe.

31. With the outbreak of the South African War in 1899, Shembe and his family were expelled from Coenraad's farm at Grabe. After the war Shembe settled at the farm of George Curwen and served as his superintendent for those who worked at night. He and his family lived there until 1906.

32. These prophetic warnings are recorded in multiple sources. See Papini, *Rise Up*, 27-29; Papini, "Carl Faye," 283; Hexham and Oosthuizen, *The Story of Isaiah Shembe, Vol. One*, 16-17, 17-19, 19-22, 22-26. Testimony of Petros M. Dhlomo, Khaya S. Ndelu, and Jeslinah Mchunu.

33. The account of these experiences can be found in Hexham and Oosthuizen, *The Story of Isaiah Shembe, Vol. One*, 19-22, 22-26, 26-28. Testimony of Petros M. Dhlomo, Khaya S. Ndelu, and Jeslinah Mchunu; and Papini, "Carl Faye," 271, 273, 275, 283.

34. Dube, "A Man Should Not Commit Suicide," in chapter 3.

35. This prophetic account can be found in Hexham and Oosthuizen, *The Story of Isaiah Shembe, Vol. One*, 19-21. Testimony of Petros M. Dhlomo and Muntuwezizwe Buthelezi; Papini, *Rise Up*, 28-29; Papini, "Carl Faye's Transcript," 271, 273, 275.

36. Dube, "A Very Gracious Voice," in chapter 4.

37. Papini, "Carl Faye's Transcript," 271, 273, 275. Versions of this narrative can also be found in Papini, *Rise Up*, 27-28, and Hexham and Oosthuizen, *The Story of Isaiah Shembe, Vol. One*, 17-19. Testimony of Petros M. Dhlomo.

38. For examples of other African prophets who resisted their calling, see Robert R. Edgar and Hilary Sapire, *African Apocalypse: The Story of Nontetha Nkwenkwe, a Twentieth-Century South African Prophet* (Athens: Ohio University Press; Johannesburg: Witwatersrand University Press, 2000), 17, 73; Marilyn Robinson Waldman and Robert M. Baum, "Innovation as renovation: The 'prophet' as agent of change," in *Innovation in Religious Traditions*, eds. Michael A. Williams, et. al. (Berlin: Mouton de Gruyter, 1992), 267; and Marie-Louise Martin, *Kimbangu: An African Prophet and His Church* (Oxford: Basil Blackwood, 1971), 44.

39. David E. Aune, *Prophecy in Early Christianity and the Ancient Mediterranean World* (Grand Rapids, MI: William B. Eerdmans Pub. Co., 1983), 189-200; Hourihane, "Introduction," in *Looking Beyond*, xvi; Moreira, *Dreams, Visions, and Spiritual Authority*, 71, 142, 205-206.

40. There is no evidence that Shembe and Leshega were in communication after 1910. Elizabeth Gunner, *The Man of Heaven and the Beautiful Ones of God* (Leiden: E. J. Brill, 2002), 20; and Liz Gunner, "Hidden Stories and the Light of New Day: A Zulu Manuscript and Its Place in South African Writing," *Research in African Literatures* 31, no. 2 (Summer 2000): 8.

41. See six such testimonies in Hexham and Oosthuizen, *The Story of Isaiah Shembe, Vol. One*, 43-47, 48-51. Testimonies of Petros M. Dhlomo, Muntuwezizwe Buthelezi, and Linah Mntungwa. Shembe offers a brief discussion of this period in Papini, "Carl Faye," 277.

42. For theoretical discussions of how prophecy can be used to legitimate a religion see Carol Ann Muller, "Nazarite Song, Dance, and Dreams: The Sacralization of Time, Space, and the Female Body in South Africa," (Ph.D. diss., New York University, 1994), 180, 185; Papini, *Rise Up*, 18; and Douglas H. Johnson, *Nuer Prophets: A History of Prophecy from the Upper Nile in the Nineteenth and Twentieth Centuries* (Oxford: Clarendon Press, 1994), ix; James R. Lewis, *Legitimating New Religions* (New Brunswick, NJ: Rutgers University Press, 2003), 13-14; and Bromley, "Making Sense of Scientology," 88-89.

43. B. E. Ngobese, "The Concept of the Trinity among the Amanazaretha," in *Empirical Studies of African Independent/Indigenous Churches*, eds. G. C. Oosthuizen and Irving Hexham (Lewiston, NY: Edwin Mellen Press, 1992), 94.

44. David G. Bromley and Rachel S. Bobbitt, "Challenges to charismatic authority in the Unificationist Movement," in *Sacred Schisms: How Religions Divide*, eds. James R. Lewis and Sarah M. Lewis (Cambridge: Cambridge University Press, 2009), 130.

45. Matthew Kustenbauder, "Believing in the Black Messiah: The Legio Maria Church in an African Christian Landscape," *Nova Religio* 13, no. 1 (August 2009): 15-16, 32.

46. Kustenbauder, "Believing in the Black Messiah," 18-19. It seems likely that the members of Legio Maria are evoking the story of how Moses was "found" in Exodus 2:2-7.

47. Based upon verse 33:40 of the Qur'an, Islamic theology insists that Muhammad was the final culmination of the chain of prophets sent by God. While this belief has dampened prophetic claims within Islam, when compared to a more prophetic religion like Christianity, it has not prevented it. Those making prophetic claims reconcile their prophetic experiences with standard Islam in one of three ways. First, some claimed that they are a "messenger" and not a "prophet." In this way they can claim to be receiving messages from God or Muhammad, without challenging Islamic theology. Bamba employed this strategy. Second, some explained their prophetic abilities through the concept of the Mahdi, the Guided One. Third, others claimed that their version of Islam is the correct version of Islam. They argue that their prophetic experiences verify the fact that they are the revealer of truth from God and are therefore a legitimate prophet, and discount those who doubt them as impure Muslims. See Joel E. Tishken, "The History of Prophecy in West Africa: Indigenous, Islamic, and Christian," *History Compass* 5, no. 5 (2007): 1471-1474.

48. Christian Coulon, "The *Grand Magal* in Touba: A Religious Festival of the Mouride Brotherhood of Senegal," *African Affairs* 98 (1999): 198-200; Cheikh Anta Babou, *Fighting the Greater Jihad: Amadu Bamba and the Founding of the Muridiyya of Senegal, 1853-1913* (Athens: Ohio University Press, 2007), 183.

49. Jules-Rosette wrote of the legitimating power of retroactive interpretations of dreams in the Church of John Maranke. See Bennetta Jules-Rosette, *African Apostles: Ritual and Conversion in the Church of John Maranke* (Ithaca, NY: Cornell University Press, 1975), 61, 72.

50. E. Gunner, "The Word, the Book and the Zulu Church of Nazareth," In *Oral Tradition and Literacy: Changing Visions of the World*, eds. R. A. Whitaker and E. R. Sienaert (Durban: Natal University Documentation and Research Centre, 1986), 179-188; and Gunner, "Hidden Stories and the Light of New Day," 1, 10.

51. Joel Cabrita, "Texts, Authority, and Community in the South African 'Ibandla lamaNazaretha' (Church of the Nazaretha), 1910-1976," *Journal of Religion in Africa* 40 (2010): 65-66; Bengt Sundkler, *Zulu Zion and some Swazi Zionists* (Oxford: Oxford University Press, 1976), 186; Bengt Sundkler, *Bantu Prophets in South Africa*, (1948, repr., London: Oxford University Press, 1961), 194; Absolom Vilakazi, with Bongani Mthethwa and Mthembeni Mpanza, *Shembe: The Revitalization of African Society* (Johannesburg: Skotaville, 1986), 140; Muller, "Nazarite Song, Dance and Dreams," 175.

52. Thomas W. Overholt, "Prophecy: The Problem of Cross-Cultural Comparison," in *Anthropological Approaches to the Old Testament*, ed. Bernhard Lang (Philadelphia: Fortress; London: SPCK, 1985), 78. This process is identical to what happened in early Christianity as well, where the accumulation of Acts, canonical and apocryphal, generated legitimacy for the new religion and its founder. Personal communication, Eugene V. Gallagher to Joel E. Tishken, 23 February 2012.

53. B. N. Mthethwa, "Shembe's Hymnody and the Ethical Standards and Worldview of the AmaNazaretha," in *Empirical Studies of African Independent/Indigenous Churches*, eds. G. C. Oosthuizen and Irving Hexham (Lewiston, NY: Edwin Mellen Press, 1992), 240; Sundkler, *Zulu Zion*, 161.

54. Lewis R. Rambo, *Understanding Religious Conversion* (New Haven, CT: Yale University Press, 1993), 30-40.

55. Simbandumwe, *A Socio-Religious and Political Analysis*, 263.

56. Hexham and Oosthuizen, *The Story of Isaiah Shembe, Vol., One*, 92-93. Testimony of Esther Zungu and Sindile Cebekhulu.

57. See "No Nazaretha Christian Will Be Killed by a Snake" in Hexham and Oosthuizen, *The Story of Isaiah Shembe, Vol. One*, 120-25, for four such stories, one undated, one from 1913, and two from the 1930s.

58. For two examples see the testimony of Shembe purportedly resurrecting a child in Hexham and Oosthuizen, *The Story of Isaiah Shembe, Vol. One*, 138-39. Testimony of Thomas Makhathini; and knowing a source of underground water in Hexham and Oosthuizen, *The Story of Isaiah Shembe, Vol. One*, 90. Testimony of Thandekile Shembe.

59. Ngobese, "The Concept of the Trinity among the Amanazaretha," 94; Gunner, "The Word, the Book and the Zulu Church of Nazareth," 182.

60. Hoehler-Fatton argues the same for members of Roho religion. See Cynthia Hoehler-Fatton, *Women of Fire and Spirit: History, Faith, and Gender in Roho Religion in Western Kenya* (Oxford: Oxford University Press, 1996), 209. Similarly, Porter contends that historians must take theology and religion seriously when studying missionaries and not dismiss their motivations as simply politically inspired. See Andrew Porter, *Religion versus Empire? British Overseas Protestant Missionaries and Overseas Expansion, 1700-1914* (Manchester: Manchester University Press, 2004), 11.

61. Joel Robbins recently critiqued this scholarly approach as the study of "crypto-religion," stating that such scholars doubted the power and sincerity of conversions, instead assuming that the power of cultural continuity was so great that the primary religious commitment of anyone in a colonial context was to their traditional faith. Such converts, then, should not be counted as Christians according to this crypto-religious approach. Additionally, the traditional religious allegiance of such insincerely converted individuals provided a latent source for resistance. See Joel Robbins, "Crypto-Religion and the Study of Cultural Mixtures: Anthropology, Value, and the Nature of Syncretism," *Journal of the American Academy of Religion* 79, no. 2 (2011): 410-414, 421.

62. For an example of such an argument see, B. I. Sharevskaia, "Toward a Typology of Anticolonial Religious-Political Movements in Tropical Africa," *Anthropology & Archeology of Eurasia* 15, no. 1 (1974): 100, who concludes that "true" religion can only be found in a minority of seemingly religious movements. The rest are actually expressions of political protest.

63. Terence O. Ranger, "Religious Movements and Politics in Sub-Saharan Africa," *African Studies Review* 29, no. 2 (1986): 51; David J. Hufford, "Beings Without Bodies: An Experience-Centered Theory of the Belief in Spirits," in *Out of the Ordinary: Folklore and the Supernatural*, ed. Barbara Walker (Logan: Utah State University Press, 1995), 11, 16, 34.

64. Gerald O. West, "Reading Shembe 'Re-membering' the Bible: Isaiah Shembe's Instructions on Adultery," *Neotestamentica* 40, no. 1 (2006): 178-179.

Chapter IV

1. Irving Hexham and G. C. Oosthuizen, eds., trans. Hans-Jürgen Becken, *The Story of Isaiah Shembe, Volume One: History and Traditions Centered on Ekuphakameni and Mount Nhlangakazi* (Lewiston, NY: Edwin Mellen Press, 1996), 71-72. Testimony of Dainah Shembe.

2. The phrase "margins to maneuver" is used by Umar in illustrating the space Muslims had in northern colonial Nigeria amid the "firm yet partial" rule of the British. Muhammad S. Umar, *Islam and Colonialism: Intellectual Responses of Muslims of Northern Nigeria to British Colonial Rule* (Leiden: E. J. Brill, 2006), 7.

3. Prior to union, Natal had four "native" districts, each administered by co-equal district native commissioners. Following the Union of South Africa in 1910, the same year the church was founded, Natal had a single chief native commissioner and various district officers, all under the supervision of the federal Native Affairs Department. See Howard Rogers, *Native Administration in South Africa* (1933, repr., Westport, CN: Negro Universities Press, 1970), 4-16.

4. CNC 2155/12/24, Kessel to Magistrate, 10 April 1913.

5. General Missionary Secretary of the Methodist Church of South Africa, Rev. Allen Lea, called Bulhoek a tragic yet "sad instance of the blending of a poor understanding of the Christian Religion with a foolish desire to get rid of the white man's control." Allen Lea, *The Native Separatist Church Movement in South Africa* (Cape Town: Juta & Co. Ltd., 1924), 15.

6. NTS 1431 24/214, Harrison to CNC, 24 April 1922.

7. NTS 1431 24/214, Sgt. Monger to District Officer, 13 Nov. 1922.

8. NTS 1431 24/214, Sgt. Masimini Zulu to Chas. McKenzie, Magistrate, Ndwedwe, 13 February 1922.

9. See CNC 562/1919, Roach to CNC, 26 May 1919; AGO 610/1913, Harrison to Attorney General, 24 Sept. 1913; and NTS 1431 24/214 Part II, Gerson to Secretary for Native Affairs, 28 June 1950.

10. Karen Brown, "The Function of Dress and Ritual in the Nazareth Baptist Church of Isaiah Shembe (South Africa)," (Ph.D. diss., Indiana University, 1995), 81.

11. NTS 1431 24/214, Interview with Isaiah Tshembe, 15 January 1923.

12. NTS 1431 24/214, Craddock to District Officer, 10 September 1921.

13. NTS 1431 24/414, Statement of Petros Majosi ka Silomo, 14 March 1922.

14. NTS 1431 24/214, Magistrate to CNC, 15 March 1922.

15. NTS 1431 24/214, Craddock to District Officer Verulam, 10 September 1921.

16. NTS 1431 24/214, Craddock to District Commandant, 31 July 1922.

17. Bent continues to remark from jail about how the situations that brought him to trial were not illegal and were within the bounds of a Christian leader. See his remarks on his website "Wayne Bent aka Michael Travesser" 22 October 2012, <http://www.waynebent.com/>. Accessed 10 November 2012.

18. For more on The Lord Our Righteousness Church see Eddie Stafford and Tim Hopper, *Inside a Cult* (Washington D. C.: National Geographic Channel, 2008) and Tim Hopper, *Inside a Cult: Messiah on Trial* (Washington D. C.: National Geographic Channel, 2009). There are also a number of news articles about the court case from May 2008, including: "Accusations Against Sect in New Mexico," Associated Press, 4 May 2008 and "Church leader arrested on sex charges in northeast N.M.," Associated Press, 6 May 2008.

19. In June 2011 the New Mexico Court of Appeals overturned the 2008 convictions having determined that the grand jury was not legally assembled. The Supreme Court of the State of New Mexico overturned the ruling of the appellate court and the criminal charges were reinstated on 22 October 2012.

20. Carol Ann Muller, "Nazarite Song, Dance, and Dreams: The Sacralization of Time, Space, and the Female Body in South Africa," (Ph.D. diss., New York University, 1994), 49; Carol Ann Muller, *Rituals of Fertility and the Sacrifice of Desire* (Chicago: University of Chicago Press, 1999), 21.

21. NTS 1431 24/214, Wheelwright to Secretary for Native Affairs, 8 September 1922.

22. NTS 1431 24/214, Statement of Dhlamini, 31 January 1923.

23. VLM 3/3/3/4, Wells to Lugg, 22 February 1929.

24. NTS 1431 24/214, Magistrate to CNC, 22 September 1915.

25. NTS 1431 24/214, Statement of Chief Mlokotwa, 14 March 1922; Statement of Mshayankomo ka Magolwane Jiyana, 14 March 1922.

26. NTS 1431 24/214, Statement by Setshebe Mbhele ka Ndadano, 20 September 1915.

27. NTS 1431 24/214, Craddock to District Commandant, 31 July 1922.

28. NTS 1431 24/214, McKenzie to CNC, 22 January 1923.

29. NTS 1431 24/214, Craddock to District Commandant, 31 July 1922.

30. NTS 1431 24/214, Wheelwright to SNA, 8 September 1922.

31. NTS 1431 24/214, Interviewed [sic] with Isaiah Tshembe, 15 January 1923. Weber notes that it is common for founding prophets to shirk traditional economic behavior because doing so legitimizes their prophetic calling. Max Weber, *Max Weber on Charisma and Institution Building*, ed. S. N. Eisenstadt (Chicago: University of Chicago Press, 1968), 21, 52, 255.

32. NTS 1431 24/214, Interviewed [sic] with Isaiah Tshembe, 15 January 1923.

33. NTS 1431 24/214, Interviewed [sic] with Isaiah Tshembe, 15 January 1923.

34. As defined in the famous study by James C. Scott, a public transcript refers to the "encounter of the public transcript of the dominant with the public transcript of the subordinate," and a hidden one to "discourse that takes place 'offstage' beyond direct observation by powerholders." James C. Scott, *Domination and the Arts of Resistance: Hidden Transcripts* (New Haven, CT: Yale University Press, 1990), 4-5, 13-15.

35. Sherry B. Ortner, *Anthropology and Social Theory: Culture, Power, and the Acting Subject* (Durham, NC: Duke University Press, 2006), 48-49.

36. For information on Chilembwe, see George Shepperson and Thomas Price, *Independent African: John Chilembwe and the Origins, Setting, and Significance of the Nyasaland Native Uprising of 1915* (Edinburgh: Edinburgh University Press, 1958); on Mgijima, see Robert Edgar, *Because they Chose the Plan of God: The Story of the Bulhoek Massacre* (Johannesburg: Raven Press, 1988); and on Mpadi, see Wyatt MacGaffey, *Modern Kongo Prophets* (Bloomington: Indiana University Press, 1983), 41-45, 58-59, 218-223.

37. "To our famous Chief Mambuka Mthiyane of Mpuza at Vulindlebe. According to Interpretation: at Mandlazini, December 4, 1932" in Irving Hexham, ed., trans. Londa Shembe and Hans-Jürgen Becken, *The Scriptures of the amaNazaretha of EKuphaKameni: Selected Writings of the Zulu Prophets Isaiah and Londa Shembe* (Calgary: University of Calgary Press, 1994), 38-39.

38. "The Commandments of Shembe, Servant of Suffering," [Y73] *Catechism of the Nazarites*, uncatalogued, Durban Local History Museums, Durban, South Africa.

39. John Comaroff and Jean Comaroff, *Of Revelation and Revolution: The Dialectics of Modernity on a South African Frontier, Volume Two* (Chicago: University of Chicago Press, 1999), 365.

40. See Michael F. Brown, "On Resisting Resistance," *American Anthropologist* 98, no. 4 (1996): 733; Sherry B. Ortner, "Resistance and the Problem of Ethnographic Refusal," *Comparative Studies in Society and History* 37, no. 1 (January 1995): 179, 186; and Lila Abu-Lughod, "The Romance of Resistance: Tracing Transformations of Power through Bedouin Women," *American Ethnologist* 17, no. 1 (February 1990): 42.

41. Fields makes a similar case for the political cognizance of Watchtower members within Central Africa. See Karen E. Fields, *Revival and Rebellion in Colonial Central Africa* (London: Heinemann, 1997), 272-274, 283-284.

42. "Shembe's Prayer in Remembrance of His Nation," [Y16] *Catechism.*

43. "A Prayer for the Day of Dingane," [Y31] *Catechism.*

44. Andreas Heuser and Irving Hexham, eds., trans. Hans-Jürgen Becken, *The Hymns and Sabbath Liturgy for Morning and Evening Prayer of Isaiah Shembe's amaNazarites, Volume Five* (Lewiston, NY: The Edwin Mellen Press, 2005), 56-57.

45. Heuser and Hexham, *The Hymns and Sabbath Liturgy*, 84-85.

46. Hexham and Oosthuizen, *The Story of Isaiah Shembe, Vol. One*, 157, 159-160. Testimonies of Hlanganisumuzi David Mncwanga and Lotha Zuma.

47. Hexham and Oosthuizen, *The Story of Isaiah Shembe, Vol. One*, 94. Testimonies of Thembekile Mhlongo and Petros M. Dhlomo.

48. Hexham and Oosthuizen, *The Story of Isaiah Shembe, Vol. One*, 94. Testimonies of Thembekile Mhlongo and Petros M. Dhlomo.

49. All the details of this meeting come from NTS 1431 24/214. Interviewed [sic] with Isaiah Tshembe, 15 January 1923.

50. NTS 1431, 24/214. Statement of Native Constable Dhlamvuza Dhlamini to Magistrate Chas. McKenzie, Ndwedwe, 31 January 1923.

51. NTS 1431, 24/214 Assistant Health Officer to Secretary for Public Health, 9 December 1926, as cited in Cabrita, "Theological Biography," 194, nts 624-627.

52. The details regarding the vaccination controversy can be found in Hexham, *The Story of Isaiah Shembe, Vol. One*, 145-151. Testimony of John Mabuyakhulu.

53. NTS 1431, 24/214 Magistrate Verulam to Assistant Health Officer, 26 April 1929, as cited in Cabrita, *Theological Biography*, 195, n. 630.

54. A. W. G. Champion and R. R. R. Dhlomo, ed. M. W. Swanson, trans. E. R. Dahle and A. T. Cope, *The Views of Mahlathi: Writings of A. W. G. Champion, a Black South African: with a Biography of A. W. G. Champion* (Pietermaritzburg: University of Natal Press; Durban: Killie Campbell Africana Library, 1982), 23.

55. It was not until 1944 that Galilee Shembe finally relented to vaccinations, when a different political climate provided him the choice of either complying or having his congregation subjected to forced vaccinations.

56. NTS 3192 125/307, C. C. Allen, October 1922.

57. NTS 1431 24/214, CNC to SNA, 22 September 1922.

58. URU 1225/2463, Minute, 11 August 1931; and URU 22892/1081 Minute, 13 August 1929, as cited in Robert Papini, "Carl Faye's Transcript of Isaiah Shembe's Testimony on his Early Life and Calling," *Journal of Religion in Africa* 29, no. 3 (1999): 251 nts. 36 and 37.

59. Joshua Bheki Mzizi, "Images of Isaiah Shembe: An Appraisal of the Views of Mthembeni Mpanza," *Missionalia* 32, no. 2 (August 2004): 207.

60. "A Letter of Shembe written at Zibone on the Sabbath, 22 August 1931," [Y76] *Catechism*. This testimony is also preserved in the copybook of Imilando Nemithetho's "Histories and Laws." See "Sabbath Maxims on the Morning of 22nd day of August 1931," in Elizabeth Gunner, *The Man of Heaven and the Beautiful Ones of God* (Leiden: E. J. Brill, 2002), 121.

61. See the dream that inspired Shembe's prediction of future violence in South Africa and the protection that church gowns would provide in Carol Ann Muller, "Nazarite Song, Dance, and Dreams: The Sacralization of Time, Space, and the Female Body in South Africa" (Ph.D. diss., New York University, 1994), 107-108.

62. When German theologian Hans-Jürgen Becken asked Amos Shembe, in 1989, to view the mission stations in Zululand, Shembe's letter of 1931 was brought forth. When a theologian made the request to view the mission stations, it was believed Shembe's prediction about the destroyed temple locations had come true decades later. H.-J. Becken, "I Love to Tell the Story: Oral History in the Nazaretha Church," in *Empirical Studies of African Independent/Indigenous Churches*, eds. G. C. Oosthuizen and Irving Hexham (Lewiston, NY: Edwin Mellen Press, 1992), 34.

63. See Hexham and Oosthuizen, *The Story of Isaiah Shembe, Vol. One*, 69-72. Testimonies of Petros M. Dhlomo, Linah Mntungwa, and Dinah Shembe; "Prayer for the Confession of Sins at Ekuphakameni II," [Y26] *Catechism*, and "Prayer of Shembe at Linda Home," [Y18] *Catechism*. For a discussion of this feeling of contestation within the church's *izibongo*, see Elizabeth Gunner, "Power House, Prison House–An Oral Genre and Its Use in Isaiah Shembe's Nazareth Baptist Church," *Journal of Southern African Studies* 14, no. 2 (January 1988): 212-221.

64. "Herd Boy Turns Healer," Unidentified newspaper, 27 July 1927; clipping in NTS 1431 24/214.

65. "Native 'Prophet's' Large Following." *District Notes & News*, 30 July 1929.

66. Papini, "Carl Faye's Transcript," 250.

67. VLM 3/3/3/4 file 2/8/6 Wells to Lugg, 22 February 1929, p. 3. Shembe had called upon Champion's legal advice in the mid-1920s, but by 1928 the ICU had begun to break up following expulsion of Communists in 1926 and a leadership struggle between Champion and Clement Kadalie.

68. Nattie Wells, *Natal Mercury*, 30 July 1929. Note the use of her language by the *Illustrated London News* article from 1930.

69. KCAL, Uncat Mss: Shembe Festival, date unknown. The typeface and content suggest it is likely from the 1940s.

70. Esther Roberts, "Shembe: The Man and his Work," ed. Robert Papini, 1999 (Master's thesis, University of South Africa, 1936), 25. All citations of Roberts refers to this unpublished version edited by Robert Papini in 1999.

71. Roberts, "Shembe: The Man and his Work," 43.

72. Liz Gunner, "Testimonies of Dispossession and Repossession: Writing about the South African Prophet Isaiah Shembe," *Bulletin of the John Rylands Library of Manchester* 73, no. 3 (Autumn 1991): 102; Gunner, "Power House," 214; Papini, "Carl Faye's Transcript," 253, 255.

73. Adam Payne, "A Prophet among the Zulus: Shembe a Power for Peace and a Restraining Influence," *Illustrated London News*, 8 February 1930, 203-4.

74. Joel Marie Cabrita, "A Theological Biography of Isaiah Shembe, c. 1870-1935" (Ph.D. diss., University of Cambridge, 2008), 86.

75. Cabrita, "Theological Biography," 87.

76. Hexham and Oosthuizen, *The Story of Isaiah Shembe*, Vol. One, 158-59. Testimony of John Mabuyakhulu.

77. "Shembe's Prayer in Remembrance of His Nation," [Y16] *Catechism*.

78. Hexham, *Scriptures of the amaNazaretha*, 16.

79. Hexham and Oosthuizen, *The Story of Isaiah Shembe*, Vol. One, 53. Author unknown.

80. Roberts, "Shembe," 25, 41.

81. Brown, "The Function of Dress," 59. Galilee Shembe made an estimate of 40,000 to Esther Roberts. See Roberts, "Shembe," 42.

82. Hexham and Oosthuizen, *The Story of Isaiah Shembe*, Vol. One, 241. Testimony of Ellen Mngomezulu.

83. Hexham and Oosthuizen, *The Story of Isaiah Shembe*, Vol. One, 97, 236, 240. Testimonies of Petros M. Dhlomo, Selina Nomahashi Mpanza, Thuthwase Emmah Samarian Mthethwa, Dainah Shembe, Nongilishi Nokwanela Mdluli, Muntuwezizwe Buthelezi, and Galilee Shembe.

84. John L. Dube, "Shembe Passes Away," in chapter 23 of *Ushembe* (Pietermaritzburg: Shuter and Shooter, 1936), translated into English by Hans-Jürgen Becken, n. p., 1993; Hexham and Oosthuizen, *The Story of Isaiah Shembe*, Vol. 1, 239-41. Testimonies of Thuthwase Emmah Samarian Mthethwa, Dainah Shembe, Nongilishi Nokwanela Mdluli, Muntuwezizwe Buthelezi, and Galilee Shembe.

85. James Fernandez, "Precincts of the Prophet: A Day with Johannes Galilee Shembe," *Journal of Religion in Africa* 5, no. 1 (1973): 44; *Natal Mercury*, 3 May 1935 & 6 May 1935; *Sunday Times*, 5 May 1935; *Rand Daily Mail*, 6 May 1935.

86. Hexham and Oosthuizen, *The Story of Isaiah Shembe*, Vol. One, 254-55. Testimonies of Galilee Shembe, Muntuwezizwe Buthelezi, and Petros M. Dhlomo.

87. Hymn 71 confirms Shembe's existence as an eternal spirit. The hymn refers to Shembe being blessed by the Lord after creation but "before the mountains were hardened" or the "springs of water had spurt so powerfully." See Andreas Heuser and Irving Hexham, eds., trans. Hans-Jürgen Becken, *The Hymns and Sabbath Liturgy for Morning and Evening Prayer of Isaiah Shembe's amaNazarites, Volume Five* (Lewiston, NY: Edwin Mellen Press, 2005), 59-60.

88. Absolom Vilakazi, with Bongani Mthethwa and Mthembeni Mpanza, *Shembe: The Revitalization of African Society* (Johannesburg: Skotaville, 1986), 51-52.

89. Muller, "Nazarite Song, Dance, and Dreams," 169.

90. H. B. Mkhize, "The Umthandazi–Prayer-Healer," in *Afro-Christian Religion and Healing in Southern Africa*, eds. G. C. Oosthuizen et. al. (Lewiston, NY: Edwin Mellen Press, 1989), 286, 288.

91. Hexham and Oosthuizen, *The Story of Isaiah Shembe*, Vol. One, 19-20. Testimony of Josiah Mthembu.

92. Joel E. Tishken, "Whose Nazareth Baptist Church? Prophecy, Power, and Schism in South Africa," *Nova Religio* 9, no. 4 (May 2006): 93-94.

93. J. Galilee Shembe, comp., *Izihlabelelo zaManazaretha* (1940, 5th ed., repr., n.p., 1990), 167.

Chapter V

1. Irving Hexham and G. C. Oosthuizen, eds., trans. Hans-Jürgen Becken, *The Story of Isaiah Shembe, Volume One: History and Traditions Centered on Ekuphakameni and Mount Nhlangakazi* (Lewiston, NY: Edwin Mellen Press, 1996), 103. Testimony of Daniel Dube.

2. I am not the only scholar who has commented upon the church's geography. But whereas I am arguing that the map of Shembe and the Nazareth Baptist Church was a new invention based upon their new identity as God's chosen, Gunner sees it as resistance to the white world grounded within indigenous notions of landscape. See Liz Gunner, "Remapping land and remaking culture: memory and landscape in 20th-century South Africa," *Journal of Historical Geography* 31 (2005): 285-286, 289.

3. Hexham and Oosthuizen, *The Story of Isaiah Shembe, Vol. One*, 81. Testimony of Petros M. Dhlomo.

4. Hexham and Oosthuizen, *The Story of Isaiah Shembe, Vol. One*, 52-53. Testimony of Daniel Dube.

5. Mthembeni P. Mpanza, "The Biography of Isaiah Shembe," 25. Durban Local History Museums, accession number 98/653.

6. Liz Gunner, "Hidden Stories and the Light of New Day: A Zulu Manuscript and Its Place in South African Writing," *Research in African Literatures* 31, no. 2 (Summer 2000): 8.

7. Robert Papini, "Carl Faye's Transcript of Isaiah Shembe's Testimony on his Early Life and Calling," *Journal of Religion in Africa* 29, no. 3 (1999): 279.

8. Papini "Carl Faye's Transcript," 265.

9. Karen Brown, "The Function of Dress and Ritual in the Nazareth Baptist Church of Isaiah Shembe (South Africa)" (Ph.D. diss., Indiana University, 1995), 58 n. 4.

10. Hexham and Oosthuizen, *The Story of Isaiah Shembe, Vol. One*, 87. Testimony of Petros M. Dhlomo.

11. "Laws to Cleanse People at Ekuphakameni, 7 August 1932," [Y79] *Catechism of the Nazarites*, uncatalogued, Durban Local History Museums.

12. Hexham and Oosthuizen, *The Story of Isaiah Shembe, Vol. One*, 89. Testimony of Petros M. Dhlomo.

13. Hexham and Oosthuizen, *The Story of Isaiah Shembe, Vol. One*, 115-116. Testimony of Selina Nomahashi Mpanza.

14. "Laws to Cleanse People at Ekuphakameni, 7 August 1932," [Y79] *Catechism*.

15. "Prayer for the Confession of Sins at Ekuphakameni," [Y26] *Catechism*.

16. Carol Muller, "'Written' into the Book of Life: Nazarite Women's Performance Inscribed as Spiritual Text in 'Ibandla lamaNazaretha," *Research in African Literatures* 28, no. 1 (1997): 6.

17. See the testimonies of Petros M. Dhlomo, Muntuwezizwe Buthelezi, Johannes Duma, and Solomon Mdluli in Hexham and Oosthuizen, *The Story of Isaiah Shembe, Vol. One*, 79-84; Mthembeni P. Mpanza, "The Biography of Isaiah Shembe," 46; and Evangelist Khaya Ndelu in Robert Papini, *Rise Up and Dance and Praise God* (Durban: Local History Museum, 1992), 26.

18. In this particular vision, Shembe reported the heavenly spirits wearing white robes tied by belts (black or gold belts depending on the tradition) over their chests. The belts were not reported in other visions of the uniform, nor did Shembe implement them as part of the *umnazaretha* for the church.

19. Hexham and Oosthuizen, *The Story of Isaiah Shembe, Vol. One*, 81. Testimony of Petros M. Dhlomo.

20. Hexham and Oosthuizen, *The Story of Isaiah Shembe, Vol. One*, 82. Testimony of Johannes Duma.

21. Hexham and Oosthuizen, *The Story of Isaiah Shembe, Vol. One*, 84-85. Testimony of Petros M. Dhlomo.

22. Joel E. Tishken, "Whose Nazareth Baptist Church? Prophecy, Power, and Schism in South Africa," *Nova Religio* 9, no. 4 (May 2006): 93-94.

23. Hexham and Oosthuizen, *The Story of Isaiah Shembe, Vol. One*, 86. Testimony of Petros M. Dhlomo.

24. Hexham and Oosthuizen, *The Story of Isaiah Shembe, Vol. One*, 90. Testimony of Thandekile Shembe.

25. Modern Western medicine considers suction of the wound to be an outmoded technique that has little or no impact, but can introduce the toxin into the mouth of the extractor, or bacteria from the extractor's mouth into the wound, posing a risk for gangrene.

26. Hexham and Oosthuizen, *The Story of Isaiah Shembe, Vol. One*, 91. Testimony of Phasika Mhlongo.

27. Hexham and Oosthuizen, *The Story of Isaiah Shembe, Vol. One*, 91. Testimony of Phasika Mhlongo.

28. G. C. Oosthuizen, "The Theology of Londa Shembe and the amaNazaretha of EKuphaKameni," in *The Scriptures of the amaNazaretha of EKuphaKameni: Selected Writings of the Zulu Prophets Isaiah and Londa Shembe*, ed. Irving Hexham, trans. Londa Shembe and Hans-Jürgen Becken (Calgary: University of Calgary Press, 1994), xxvii-xxviii. Though I have done my best to locate the text of this prophecy, I have been unable to secure the original referred to by Oosthuizen. While I do not generally agree with Oosthuizen's interpretation of the Nazareth Baptist Church, I would certainly not contest his integrity as a scholar and researcher, and trust Oosthuizen's word that such a prophecy existed. I ask the reader to overlook the fact that I have not secured the exact words of the prophecy, and join me in trusting Oosthuizen that Shembe had a vision in 1913 that blessed his Sabbatarian position.

29. "The Biblical Chapters Concerning the Sabbath," in KCAL: Album: African Religions: Shembe, Londa.

30. Isaiah 58:13, "If you refrain from trampling the sabbath, from pursuing your own interests on my holy day; if you call the sabbath a delight and the holy day of the Lord honorable; if you honor it, not going your own ways, serving your own interests, or pursuing your own affairs" NRSV

31. Deuteronomy 5:12, "Observe the sabbath day and keep it holy, as the Lord your God commanded you."

32. Exodus 16:25, Moses said, "Eat it today, for today is a sabbath to the Lord; today you will not find it in the field."

33. Exodus 35:1-3, "Moses assembled all the congregation of the Israelites and said to them: These are the things that the Lord has commanded you to do: Six days shall work be done, but on the seventh day you shall have a holy sabbath of solemn rest to the Lord; whoever does any work on it shall be put to death. You shall kindle no fire in all your dwellings on the sabbath day."

34. Irving Hexham and G. C. Oosthuizen, eds., trans. Hans-Jürgen Becken, *The Story of Isaiah Shembe, Volume Two: Early Regional Traditions of the Acts of the Nazarites* (Lewiston, NY: Edwin Mellen Press, 1999), 144-145. Testimony of Aaron Magwaza.

35. "The Biblical Chapters Concerning the Sabbath," in KCAL: Album: African Religions: Shembe, Londa.

36. Exodus 31:14-16, "You shall keep the sabbath, because it is holy for you; everyone who profanes it shall be put to death; whoever does any work on it shall be cut off from among the people. Six days shall work be done, but the seventh day is a sabbath of solemn rest, holy to the Lord; whoever does any work on the sabbath day shall be put to death.

Therefore the Israelites shall keep the sabbath, observing the sabbath throughout their generations, as a perpetual covenant."

37. Numbers 15:32-36, "When the Israelites were in the wilderness, they found a man gathering sticks on the sabbath day. Those who found him gathering sticks brought him to Moses, Aaron, and to the whole congregation. They put him in custody, because it was not clear what should be done to him. Then the Lord said to Moses, 'The man shall be put to death; all the congregation shall stone him outside the camp.' The whole congregation brought him outside the camp and stoned him to death, just as the Lord had commanded Moses."

38. Andreas Heuser and Irving Hexham, eds., trans. Hans-Jürgen Becken, *The Hymns and Sabbath Liturgy for Morning and Evening Prayer of Isaiah Shembe's amaNazarites, Volume Five* (Lewiston, NY: The Edwin Mellen Press, 2005), 144-145.

39. The term *nazir/naziyr* is a noun meaning "one consecrated" that derives from the verbal root *nazar* meaning "to separate, or to consecrate." The Zulu translation of the Bible uses the term *somNaziri* for nazirite. See *Ibhayibheli Elingcwele* (Goodwood, South Africa: National Book Printers, 1999), 163. Other bibilical translations, including the King James Version, use the spelling *nazarite*. James Strong notes that *nazarite* is a false alliteration with Nazareth. It is possible that Shembe reproduced the same false alliteration to Nazareth himself when choosing the spelling *nazarite*, which seems likely given the church's name. However, given that the spelling can be found in other translations of the Bible, it is also possible that the spelling *nazarite* was in circulation in South Africa and picked up by Shembe. See term no. 5139 in James Strong, *A Concise Dictionary of the words in the Hebrew Bible with their rendering in the Authorized English Version* (Nashville: Abingdon-Cokesbury Press, 1890), 77.

40. Numbers 6:2, "Speak to the Israelites and say to them: 'When either men or women make a special vow, the vow of a nazirite, to separate themselves to the Lord'"

41. "The Law governing Leaders who want to be married," [Y74] *Catechism.*

42. Eileen Jensen Krige, *The Social System of the Zulu*, 3rd ed. (Pietermaritzburg: Shuter and Shooter, 1957), 388.

43. Heuser and Hexham, *The Hymns and Sabbath Liturgy*, 52.

44. Hexham and Oosthuizen, *The Story of Isaiah Shembe, Vol. One*, 101. Testimony of Johannes Galilee Shembe; and Response 8 in "Catechism of the Nazarites" says "God said that to Moses. Even Jesus did not wear shoes, he was barefooted when baptised [Exodus 3:5]. And Shembe says we must take off our shoes in the holy place."

45. Exodus 3:5, "Then he said, 'Come no closer! Remove the sandals from your feet, for the place on which you are standing is holy ground.'" The "Statute" cites Exodus 3:2-3, which tells the story of the burning bush, but it is verse 5 that contains the command about removing sandals. The "Catechism of the Nazarites" cites the correct verse for the quote. It is unclear which verse Shembe originally cited.

46. Joshua 5:14, "He replied, 'Neither; but as commander of the army of the Lord I have now come.' And Joshua fell on his face to the earth and worshiped, and he said to him, 'What do you command your servant, my lord?'"

47. "Reminder of the Statute," no. 78 in section titled "Footwear." *Catechism.*

48. "Catechism of the Nazarites," *Catechism.*

49. David Barrett, *Schism and Renewal: An Analysis of Six Thousand Contemporary Religious Movements* (Nairobi: Oxford University Press, 1968), 184; H. W. Turner, "A Typology for African Religious Movements," *Journal of Religion in Africa* 1, no. 1 (1967): 6-10, 33.

50. Bart D. Ehrman, *Lost Christianities: The Battle for Scripture and the Faiths We Never Knew* (Oxford: Oxford University Press, 2003), 96-103.

51. See Nicole Andersen and Scott London, "South Africa's Newest 'Jews': The Moemedi Pentecostal Church and Jewish Identity," *Nova Religio* 13, no. 1 (2009): 92-105, for a Zionist group that does self-identify as Jews.

52. Carol Ann Muller, "Nazarite Song, Dance, and Dreams: The Sacralization of Time, Space, and the Female Body in South Africa" (Ph.D. diss., New York University, 1994), 131.

53. Nellie Wells, "Notes for film" (Film: *Dancin' up dem golden stairs*, c1930-34; 5 mins.), video copy accession number 65/392.

54. For three such instances see Donald M'Timkulu, "Some Aspects of Zulu Religion," in *African Religions: A Symposium*, ed. Newell S. Booth (New York: NOK Publishers, 1977), 25; Absolom Vilakazi, with Bongani Mthethwa and Mthembeni Mpanza, *Shembe: The Revitalization of African Society* (Johannesburg: Skotaville, 1986), 155-156; and Duncan Brown, "Orality and Christianity: The Hymns of Isaiah Shembe and the Church of the Nazarites," *Current Writing* 7, no. 2 (1995): 76-80.

55. Hexham and Oosthuizen, *The Story of Isaiah Shembe, Volume Two*, 244. Testimony of Hlanganisumuzi David Mncwanga. See also Hexham and Oosthuizen, *The Story of Isaiah Shembe, Vol. One*, 155. Testimony of Sheleni Ngubane and Hexham and Oosthuizen, *The Story of Isaiah Shembe, Vol. One*, 157. Testimony of Hlanganisumuzi David Mncwanga.

56. For more on the souring of relations between Shembe and King Solomon see Joel Cabrita, "Isaiah Shembe's Theological Nationalism, 1920s-1935," *Journal of Southern African Studies* 35, no. 3 (September 2009): 614-620.

57. Nicolas Cope, *To Bind the Nation: Solomon kaDinuzulu and Zulu Nationalism, 1913-1933* (Pietermaritzburg: University of Natal Press, 1993), 111.

58. Andreas Heuser, "Contested Charisma: Reflections on the Appearance and Disappearance of Female Visionary Power in a South African Independent Church," *Zeitschrift für Globalgerschichte und vergleichende Gesellschaftsforchung* 17, nos. 5/6 (2007): 82-83.

59. For a theoretical articulation of scholarly failures to appreciate the creative and innovative uses of indigenous cultures see Sherry B. Ortner, "Resistance and the Problem of Ethnographic Refusal," *Comparative Studies in Society and History* 37, no. 1 (January 1995): 186, 190-191.

60. For examples of scholarship that has argued that the church should be seen a stronghold of cultural resistance see Carol Ann Muller, *Rituals of Fertility and the Sacrifice of Desire* (Chicago: University of Chicago Press, 1999), 18-20, 65; Elizabeth Gunner, *The Man of Heaven and the Beautiful Ones of God* (Leiden: E. J. Brill, 2002), 7-9; and Robert Papini, "The Nazareth Scotch: Dance Uniform as Admonitory Infrapolitics for an Eikonic Zion City in Early Union Natal," *Southern African Humanities* 14 (December 2002): 79-80, 82-83.

61. Wells, "Notes for film."

62. Andreas Heuser, "Experiments in an Independent African Satyagraha: Gandhi, Shembe and the Roots of Passive Resistance in South Africa," in *Religion and the Political Imagination in a Changing South Africa*, eds. Gordon Mitchell and Eve Mullen (Munster: Waxmann, 2002), 85.

63. Hexham and Oosthuizen, *The Story of Isaiah Shembe, Vol. One*, 81. Testimony of Petros M. Dhlomo. In the early years of the church, Shembe and his congregation used the Zulu term *nsundu*, or brown, to refer to Africans more often than *omnyama*, or black. Both terms can be used to mean dark-skinned person.

64. Brown, "Orality and Christianity," 88.

65. Esther L. Roberts, "Shembe: The Man and his Work," ed. Robert Papini, 1999. (Master's thesis, University of South Africa, 1936), 25. Roberts estimated that the church had around 200 Indian and Coloured members in the early 1930s. Though not huge in number, their very presence does suggest that at least some individuals understood Shembe's message about God's "brown" people to mean not just all African ethnicities, but all non-whites.

66. Hexham and Oosthuizen, *The Story of Isaiah Shembe, Vol. One*, 81. Testimony of Petros M. Dhlomo.

Chapter VI

1.   Irving Hexham and G. C. Oosthuizen, eds., trans. Hans-Jürgen Becken, *The Story of Isaiah Shembe, Volume One: History and Traditions Centered on Ekuphakameni and Mount Nhlangakazi* (Lewiston, NY: Edwin Mellen Press, 1996), 135-136. Testimony of Abednego Josiah Mthembu.

2.   B. E. Ngobese, "The Concept of the Trinity among the Amanazaretha," in *Empirical Studies of African Independent/Indigenous Churches*, eds. G. C. Oosthuizen and Irving Hexham (Lewiston, NY: Edwin Mellen Press, 1992), 94.

3.   Sacraments serve the same kind of reinforcing role to faith, ideology, and communal identity throughout Christendom. Alister E. McGrath, *Christian Theology: An Introduction*, 4th ed. (Oxford: Blackwell, 2007), 426-430.

4.   Irving Hexham and G. C. Oosthuizen, eds., trans. by Hans-Jürgen Becken, *The Story of Isaiah Shembe, Volume Two: Early Regional Traditions of the Acts of the Nazarites* (Lewiston, NY: Edwin Mellen Press, 1999), 16. Testimony of Petros M. Dhlomo.

5.   John 15:10, "If you keep my commandments, you will abide in my love, just as I have kept my Father's commandments and abide in his love." NRSV

6.   Matthew 26:20, "When it was evening, he took his place with the twelve...."

7.   1 Corinthians 11:23, "For I received from the Lord what I also handed on to you, that the Lord Jesus on the night when he was betrayed took a loaf of bread...."

8.   "Native 'Prophet's' Large Following." *District Notes & News*, 30 July 1929; John L. Dube, "Shembe Passes Away," in chapter 11 of *Ushembe* (Pietermaritzburg: Shuter and Shooter, 1936), translated into English by Hans-Jürgen Becken, n. p., 1993.

9.   Question 1 in "The Statute of the Lord's Supper." *Catechism of the Nazarites*, uncatalogued, Durban Local History Museums, Durban, South Africa.

10. See Questions 2, 13, 17, and 18 in "The Statute of the Lord's Supper."

11. See Question 2 in "The Statute of the Lord's Supper."

12. John 13:14-15, "So if I, your Lord and Teacher, have washed your feet, you also ought to wash one another's feet. For I have set you an example, that you also should do as I have done to you."

13. Mthembeni P. Mpanza, "The Biography of Isaiah Shembe," 20, accession number 98/653, Durban Local History Museums, Durban, South Africa.

14. Dube, "Shembe and Work," chapter 19.

15. "The Council of Trent," in *Documents of the Christian Church*, 3rd edition, eds. Henry Bettenson and Chris Maunder (Oxford: Oxford University Press, 1999), 278.

16. Lamula was ordained by the Norwegian Mission Society in 1915, a Lutheran organization. He left the NMS in 1926 and created his own Ethiopianist church, the United Native

National Church of Christ, which remained Lutheran in theology. Because this testimony is undated, it is not possible to know which church Lamula was a part of at the time of his conversation with Shembe, but his theology would have been largely similar in either case. Paul la Hausse de Lalouvière, *Restless Identities: Signatures of Nationalism, Zulu Ethnicity, and History in the Lives of Petros Lamula (c. 1881-1948) and Lymon Maling (1889-c. 1936)* (Scottsville, South Africa: University of Natal Press, 2000), 129.

17. Hexham and Oosthuizen, eds., *The Story of Isaiah Shembe*, Vol. One, 131. Testimony of Solomon Mdluli. Biltong is a cured meat, akin to jerky, but with different spices and ingredients, and is made from a variety of meats.

18. Hexham and Oosthuizen, eds., *The Story of Isaiah Shembe*, Vol. One, 131. Testimony of Muntuwezizwe Buthelezi.

19. McGrath, *Christian Theology*, 440.

20. Hexham and Oosthuizen, *The Story of Isaiah Shembe*, Vol. One, 130-131. Testimony of Solomon Mdluli.

21. Hexham and Oosthuizen, *The Story of Isaiah Shembe*, Vol. One, 131. Testimony of Muntuwezizwe Buthelezi.

22. Hexham and Oosthuizen, *The Story of Isaiah Shembe*, Vol. One, 131. Testimony of Solomon Mdluli.

23. John 3:23, "John also was baptizing at Aenon near Salim because water was abundant there; and people kept coming and were being baptized."

24. Matthew 3:13-17, "Then Jesus came from Galilee to John at the Jordan, to be baptized by him. John would have prevented him, saying, 'I need to be baptized by you, and do you come to me?' But Jesus answered him, 'Let it be so now; for it is proper for us in this way to fulfill all righteousness.' Then he consented. And when Jesus had been baptized, just as he came up from the water, suddenly the heavens were opened to him and he saw the Spirit of God descending like a dove and alighting on him. And a voice from heaven said, 'This is my Son, the Beloved, with whom I am well pleased.'"

25. While Shembe typically conducted baptisms in fresh water rivers, he did baptize members in salt water (the Indian Ocean) on several occasions. See "Shembe comes to Natal," in Hexham and Oosthuizen, *The Story of Isaiah Shembe*, Vol. One, 42-43. Testimony of Bheki-Mkhize.

26. Question 1 in "The Statute of Baptism," *Catechism*.

27. Hexham and Oosthuizen, *The Story of Isaiah Shembe*, Vol. One, 33. Testimony of Johannes Galilee Shembe.

28. Hexham and Oosthuizen, *The Story of Isaiah Shembe*, Vol. One, 31. Testimony of Petros M. Dhlomo.

29. Dube, "The Baptism of Shembe," chapter 1.

30. A 1916 Groutville mission report names the head of the station as one Pastor Goba. See Joel Marie Cabrita, "A Theological Biography of Isaiah Shembe, c. 1870-1935," (Ph.D. diss., University of Cambridge, 2008), 159, nt 178.

31. Hexham and Oosthuizen, *The Story of Isaiah Shembe*, Vol. Two, 120-121. Testimony of Timothy Khuzwayo.

32. Question 2, "Catechism of the Nazarites."

33. Hexham and Oosthuizen, *The Story of Isaiah Shembe*, Vol. One, 31-33. Testimony of Khaya S. Ndelu.

34. Hexham and Oosthuizen, *The Story of Isaiah Shembe*, Vol. One, 42. Testimony of Bheki Mkhize.

35. Hexham and Oosthuizen, *The Story of Isaiah Shembe, Vol. One*, 125-126. Testimony of Edmond Dladla and Petros Dhlomo.

36. Hexham and Oosthuizen, *The Story of Isaiah Shembe, Vol. One*, 126-127. Testimony of Thomas Makhathini.

37. Hexham and Oosthuizen, *The Story of Isaiah Shembe, Vol. One*, 127-129. Testimonies of Thomas Makhathini and Azariah Mthiyane.

38. Paragraph 3, "Statute of Baptism."

39. Robert Papini, "Dance Uniform History in the Church of the Nazareth Baptists: The Move to Tradition," *African Arts* 37, no. 3 (Autumn 2004): 49.

40. Psalm 150:1-6, "Praise the Lord! Praise God in his sanctuary; praise him in his mighty firmament! Praise him for his mighty deeds; praise him according to his surpassing greatness! Praise him with trumpet sound; praise him with lute and harp! Praise him with tambourine and dance; praise him with strings and pipe! Praise him with clanging cymbals; praise him with loud clashing cymbals! Let everything that breathes praise the Lord! Praise the Lord!"

41. Papini, "Dance Uniform History," 56.

42. See Peter Larlham, "Festivals of the Nazareth Baptist Church," *The Drama Review* 25, no. 4 (Winter 1981): 59-74; Carol Ann Muller, "Nazarite Song, Dance, and Dreams: The Sacralization of Time, Space, and the Female Body in South Africa," (Ph.D. diss., New York University, 1994); Robert Papini, "The Nazareth Scotch: Dance Uniform as Admonitory Infrapolitics for an Eikonic Zion City in Early Union Natal," *Southern African Humanities* 14 (December 2002): 79-106; and Papini, "Dance Uniform History," 48-61, 90-92.

43. James W. Fernandez, "Precincts of the Prophet: A Day with Johannes Galilee Shembe," *Journal of Religion in Africa* 5, no. 1 (1973): 42; H. J. Becken, "The Nazareth Baptist Church of Shembe," in *Our Approach to the Independent Church Movement in South Africa*, ed. Lutheran Theological College (Mapumulo: Lutheran Theological College, Missiological Institute; Christian Institute of Southern Africa, 1965), 105.

44. Robert Papini, *Rise Up and Dance and Praise God* (Durban: Local History Museum, 1992), 18.

45. Larlham, "Festivals," 72.

46. Native Economic Commission, 1931, pg. 6544. CNC 22/635.

47. B. N. Mthethwa, "Music and Dance as Therapy in African Traditional Societies with Special Reference to the iBandla lamaNazaretha," in *Afro-Christian Religions and Healing in Southern Africa*, eds. G. C. Oosthuizen, et. al., (Lewiston, NY: Edwin Mellen Press, 1991), 249-250.

48. Mthethwa, "Music and Dance as Therapy," 251; Interview with Nkosinathi Sithole by Joel Marie Cabrita, 15 September 2006, in Cabrita, "A Theological Biography of Isaiah Shembe," 216, n. 693.

49. This is the argument of Muller, "Nazarite Song, Dance, and Dreams," 187, and Papini, "Dance Uniform History," 49.

50. Sherry B. Ortner, "Resistance and the Problem of Ethnographic Refusal," *Comparative Studies in Society and History* 37, no. 1 (January 1995), 180-183.

51. Joel Cabrita, "Isaiah Shembe's Theological Nationalism, 1920s-1935," *Journal of Southern African Studies* 35, no. 3 (September 2009), 621; Papini, "Dance Uniform History," 59.

52. Papini, "The Nazareth Scotch," 79.

53. Papini, "Dance Uniform History," 51.

54. Larlham, "Festivals," 70.

55. Cabrita, "A Theological Biography of Isaiah Shembe," 91.

56. Hexham and Oosthuizen, *The Story of Isaiah Shembe, Vol. One*, 6-7. Testimony of Petros M. Dhlomo, Muntuwezizwe Buthelezi, and Khaya S. Ndelu.

57. Thomas W. Overholt, "The Ghost Dance of 1890 and the Nature of the Prophetic Process," *Ethnohistory* 21, no. 1 (1974): 38.

58. Hexham and Oosthuizen, *The Story of Isaiah Shembe, Vol. One*, 22-26. Testimony of Petros M. Dhlomo, Khaya S. Ndelu, and Jeslinah Mchunu; Papini, "Carl Faye's Transcript," 271, 273.

59. Hexham and Oosthuizen, *The Story of Isaiah Shembe, Vol. One*, 79-84. Testimonies of Petros M. Dhlomo, Muntuwezizwe Buthelezi, Johannes Duma, and Solomon Mdluli; Mpanza, "The Biography of Isaiah Shembe," 46; and Evangelist Khaya Ndelu in Papini, *Rise Up*, 26.

60. Brown, "Function of Dress and Ritual," 34.

61. See the full transcript of Shembe's account of this prophetic experience in chapter 2.

62. Hexham and Oosthuizen, *The Story of Isaiah Shembe, Vol. One*, 79-84. Testimonies of Petros M. Dhlomo, Muntuwezizwe Buthelezi, Johannes Duma, and Solomon Mdluli.

63. Muller, "Nazarite Song, Dance, and Dreams," 107, 159.

64. This particular version is the testimonial of Daniel Dube in Hexham and Oosthuizen, *The Story of Isaiah Shembe, Vol. One*, 40. It is in Galilee Shembe's testimony that Nkabinde is identified as John the Baptist. Hexham and Oosthuizen, *The Story of Isaiah Shembe, Vol. One*, 39.

65. Hexham and Oosthuizen, *The Story of Isaiah Shembe, Vol. One*, 64-54. Testimony of Gertie Mbambo.

66. Hexham and Oosthuizen, *The Story of Isaiah Shembe, Vol. One*, 135-136. Testimony of Abednego Josiah Mthembu.

Chapter VII

1. Robin M. Petersen, "The AICs and the TRC," in *Facing the Truth: South African Faith Communities and the Truth & Reconciliation Commission*, eds. James Cochran, John de Gruchy, and Stephen Martin (Cape Town: David Philip; Athens: Ohio University Press, 1999), 117; Lyn S. Graybill, *Religion and Resistance Politics in South Africa* (Westport, CT; London: Praeger, 1995), 60.

2. See Robert I. Rotberg, *The Rise of Nationalism in Central Africa: The Making of Malawi and Zambia, 1873-1964,* (Cambridge: Harvard University Press, 1965), 142-147; Paul Bohannan, *Africa and Africans* (Garden City, NY: Natural History Press, 1964); and Frederick Burkewood Welbourn, *East African Rebels: A Study of some Independent Churches* (London: SCM Press, 1961).

3. Absolom Vilakazi, with Bongani Mthethwa and Mthembeni Mpanza, *Shembe: The Revitalization of African Society* (Johannesburg: Skotaville, 1986), x-xi, 88-116, 153-158.

4. Sundkler argued that Zionist churches were examples of heretical Christianity and weak acculturation, bridges that brought Africans back to heathenism. In the case of the Nazareth Baptist Church, he said Shembe had replaced Christ and was worshiped as a messiah. Bengt Sundkler, *Bantu Prophets in South Africa* (1948, repr., London: Oxford University Press, 1961), 297.

5. Oosthuizen insisted that Shembe had replaced God entirely, not just the position of Christ as Sundkler contended. Oosthuizen further stated that the Nazareth Baptist Church was a Zuluized, non-Christian religion that was a syncretic blend derived from a poor understanding of both Zulu indigenous religion and Christianity. G. C. Oosthuizen, *Theology of a South African Messiah: An Analysis of the Hymnal of the Church of the Nazarites* (Leiden: E. J. Brill, 1967), 10, 19, 25, 32, 34, 56.

6. See Vilakazi, Mthethwa, and Mpanza, *Shembe*, x-xi, 88-116, 153-158 for their remarks upon this debate.

7. Gerald O. West, "Reading Shembe 'Re-membering' the Bible: Isaiah Shembe's Instructions on Adultery," *Neotestamenica* 40, no. 1 (2006): 169, 176. In the scholarly quest to glorify all things subaltern and indigenous, while condemning the evils of Westernization, scholars often miss or purposefully ignore the fact that subjects often use colonial cultures and resist indigenous ones. Sherry B. Ortner, "Resistance and the Problem of Ethnographic Refusal," *Comparative Studies in Society and History* 37, no. 1 (January 1995): 186, 190-191.

8. When scholars focus upon resistance and power, they can readily miss or misread the creative responses people generate. See Michael F. Brown, "On Resisting Resistance," *American Anthropologist* 98, no. 4 (1996): 733; Sherry B. Ortner, "Resistance and the Problem of Ethnographic Refusal," *Comparative Studies in Society and History* 37, no. 1 (January 1995): 179, 186; and Lila Abu-Lughod, "The Romance of Resistance: Tracing Transformations of Power through Bedouin Women," *American Ethnologist* 17, no. 1 (February 1990): 42.

9. The most well-known include Itumeleng Mosala and Buti Tlhagale, eds., *The Unquestionable Right to be Free: Black Theology from South Africa* (Maryknoll, NY: Orbis Books, 1986); Bonganjalo Goba, *An Agenda for Black Theology: Hermeneutics for Social Change* (Johannesburg: Skotaville, 1988); and Desmond Tutu, ed. John Webster, *Crying in the Wilderness: The Struggle for Justice in South Africa* (Grand Rapids, MI: W.B. Eerdmans, 1982).

10. See chapter five, "Challenge to Action," in *The Kairos Document: Challenge to the Church, A Theological Comment on the Political Crisis in South Africa*, foreword by John W. de Gruchy (Braamfontein: Kairos Theologians, 1985), 47-51.

11. Dwight N. Hopkins, *Black Theology USA and South Africa: Politics, Culture, and Liberation* (Maryknoll, NY: Orbis Books, 1989), 119-120. For examples of such critiques see John W. de Gruchy, *The Church Struggle in South Africa* (Grand Rapids, MI: W.B. Eerdmans, 1979), 47; Bonganjalo Goba, *An Agenda for Black Theology: Hermeneutics for Social Change* (Johannesburg: Skotaville, 1988), 64; and Peter Walshe, *Prophetic Christianity and the Liberation Movement in South Africa* (Pietermaritzburg: Cluster Publications, 1995), 110.

12. Such claims of acquiescence were not solely from the perspective of theology. For some other perspectives see Nicholas Petryszak, "The Dynamics of Acquiescence in South Africa," *African Affairs* 75, no. 301 (October 1976): 459; Allister Sparks, *The Mind of South Africa* (New York: Alfred A. Knopf, 1990), 293; and Matthew Schoffeleers, "Ritual Healing and Political Acquiescence: The Case of the Zionist Churches in Southern Africa," *Africa* 60, no. 1 (1991): 1-25.

13. Ortner, "Resistance and the Problem of Ethnographic Refusal," 179.

14. Scholars have demonstrated that the political posture of a religion's practitioners may not necessarily have any relationship to a state's degree of repressiveness. Repressive states do not produce more resistant or acquiescent postures among the population than less repressive ones. See Schoffeleers, "Ritual Healing and Political Acquiescence," 1; and Kaja Finkler, *Spiritual Healers in Mexico: Successes and Failures of Alternative Therapeutics* (New York: Praeger, 1985), 16-19.

15. Robert Papini to Joel E. Tishken, personal communication, 14 June 2011. As a researcher for the Durban Local History Museum, Papini visited the church regularly in the 1990s. He witnessed this behavior consistently, where politics was left outside the boundaries of the church grounds.

16. Robert Papini to Joel E. Tishken, personal communication, 14 June 2011.

17. Jean Comaroff, *Body of Power, Spirit of Resistance: The Culture and History of a South African People* (Chicago: University of Chicago Press, 1985), 188-199, 260-262; and James C. Scott, *Domination and the Arts of Resistance: Hidden Transcripts* (New Haven, CT: Yale University Press, 1990), 4-5, 13-15; Linda Elaine Thomas, *Under the Canopy: Ritual Process and Spiritual Resilience in South Africa* (Columbia: University of South Carolina Press, 1999), 86-122.

18. Duncan Brown, "Orality and Christianity: The Hymns of Isaiah Shembe and the Church of the Nazarites," *Current Writing* 7, no. 2 (1995): 69-70; Carol Ann Muller, *Rituals of Fertility and the Sacrifice of Desire* (Chicago: University of Chicago Press, 1999), 18-20, 65; Carol Ann Muller, "Nazarite Song, Dance, and Dreams: The Sacralization of Time, Space, and the Female Body in South Africa" (Ph.D. diss., New York University, 1994), 46-47, 187; Elizabeth Gunner, *The Man of Heaven and the Beautiful Ones of God* (Leiden: E. J. Brill, 2002), 7-9; and Robert Papini, "The Nazareth Scotch: Dance Uniform as Admonitory Infrapolitics for an Eikonic Zion City in Early Union Natal," *Southern African Humanities* 14 (December 2002): 79-80, 82-83.

19. Robert J. Houle, *Making African Christianity: Africans Reimagining Their Faith in Colonial South Africa* (Bethlehem, PA: Lehigh University Press, 2011), xxiv; Paul S. Landau, "Hegemony and History in Jean and John L. Comaroff's *Of Revelation and Revolution*," *Africa* 70, no. 3 (2000): 512; Brown, "On Resisting Resistance," 730; Thomas O. Beidelman, review of Jean Comaroff, *Body of Power, Spirit of Resistance, Ethnohistory* 33, no. 3 (1986): 332; J. Kiernan, review of Jean Comaroff, *Body of Power, Spirit of Resistance, Africa* 57, no. 1 (1987): 132.

20. Comaroff, *Body of Power, Spirit of Resistance,* 243-244.

21. Marshall Sahlins, *Waiting for Foucault, still* (Chicago: Prickly Paradigm Press, 2002), 20-23.

22. Allen Isaacman, "Peasants and Rural Social Protest in Africa," *African Studies Review* 33, no. 2 (September 1990): 11-12. Brown argues that resistance is applied to many situations where it does not belong so that privileged scholars may express sympathy with the unprivileged and demonstrate that they are not politically naïve or morally insensitive. See Brown, "On Resisting Resistance," 733-734.

23. Using American practitioners of channeling, Brown shows how a resistance paradigm distorts the goals of those who participate. Within the minds of many female practitioners of channeling, the non-conformist gender roles involved are not being used as a means to celebrate femininity or resist male domination, but rather to transcend gender and engage in spiritual androgyny. Brown, "On Resisting Resistance," 732, 733.

24. Nkosinathi Sithole, "Acquiescence or Resistance? The Role of the AIC in the Struggle Against Apartheid," *Journal of Theology for Southern Africa* 137 (July 2010): 107.

25. It was Papini who first applied the term involutionist to the Nazareth Baptist Church. Robert Papini to Joel E. Tishken, personal communication, 14 June 2011.

26. Fields notes how leaders and members of Central African Watchtower movements also wove imperialism into their own interpretative narrative based on prophecy. In the case of Watchtower, however, leaders and members believed the colonial order would end through an imminent apocalypse. These waves of millenarian fever raised many "queer alarms" and "queer rebellions" and were interpreted as challenges to the maintenance of colonial order by colonial officials. Karen E. Fields, *Revival and Rebellion in Colonial Central*

Africa (London: Heinemann, 1997), 4-9, 272-274, 283-284. The memberships of Watchtower and the Nazareth Baptist Church both possessed prophetic worldviews, but their differing interpretations of empire's theological significance produced different postures to colonialism. For the first, looking forward to the demise of empire was something to celebrate as part of the upcoming apocalypse, while for the second, colonialism was something that must be endured as a form of penance.

27. Muhammad S. Umar, *Islam and Colonialism: Intellectual Responses of Muslims of Northern Nigeria to British Colonial Rule* (Leiden: E. J. Brill, 2006), 208.

28. Joseph Diangienda, "Église et Politique," *Cahiers de Réconciliation* 5, no. 6 (Mai-Juin 1966): 40.

29. Ntuma, Kuyowa, and Mbandhla to Rev. George Cameron, 2 June 1923, in Cecilia Irvine, "The Birth of the Kimbanguist Movement in the Bas-Zaire 1921," *Journal of Religion in Africa* 6, no. 1 (1974): 75.

30. Donald MacKay and Daniel Ntoni-Nzinga, "Kimbangu's Interlocutor: Nyuvudi's *Nsamu Miangunza (The Story of the Prophets)*," *Journal of Religion in Africa* 23, no. 3 (1993): 243. This text comes from a biography written by one of Kimbangu's earliest disciples, Paul Nyuvudi.

31. John 17:14, "I have given them your word, and the world has hated them because they do not belong to the world, just as I do not belong to the world." NRSV

32. Explanation of both of these events can be found in "The Catechism of Kimbangu," in John M. Janzen and Wyatt MacGaffey, eds., *An Anthology of Kongo Religion: Primary Texts from Lower Zaire* (Lawrence: University of Kansas Press, 1974), 126-127

33. N. H. Ngada, *Speaking for Ourselves* (Braamfontein: Institute for Contextual Theology, 1985), 30-31.

34. The CPSA was banned by the Apartheid government in 1950, and relaunched in 1953 as the South African Communist Party, an underground organization.

35. See Simon Adams, *Comrade Minister: The South African Communist Party and the Transition from Apartheid to Democracy* (Huntington, NY: Nova Science Pub. Inc., 2001), 24-28.

36. Andreas Heuser, "Memory Tales: Representations of Shembe in the Cultural Discourse of African Renaissance," *Journal of Religion in Africa* 35, no. 3 (2005): 362-367.

37. Heuser, "Memory Tales," 367.

38. All my information on the Zion Christian Church comes from their testimony at: "Truth and Reconciliation Commission, Faith Community Hearings, 17-19 November 1997," <http://www.justice.gov.za/trc/special/faith/faith_b.htm>. Accessed 15 January 2012.

39. Allan Anderson, "The Lekganyanes and Prophecy in the Zion Christian Church," *Journal of Religion in Africa* 29, no. 3 (1985): 293.

40. Mthembeni P. Mpanza, "Submission to the Truth and Reconciliation Commission by Ibandla lamaNazaretha on the 18th November 1997: East London," (n.p., n.d.).

41. Mpanza, "Submission to the Truth and Reconciliation Commission."

42. Mpanza, "Submission to the Truth and Reconciliation Commission."

43. Robin M. Petersen, "The AICs and the TRC," in *Facing the Truth: South African Faith Communities and the Truth & Reconciliation Commission*, eds. James Cochran, John de Gruchy, and Stephen Martin (Cape Town: David Philip; Athens: Ohio University Press, 1999), 121.

Bibliography

Archival Sources

National Archives Repository (SAB), Pretoria, South Africa
    Secretary for Native Affairs (NTS), Correspondence, 1915-1952.
Pietermaritzburg (Natal) Archives Repository (NAB), Pietermaritzburg, South Africa
    Chief Native Commissioner (CNC), Correspondence, 1912-1938.
    Office of the Attorney General (AGO), Correspondence, 1913.
Durban Local History Museums, Durban, South Africa
    Catechism of the Nazarites. Uncatalogued.
    "Memela." Accession number 98/655.
    Mpanza, Mthembeni P. "The Biography of Isaiah Shembe." Accession number 98/653.
    Wells, Nellie. "Notes for film." Film: Dancin' up dem golden stairs, c1930-34; 5 mins., video copy accession number 65/392.
Killie Campbell Africana Library (KCAL), Durban, South Africa
    Album: African Religions: Shembe, Londa.
    Shembe File 8637.
    Uncat Mss.: Shembe Festival.

Oral Traditions

Gunner, Elizabeth. *The Man of Heaven and the Beautiful Ones of God*. Leiden: E. J. Brill, 2002.

Heuser, Andreas and Irving Hexham, eds. Translated by Hans-Jürgen Becken. *The Hymns and Sabbath Liturgy for Morning and Evening Prayer of Isaiah Shembe's amaNazarites, Volume Five*. Lewiston, NY: Edwin Mellen Press, 2005.

Hexham, Irving, ed. Translated by Londa Shembe and Hans-Jürgen Becken. *The Scriptures of the amaNazaretha of EKuphaKameni: Selected Writings of the Zulu Prophets Isaiah and Londa Shembe*. Calgary: University of Calgary Press, 1994.

Hexham, Irving and G. C. Oosthuizen, eds. Translated by Hans-Jürgen Becken. *The Story of Isaiah Shembe, Volume One: History and Traditions Centered on Ekuphakameni and Mount Nhlangakazi*. Lewiston, NY: Edwin Mellen Press, 1996.

——. Translated by Hans-Jürgen Becken. *The Story of Isaiah Shembe, Volume Two: Early Regional Traditions of the Acts of the Nazarites*. Lewiston, NY: Edwin Mellen Press, 1999.

——. Translated by Hans-Jürgen Becken. *The Story of Isaiah Shembe, Volume Three: The Continuing Story of the Sun and the Moon. Oral Testimony and the Sacred History of the AMA-Nazarites*

Under the Leadership of Bishops Johannes Galilee Shembe and Amos Shembe. Lewiston, NY: Edwin Mellen Press, 2001.

Papini, Robert and Irving Hexham, eds. *The Catechism of the Nazarites and Related Writings, Volume Four*. Lewiston, NY: Edwin Mellen Press, 2002.

Published Sources

Abu-Lughod, Lila. "The Romance of Resistance: Tracing Transformations of Power through Bedouin Women." *American Ethnologist* 17, no. 1 (February 1990): 41-55.

Adams, Simon. *Comrade Minister: The South African Communist Party and the Transition from Apartheid to Democracy*. Huntington, NY: Nova Science, 2001.

Allina-Pisano, Eric. "Resistance and the Social History of Africa." *Journal of Social History* 37, no. 1 (Fall 2003): 187-198.

Anderson, Allan H. "The Lekganyanes and Prophecy in the Zion Christian Church." *Journal of Religion in Africa* 29, no. 3 (1999): 285-312.

Andersen, Nicole and Scott London. "South Africa's Newest 'Jews': The Moemedi Pentecostal Church and Jewish Identity." *Nova Religio* 13, no. 1 (2009): 92-105.

Andersson, Effraim. *Messianic Popular Movements in the Lower Congo*. Uppsala: Almquist and Wiksells, 1958.

Ashforth, Adam. *Witchcraft, Violence, and Democracy in South Africa*. Chicago: University of Chicago Press, 2005.

Aune, David E. *Prophecy in Early Christianity and the Ancient Mediterranean World*. Grand Rapids, MI: William B. Eerdmans, 1983.

Babou, Cheikh Anta. *Fighting the Greater Jihad: Amadu Bamba and the Founding of the Muridiyya of Senegal, 1853-1913*. Athens: Ohio University Press, 2007.

Balandier, Georges. "Messianism and Nationalism in Black Africa." In *Africa: Social Problems of Change and Conflict*, edited by Pierre L. Van Berghe, 443-460. San Francisco: Chandler Pub. Co., 1965.

Barber, Karin. "Introduction: Hidden Innovators in Africa." In *Africa's Hidden Histories: Everyday Literacy and the Making of the Self*, edited by Karin Barber, 1-24. Bloomington: Indiana University Press, 2006.

Barrett, David B. *Schism and Renewal in Africa: An Analysis of Six Thousand Contemporary Religious Movements*. Nairobi: Oxford University Press, 1968.

Becken, Hans-Jürgen. "The Nazareth Baptist Church of Shembe." In *Our Approach to the Independent Church Movement in South Africa*, edited by Lutheran Theological College, 101-114. Mapumulo: Lutheran Theological College, 1965.

——. *Wo der Glaube noch jung ist: Afrikanische Unabhängige Kirchen im Südlichen Afrika*. Erlangen: Verlag der Ev.-Luth. Mission, 1985.

——. "I Love to Tell the Story: Oral History in the Nazaretha Church." In *Empirical Studies of African Independent/Indigenous Churches*, edited by G. C. Oosthuizen and Irving Hexham, 29-48. Lewiston, NY: Edwin Mellen Press, 1992.

——. "The Oral History of the Ibandla lamaNazaretha." In *The Story of Isaiah Shembe, Volume One: History and Traditions Centered on Ekuphakameni and Mount Nhlangakazi*, edited by Irving Hexham and G. C. Oosthuizen, translated by Hans-Jürgen Becken, ix-xxii. Lewiston, NY: Edwin Mellen Press, 1996.

Behrend, Heike. *Alice Lakwena and the Holy Spirits: War in Northern Uganda, 1986-97*. Oxford: James Currey; Kampala: Fountain Publishers; Nairobi: EAEP; Athens: Ohio University Press, 1999.

Beidelman, Thomas O. Review of Jean Comaroff, *Body of Power, Spirit of Resistance*. *Ethnohistory* 33, no. 3 (1986): 331-333.

Bent, Wayne. "Wayne Bent aka Michael Travesser." 22 October 2012. <http://www.waynebent.com/>. Accessed 10 November 2012.

Bhabha, Homi K. "Signs Taken for Wonders: Questions of Ambivalence and Authority under a Tree outside Delhi, May 1817." *Critical Inquiry* 12, no. 1 (Autumn 1985): 144-165.

Boahen, A. Adu. *African Perspectives on Colonialism*. Baltimore: John Hopkins University Press, 1987.

Bohannan, Paul. *Africa and Africans*. Garden City, NY: Natural History Press, 1964.

Brantley, Cynthia. *The Giriama and Colonial Resistance in Kenya, 1880-1920*. Berkeley: University of California Press, 1981.

Bromley, David G. "Making Sense of Scientology: Prophetic, Contractual Religion." In *Scientology*, edited by James R. Lewis, 83-101. Oxford: Oxford University Press, 2009.

Bromley David G. and Rachel S. Bobbitt. "Challenges to Charismatic Authority in the Unificationist Movement." In *Sacred Schisms: How Religions Divide*, edited by James R. Lewis and Sarah M. Lewis, 129-146. Cambridge: Cambridge University Press, 2009.

Brown, Duncan. "Orality and Christianity: The Hymns of Isaiah Shembe and the Church of the Nazarites." *Current Writing* 7, no. 2 (1995): 69-95.

Brown, Karen. "The Function of Dress and Ritual in the Nazareth Baptist Church of Isaiah Shembe (South Africa)." Ph.D. dissertation, Indiana University, 1995.

Brown, Michael. F. "On Resisting Resistance." *American Anthropologist* 98, no.4 (December 1996): 729-735.

Burbank, Jane and Frederick Cooper. *Empires in World History: Power and the Politics of Difference*. Princeton, NJ: Princeton University Press, 2010.

Burton, Antoinette. "Introduction: On the Inadequacy and the Indispensability of the Nation." In *After the Imperial Turn: Thinking with and through the Nation*, edited by Antoinette Burton, 1-23. Durham, NC: Duke University Press, 2003.

Bushman, Richard Lyman. *Joseph Smith: Rough Stone Rolling*. New York: Alfred A. Knopf, 2005.

Cabrita, Joel Marie. "A Theological Biography of Isaiah Shembe, c. 1870-1935." Ph.D. dissertation, University of Cambridge, 2008.

——. "Isaiah Shembe's Theological Nationalism, 1920s-1935." *Journal of Southern African Studies* 35, no. 3 (September 2009): 609-625.

——. "Texts, Authority, and Community in the South African 'Ibandla lamaNazaretha' (Church of the Nazaretha), 1910-1976." *Journal of Religion in Africa* 40 (2010): 59-94.

Callaway, Henry. *The Religious System of the Amazulu in the Zulu Language with Translation into English and notes in four parts* (Facsimile reprint of 1885 ed.). Cape Town: C. Struik, 1970.

Carson, D. A., Douglas J. Moo, and Leon Morris. *An Introduction to the New Testament*. Grand Rapids, MI: Zondervan, 1992.

Carton, Benedict, John Laband, and Jabulani Sithole, eds. *Zulu Identities: Being Zulu, Past and Present*. New York: Columbia University Press, 2009.

Chafer, Tony. *The End of Empire in French West Africa: France's Successful Decolonization?* New York: Berg, 2002.

Champion, A. W. G. and R. R. R. Dhlomo, edited by M. W. Swanson, translated by E. R. Dahle and A. T. Cope. *The Views of Mahlathi: Writings of A. W. G. Champion, a Black South African: with a Biography of A. W. G. Champion.* Pietermaritzburg: University of Natal Press; Durban: Killie Campbell Africana Library, 1982.

Chidester, David. "Worldview Analysis of African Indigenous Churches." *Journal for the Study of Religion* 2, no. 1 (1989): 15-29.

Comaroff, Jean. *Body of Power, Spirit of Resistance: The Culture and History of a South African People.* Chicago: University of Chicago Press, 1985.

Comaroff, John and Jean Comaroff. *Of Revelation and Revolution: The Dialectics of Modernity on a South African Frontier, Volume Two.* Chicago: University of Chicago Press, 1999.

Cooper, Frederick. "Conflict and Connection: Rethinking Colonial African History." *The American Historical Review* 99, no. 5 (1994): 1516-1545.

——. *Africa since 1940.* Cambridge: Cambridge University Press, 2002.

——. *Colonialism in Question: Theory, Knowledge, History.* Berkeley: University of California Press, 2005.

Cope, Nicolas. *To Bind the Nation: Solomon kaDinuzulu and Zulu Nationalism, 1913-1933.* Pietermaritzburg: University of Natal Press, 1993.

Coulon, Christian. "The Grand Magal in Touba: A Religious Festival of the Mouride Brotherhood of Senegal." *African Affairs* 98 (1999): 195-210.

"The Council of Trent." In *Documents of the Christian Church*, 3rd edition, edited by Henry Bettenson and Chris Maunder, 275-282. Oxford: Oxford University Press, 1999.

Crummey, Donald, ed. *Banditry, Rebellion and Social Protest in Africa.* London: J. Currey, 1986.

Denoon, Donald. *A Trial Separation: Australia and the Decolonisation of Papua New Guinea.* Canberra: Pandanus Books, 2005.

Diangienda, Joseph. "Église et Politique." *Cahiers de Réconciliation* 5, no. 6 (Mai-Juin 1966): 40-42.

Doran, Robert. *Birth of a Worldview: Early Christianity in Its Jewish and Pagan Context.* Boulder, CO: Westview Press, 1995.

Dube, John L. *Ushembe.* Pietermaritzburg: Shuter and Shooter, 1936. Translated into English by Hans-Jürgen Becken, n. p., 1993.

Edgar, Robert. *Because They Chose the Plan of God: The Story of the Bulhoek Massacre.* Johannesburg: Raven Press, 1988.

Edgar, Robert R. and Hilary Sapire. *African Apocalypse: The Story of Nontetha Nkwenkwe, a Twentieth-Century South African Prophet.* Athens: Ohio University Press; Johannesburg: Witwatersrand University Press, 2000.

Ehrman, Bart D. *Lost Christianities: The Battle for Scripture and the Faiths We Never Knew.* New York: Oxford University Press, 2003.

——. *Lost Scriptures: Books that did not make it into the New Testament.* New York: Oxford University Press, 2003.

——. *A Brief Introduction to the New Testament.* New York: Oxford University Press, 2004.

Elliott, J. K. *The Apocryphal New Testament: A Collection of Apocryphal Christian Literature in an English Translation.* Oxford: Clarendon Press, 1993.

Etherington, Norman. "Recent Trends in the Historiography of Christianity in Southern Africa." *Journal of Southern African Studies* 22, no. 2 (1996): 201-219.

——. "Kingdoms of This World and the Next: Christian Beginnings among Zulu and Swazi." In *Christianity in South Africa: A Political, Social, and Cultural History*, edited by Richard Elphick and Rodney Davenport, 89-106. Berkeley: University of California Press, 1997.

Fernandez, James W. "Precincts of the Prophet: A Day with Johannes Galilee Shembe." *Journal of Religion in Africa* 5, no. 1 (1973): 32-53.

——. *Bwiti: An Ethnography of the Religious Imagination*. Princeton, NJ: Princeton University Press, 1982.

Fields, Karen E. *Revival and Rebellion in Colonial Central Africa*. London: Heinemann, 1997.

Finkler, Kaja. *Spiritual Healers in Mexico: Successes and Failures of Alternative Therapeutics*. New York: Praeger, 1985.

Gallagher, Eugene V. "Conversion and Salvation in the Apochryphal Acts of the Apostles." *Second Century* 8, no. 1 (Spring 1991): 13-29.

——. "Extraterrestrial Exegesis: The Raëlian Movement as a Biblical Religion." *Nova Religio* 14, no. 2 (2010): 14-33.

Gallagher, Eugene V., to Joel E. Tishken. Personal communication, 23 February 2012.

Goba, Bonganjalo. *An Agenda for Black Theology: Hermeneutics for Social Change*. Johannesburg: Skotaville, 1988.

Graham, William A. *Beyond the Written Word: Oral Aspects of Scripture in the History of Religion*. Cambridge: Cambridge University Press, 1987.

Graybill, Lyn S. *Religion and Resistance Politics in South Africa*. Westport, CT: Praeger, 1995.

Greene, Sandra E. *Sacred Sites and the Colonial Encounter: A History of Meaning and Memory in Ghana*. Bloomington: Indiana University Press, 2002.

Gregory, Brad S. *Salvation at Stake: Christian Martyrdom in Early Modern Europe*. Cambridge, MA: Harvard University Press, 1999.

Gruchy, John W. de. *The Church Struggle in South Africa*. Grand Rapids, MI: W. B. Eerdmans, 1979.

Gunner, Elizabeth. "The Word, the Book and the Zulu Church of Nazareth." In *Oral Tradition and Literacy: Changing Visions of the World*, edited by R. A. Whitaker and E. R. Sienaert, 179-188. Durban: Natal University Documentation and Research Centre, 1986.

——. "Power House, Prison House–An Oral Genre and its Use in Isaiah Shembe's Nazareth Baptist Church." *Journal of Southern African Studies* 14, no. 2 (January 1988): 204-27.

——. "Testimonies of Dispossession and Repossession: Writing about the South African Prophet Isaiah Shembe." *Bulletin of the John Rylands Library of Manchester* 73, no. 3 (Autumn 1991): 93-103.

——. "Hidden Stories and the Light of New Day: A Zulu Manuscript and Its Place in South African Writing." *Research in African Literatures* 31, no. 2 (Summer 2000): 1-16.

——. "Remapping Land and Remaking Culture: Memory and Landscape in 20th-Century South Africa." *Journal of Historical Geography* 31 (2005): 281-295.

——. "Keeping a Diary of Visions: Lazarus Phelalasekhaya Maphumulo and the Edendale Congregation of AmaNazaretha." In *Africa's Hidden Histories: Everyday Literacy and Making the Self*, edited by Karin Barber, 155-179. Bloomington: Indiana University Press, 2006.

Guy, Jeff. *The Destruction of the Zulu Kingdom: The Civil War in Zululand, 1879-1884*. London: Longman, 1979.

la Hausse de Lalouvière, Paul. *Restless Identities: Signatures of Nationalism, Zulu Ethnicity, and History in the Lives of Petros Lamula (c. 1881-1948) and Lymon Maling (1889-c. 1936)*. Scottsville, South Africa: University of Natal Press, 2000.

"Herd Boy Turns Healer." Newspaper unknown, 27 July 1927. Clipping in NTS 1431 24/214.

Hermanson, Eric. "A Brief Overview of Bible Translation in South Africa." *Acta Theologica Supplementum* 2 (2002): 6-17.

Heuser, Andreas. "Experiments in an Independent African Satyagraha: Gandhi, Shembe and the Roots of Passive Resistance in South Africa." In *Religion and the Political Imagination in a Changing South Africa*, edited by Gordon Mitchell and Eve Mullen, 73-85. Munster: Waxmann, 2002.

——. "Memory Tales: Representations of Shembe in the Cultural Discourse of African Renaissance." *Journal of Religion in Africa* 35, no. 3 (2005): 362-387.

——. "Strolling Bards of the Gospel in the War-zone of Cultural Memory: The *Hymnbook of the Nazareth Baptist Church* as the subtext of itinerant prophecy." In *The Hymns and Sabbath Liturgy for Morning and Evening Prayer of Isaiah Shembe's amaNazarites, Volume Five*, edited by Andreas Heuser and Irving Hexham, translated by Hans-Jürgen Becken, vi-xxxiii. Lewiston, NY: Edwin Mellen Press, 2005.

——. "Contested Charisma: Reflections on the Appearance and Disappearance of Female Visionary Power in a South African Independent Church." *Zeitschrift für Globalgeschichte und vergleichende Gesellschaftsforchung* 17, nos. 5/6 (2007): 76-94.

Hexham, Irving. "Introduction." In *The Scriptures of the amaNazaretha of EKuphaKameni: Selected Writings of the Zulu Prophets Isaiah and Londa Shembe*, edited by Irving Hexham, translated by Londa Shembe and Hans-Jürgen Becken, vii-xxii. Calgary: University of Calgary Press, 1994.

——. "Introduction." In *The Story of Isaiah Shembe, Volume One: History and Traditions Centered on Ekuphakameni and Mount Nhlangakazi*, edited by Irving Hexham and G. C. Oosthuizen, translated by Hans-Jürgen Becken, vii-viii. Lewiston, NY: Edwin Mellen Press, 1996.

——. "Introduction." in *The Story of Isaiah Shembe, Volume Two: Early Regional Traditions of the Acts of the Nazarites*, edited by Irving Hexham and G. C. Oosthuizen, translated by Hans-Jürgen Becken, ix-x. Lewiston, NY: Edwin Mellen Press, 1999.

——. "About the Texts and Translation." In *The Story of Isaiah Shembe, Volume Three: The Continuing Story of the Sun and the Moon. Oral Testimony and the Sacred History of the AMA-Nazarites Under the Leadership of Bishops Johannes Galilee Shembe and Amos Shembe*, edited by Irving Hexham and G. C. Oosthuizen, translated by Hans-Jürgen Becken, xiv-xv. Lewiston, NY: Edwin Mellen Press, 2001.

——. "Foreword." In *The Catechism of the Nazarites and Related Writings, Volume Four*, edited by Robert Papini and Irving Hexham, viii-xii. Lewiston, NY: Edwin Mellen Press, 2002.

Hoehler-Fatton, Cynthia. *Women of Fire and Spirit: History, Faith, and Gender in Roho Religion in Western Kenya*. Oxford: Oxford University Press, 1996.

Hofmeyr, Isabel. *The Portable Bunyan: A Transnational History of The Pilgrim's Progress*. Princeton, NJ: Princeton University Press, 2004.

Hopkins, Dwight N. *Black Theology USA and South Africa: Politics, Culture, and Liberation*. Maryknoll, NY: Orbis Books, 1989.

Houle, Robert J. *Making African Christianity: Africans Reimagining Their Faith in Colonial South Africa*. Bethlehem, PN: Lehigh University Press, 2011.

Hourihane, Colum. "Introduction." In *Looking Beyond: Visions, Dreams, and Insights in Medieval Art & History*, edited by Colum Hourihane, xv-xx. Princeton, NJ: Index of Christian Art, Princeton University, 2010.

Hufford, David J. "Beings Without Bodies: An Experience-Centered Theory of the Belief in Spirits." In *Out of the Ordinary: Folklore and the Supernatural*, edited by Barbara Walker. 11-45. Logan, UT: Utah State University Press, 1995.

Ibhayibheli Elingcwele. Goodwood, South Africa: National Book Printers, 1999.

Irvine, Cecilia. "The Birth of the Kimbanguist Movement in the Bas-Zaire 1921." *Journal of Religion in Africa* 6, no. 1 (1974): 23-76.

Isaacman, Allen. "Peasants and Rural Social Protest in Africa." *African Studies Review* 33, no. 2 (September 1990), 1-120.

Isaacman, Allen and Barbara Isaacman. *The Tradition of Resistance in Mozambique: Anti-Colonial Activity in the Zambesi Valley, 1850-1921*. London: Heinemann, 1976.

———. "Resistance and Collaboration in Southern and Central Africa, c. 1850-1920." *International Journal of African Historical Studies* 10, no. 1 (1977): 31-62.

Janzen, John M. "The Consequences of Literacy in African Religion: The Kongo Case." In *Theoretical Explorations in African Religion*, edited by Wim Van Binsbergen and Matthew Schoffeleers, 225-252. London: KPI Ltd., 1985.

Janzen, John M. and Wyatt MacGaffey. *An Anthology of Kongo Religion: Primary Texts from Lower Zaire*. Lawrence, KS: University of Kansas Press, 1974.

Johnson, Douglas H. *Nuer Prophets: A History of Prophecy from the Upper Nile in the Nineteenth and Twentieth Centuries*. Oxford: Clarendon Press, 1994.

Jules-Rosette, Bennetta. *African Apostles: Ritual and Conversion in the Church of John Maranke*. Ithaca, NY: Cornell University Press, 1975.

The Kairos Document: Challenge to the Church, A Theological Comment on the Political Crisis in South Africa, foreword by John W. de Gruchy. Braamfontein: Kairos Theologians, 1985.

Kiernan, Jim. Review of Jean Comaroff, *Body of Power, Spirit of Resistance*. *Africa* 57, no. 1 (1987): 131-132.

———. "Variations on a Christian Theme: The Healing Synthesis of Zulu Zionism." In *Syncretism/Anti-Syncretism: The Politics of Religious Synthesis*, edited by Charles Stewart and Rosalind Shaw, 69-84. London: Routledge, 1994.

Klijn, Albertus Frederik Johannes. *An Introduction to the New Testament*. Leiden: E. J. Brill, 1967.

Krige, Eileen. *The Social System of the Zulus*. 1936. 3rd ed. Pietermaritzburg: Shuter & Shooter, 1957.

Kruger, Steven F. *Dreaming in the Middle Ages*. Cambridge: Cambridge University Press, 1992.

Kustenbauder, Matthew. "Believing in the Black Messiah: The Legio Maria Church in an African Christian Landscape." *Nova Religio* 13, no. 1 (August 2009): 11-40.

Landau, Paul Stuart. *The Realm of the Word: Language, Gender, and Christianity in a Southern African Kingdom*. Portsmouth, NH: Heinemann; Cape Town: David Philip; London: James Currey, 1995.

———. "Hegemony and History in Jean and John L. Comaroff's *Of Revelation and Revolution*." *Africa* 70, no. 3 (2000): 501-519.

Lanternari, Vittorio. Translated by Lisa Sergio. *The Religions of the Oppressed: A Study of Modern Messianic Cults*. New York: Alfred A. Knopf, 1963.

Larlham, Peter. "Festivals of the Nazareth Baptist Church." *The Drama Review* 25, no. 4 (Winter 1981): 59-74.

Lea, Allen. *The Native Separatist Church Movement in South Africa*. Cape Town: Juta & Co. Ltd., 1924.

Lewis, James R. *Legitimating New Religions*. New Brunswick, NJ: Rutgers University Press, 2003.

Linden, Ian. *Catholics, Peasants, and Chewa Resistance in Nyasaland, 1889-1939*. London: Heinemann, 1974.

Lutheran Church, Missouri Synod. "Church Discipline in the Christian Congregation: A Report of the Commission on Theology and Church Relations of the Lutheran Church–Missouri Synod, November 1985." <http://www.iclnet.org/pub/resources/text/wittenberg/mosynod/web/cdis.html>. Accessed 3 March 2012.

MacGaffey, Wyatt. *Modern Kongo Prophets: Religion in a Plural Society.* Bloomington: Indiana University Press, 1983.

MacKay, Donald and Daniel Ntoni-Nzinga. "Kimbangu's Interlocutor: Nyuvudi's *Nsamu Miangunza (The Story of the Prophets).*" *Journal of Religion in Africa* 23, no. 3 (1993): 232-65.

MacMullen, Ramsay. "Two Types of Conversion to Early Christianity." *Vigiliae Christianae.* 37, no. 2 (1983): 174-192.

Mamdani, Mahmood. *Citizen and Subject: Contemporary Africa and the Legacy of Late Colonialism.* Princeton, NJ: Princeton University Press, 1996.

Marks, Shula. "Patriotism, Patriarchy and Purity: Natal and the Politics of Zulu Ethnic Consciousness." In *The Creation of Tribalism in Southern Africa,* edited by Leroy Vail, 215-240. Berkeley: University of California Press, 1989.

Martin, Marie-Louise. *Kimbangu: An African Prophet and his Church.* Oxford: Basil Blackwood, 1971.

McGrath, Alister E. *Christian Theology: An Introduction.* 1993. 4th ed. Oxford: Blackwell, 2007.

——. *Heresy: A History of Defending the Truth.* New York: HarperCollins, 2009.

Mhlongo, Nombili Joe, to Joel E. Tishken. Personal communication, 8 January 2000.

Mitchell, Robert Cameron. "Religious Protest and Social Change: The Origins of the Aladura Movement in Western Nigeria." In *Protest and Power in Black Africa,* edited by Robert I. Rotberg and Ali A. Mazrui, 458-496. New York: Oxford University Press, 1970.

Mkhize, H. B. "The Umthandazi–Prayer-Healer." In *Afro-Christian Religion and Healing in Southern Africa,* edited by G. C. Oosthuizen et. al., 283-293. Lewiston, NY: Edwin Mellen Press, 1989.

Moreira, Isabel. *Dreams, Visions, and Spiritual Authority in Merovingian Gaul.* Ithaca, NY: Cornell University Press, 2000.

Mosala, Itumeleng and Buti Tlhagale, eds., *The Unquestionable Right to be Free: Black Theology from South Africa.* Maryknoll, NY: Orbis Books, 1986.

Mpanza, Mthembeni P. "Submission to the Truth and Reconciliation Commission by Ibandla lamaNazaretha on the 18th November 1997: East London." N.p. N.d.

M'Timkulu, Donald. "Some Aspects of Zulu Religion." In *African Religions: A Symposium,* edited by Newell S. Booth, 13-30. New York: NOK Publishers, 1977.

Mthethwa, B. N. "Shembe's Hymnody and the Ethical Standards and Worldview of the AmaNazaretha." In *Empirical Studies of African Independent/Indigenous Churches,* edited by G. C. Oosthuizen and Irving Hexham, 239-57. Lewiston, NY: Edwin Mellen Press, 1992.

Muller, Carol Ann. "Nazarite Song, Dance, and Dreams: The Sacralization of Time, Space, and the Female Body in South Africa." Ph.D. dissertation, New York University, 1994.

——. "'Written' into the Book of Life: Nazarite Women's Performance Inscribed as Spiritual Text in 'Ibandla lamaNazaretha." *Research in African Literatures* 28, no. 1 (1997): 3-14.

——. *Rituals of Fertility and the Sacrifice of Desire.* Chicago: University of Chicago Press, 1999.

Mzizi, Joshua Bheki. "Images of Isaiah Shembe: An Appraisal of the Views of Mthembeni Mpanza." *Missionalia* 32, no. 2 (August 2004): 190-209.

"Native 'Prophet's' Large Following." *District Notes & News,* 30 July 1929.

Neale, Caroline. *Writing "Independent" History: African Historiography 1960-1980.* Westport: CT: Greenwood Press, 1985.

Newman, Barbara. "'Sibyl of the Rhine': Hildegard's Life and Times." In *Voice of the Living Light: Hildegard of Bingen and her World*, edited by Barbara Newman, 1-29. Berkeley: University of California Press, 1998.

———. *God and the Goddesses: Vision, Poetry, and Belief in the Middle Ages.* Philadelphia: University of Pennsylvania Press, 2003.

Ngada, N. H. *Speaking for Ourselves: Members of African Independent Churches report on their pilot study of the History and Theology of their Churches.* Braamfontein: Institute for Contextual Theology, 1985.

Ngobese, B. E. "The Concept of the Trinity among the Amanazaretha." In *Empirical Studies of African Independent/Indigenous Churches*, edited by G. C. Oosthuizen and Irving Hexham, 91-109. Lewiston, NY: Edwin Mellen Press, 1992.

Olupona, Jacob. "Introduction." In *Beyond Primitivism: Indigenous Religious Traditions and Modernity*, edited by Jacob Olupona, 1-19. London: Routledge, 2004.

Oosthuizen, G. C. *Theology of a South African Messiah: An Analysis of the Hymnal of the Church of the Nazarites.* Leiden: E. J. Brill, 1967.

———. "The Theology of Londa Shembe and the amaNazaretha of EkuphaKameni." In *The Scriptures of the amaNazaretha of EKuphaKameni: Selected Writings of the Zulu Prophets Isaiah and Londa Shembe*, edited by Irving Hexham, translated by Londa Shembe and Hans-Jürgen Becken, xxiii-xlix. Calgary: University of Calgary Press, 1994.

———. "iBandla lamaNazaretha uNkuluknulu KaGcwesna." N. p.: N. d.

Opoku, K. Asare. "Religion in Africa during the colonial era." In *UNESCO General History of Africa, Volume VII: Africa under Colonial Domination 1880-1935*, edited by A. Adu Boahen, 508-538. Paris: UNESCO; London: Heinemann; Berkeley: University of California Press, 1985.

Ortner, Sherry B. "Resistance and the Problem of Ethnographic Refusal." *Comparative Studies in Society and History* 37, no. 1 (January 1995): 173-193.

———. *Anthropology and Social Theory: Culture, Power, and the Acting Subject.* Durham, NC: Duke University Press, 2006.

Overholt, Thomas W. "The Ghost Dance of 1890 and the Nature of the Prophetic Process." *Ethnohistory* 21, no. 1 (1974): 37-63.

———. "Prophecy: The Problem of Cross-Cultural Comparison." In *Anthropological Approaches to the Old Testament*, edited by Bernard Lang, 60-82. Philadelphia: Fortress; London: SPCK, 1985.

Papini, Robert. *Rise Up and Dance and Praise God.* Durban: The Local History Museum, 1992.

———. "Carl Faye's Transcript of Isaiah Shembe's Testimony on his Early Life and Calling." *Journal of Religion in Africa* 29, no. 3 (1999): 243-84.

———. "The Nazareth Scotch: Dance Uniform as Admonitory Infrapolitics for an Eikonic Zion City in Early Union Natal." *Southern African Humanities* 14 (December 2002): 79-106.

———. "Introduction." In *The Catechism of the Nazarites and Related Writings, Volume Four*, edited by Robert Papini and Irving Hexham. xiii-xlv. Lewiston, NY: Edwin Mellen Press, 2002.

———. "Dance Uniform History in the Church of the Nazareth Baptists: The Move to Tradition." *African Arts* 37, no. 3 (Autumn 2004): 48-61, 90-92.

Papini, Robert, to Joel E. Tishken. Personal communication, 14 June 2011.

Payne, Adam. "A Prophet among the Zulus: Shembe a Power for Peace and a Restraining Influence." *Illustrated London News*, 204, 8 February 1930.

Peterson, Derek R. *Creative Writing: Translation, Bookkeeping, and the Work of the Imagination in Colonial Kenya*. Portsmouth, NH: Heinemann, 2004.

Petersen, Robin M. "The AICs and the TRC." In *Facing the Truth: South African Faith Communities and the Truth & Reconciliation Commission*, edited by James Cochran, John de Gruchy, and Stephen Martin, 114-125. Cape Town: David Philip; Athens: Ohio University Press, 1999.

Petryszak, Nicholas. "The Dynamics of Acquiescence in South Africa." *African Affairs* 75, no. 301 (October 1976): 444-462.

Porter, Andrew. *Religion versus Empire? British Overseas Protestant Missionaries and Overseas Expansion, 1700-1914*. Manchester: Manchester University Press, 2004.

Price, Richard N. Review of Richard Gott, *Britain's Empire: Resistance, Repression and Revolt* and Kwasi Kwarteng, *Ghosts of Empire: Britain's Legacies in the Modern World*. H-Empire, H-Net Reviews. April 2012. <https://www.h-net.org/reviews/showrev.php?id=3D35775>

Rambo, Lewis R. *Understanding Religious Conversion*. New Haven, CN: Yale University Press, 1993.

Ranger, Terence O. *Revolt in Southern Rhodesia, 1896-97: A Study in African Resistance*. London: Heinemann, 1967.

——. "Connections Between 'Primary Resistance' Movements and Modern Mass Nationalism in East and Central Africa." *Journal of African History* 10, nos. 3-4 (1968): 437-53 and 631-41.

——. "The Mwana Lesa Movement of 1925." In *Themes in the Christian History of Central Africa*, edited by T. O. Ranger and John C. Weller, 45-75. Berkeley: University of California Press, 1975.

——. "Religious Movements and Politics in Sub-Saharan Africa." *African Studies Review* 29, no. 2 (1986): 1-69.

——. "The Local and the Global in Southern African Religious History." In *Conversion to Christianity: Historical and Anthropological Perspectives on a Great Transformation*, edited by Robert W. Hefner, 65-98. Berkeley: University of California Press, 1993.

Rhein, Francis Bayard. *Understanding the New Testament*. Woodbury, NY: Barron's Educational Series, 1974.

Robbins, Joel. "Crypto-Religion and the Study of Cultural Mixtures: Anthropology, Value, and the Nature of Syncretism." *Journal of the American Academy of Religion* 79, no. 2 (2011): 408-424.

Roberts, Esther L. "Shembe: The Man and his Work," edited by Robert Papini, 1999. Master's thesis, University of South Africa, 1936.

Robertson, Roland. "Globalisation or glocalisation?" *The Journal of International Communication* 1, no. 1 (1994): 33-52.

Robinson, David. "Beyond Resistance and Collaboration: Amadu Bamba and the Murids of Senegal." *Journal of Religion in Africa* 21, no. 2 (1991): 149-171.

Robinson, James McConkey, ed. *The Nag Hammadi Library in English*. 1978. 3rd ed. San Francisco: HarperCollins, 1990.

Rogers, Howard. *Native Administration in South Africa*. 1933. Reprint. Westport, CN: Negro Universities Press, 1970.

Rotberg, Robert I. *The Rise of Nationalism in Central Africa: The Making of Malawi and Zambia, 1873-1964*. Cambridge, MA: Harvard University Press, 1965.

Rotberg, Robert I. and Ali A. Mazrui, eds. *Protest and Power in Black Africa*. New York: Oxford University Press, 1970.

Sahlins, Marshall. *Waiting for Foucault, still*. Chicago: Prickly Paradigm Press, 2002.

Salim, Muhammad Ibrahim Abu and Knut S. Vikør. "The Man Who Believed in the Mahdi." *Sudanic Africa* 2 (1991): 29-52.

Schleiermacher, Friedrich. "On the Different Methods of Translation." In *German Romantic Criticism*, edited by A. Leslie Willson, 1-30. New York: Continuum, 1982.

Schoffeleers, Matthew. "Ritual Healing and Political Acquiescence: The Case of the Zionist Churches in Southern Africa." *Africa* 60, no. 1 (1991): 1-25.

Schoffeleers, Matthew and Ian Linden. "The Resistance of the Nyau Societies to the Roman Catholic Missions in Colonial Malawi." In *Historical Study of African Religion*, edited by T. O. Ranger and I. N. Kimambo, 252-273. London: Heineman, 1972.

Scott, James C. *Domination and the Arts of Resistance: Hidden Transcripts*. New Haven, CN: Yale University Press, 1990.

Seymour, Susan. "Resistance." *Anthropological Theory* 6, no. 3 (2006): 303-321.

Sharevskaia. B. I. "Toward a Typology of Anticolonial Religious-Political Movements in Tropical Africa." *Anthropology & Archeology of Eurasia* 15, no. 1 (1974): 84-102.

Shembe, J. Galilee, comp. *Izihlabelelo zaManazaretha*. 1940. 5th ed. N.p., 1990.

Shepperson, George. "The Politics of African Church Separatist Movements in British Central Africa, 1892-1914." *Africa* 24, no. 3 (1954): 233-246.

Shepperson, George and Thomas Price. *Independent African: John Chilembwe and the Origins, Setting and Significance of the Nyasaland Native Rising of 1915*. 1958. Reprint. Edinburgh: Edinburgh University Press, 1987.

Shipps, Jan. *Mormonism: The Story of a New Religious Tradition*. Urbana, IL: University of Illinois Press, 1987.

Sibisi, C. L., Personal communication to Karen Brown. In Karen Brown, "The Function of Dress and Ritual in the Nazareth Baptist Church of Isaiah Shembe (South Africa)." Ph.D. dissertation, Indiana University, 1995.

Simbandumwe, Samuel S. *A Socio-Religious and Political Analysis of the Judeo-Christian Concept of Prophetism and the Modern BaKongo and Zulu Prophet Movements*. Lewiston, NY: Edwin Mellen Press, 1993.

Sinha, Mrinalini. *Specters of Mother India: The Global Restructuring of an Empire*. Durham, NC: Duke University Press, 2006.

Sithole, Nkosinathi. "Acquiescence or Resistance? The Role of the AIC in the Struggle Against Apartheid." *Journal of Theology for Southern Africa* 137 (July 2010): 104-119.

Sparks, Allister. *The Mind of South Africa*. New York: Alfred A. Knopf, 1990.

Springhall, John. *Decolonization since 1945: The Collapse of European Overseas Empires*. New York: Palgrave, 2001.

Steinhart, Edward I. *Conflict and Collaboration: The Kingdoms of Western Uganda, 1890-1907*. Princeton, NJ: Princeton University Press, 1977.

Stewart, Susan. *Crimes of Writing: Problems in the Containment of Representation*. New York: Oxford University Press, 1991.

Stoler, Ann Laura. *Along the Archival Grain: Epistemic Anxieties and Colonial Common Sense*. Princeton, NJ: Princeton University Press, 2009.

Stoller, Paul. *Embodying Colonial Memories: Spirit Possession, Power, and the Hauka in West Africa*. London: Routledge, 1995.

Strong, James. *A Concise Dictionary of the words in the Hebrew Bible with their rendering in the Authorized English Version*. Nashville: Abingdon-Cokesbury Press, 1890.

Sundkler, Bengt. *Bantu Prophets in South Africa*. 1948. Reprint. London: Oxford University Press, 1961.

Sundkler, Bengt. *Zulu Zion and some Swazi Zionists*. Oxford: Oxford University Press, 1976.

Taiwo, Olufemi. *How Colonialism Preempted Modernity in Africa*. Bloomington: Indiana University Press, 2010.

Thomas, Keith. *Religion and the Decline of Magic*. 1971. New York: Oxford University Press, 1997.

Thomas, Linda Elaine. *Under the Canopy: Ritual Process and Spiritual Resilience in South Africa*. Columbia: University of South Carolina Press, 1999.

Tishken, Joel E. "Whose Nazareth Baptist Church? Prophecy, Power, and Schism in South Africa." *Nova Religio* 9, no. 4 (May 2006): 79-97.

———. "The History of Prophecy in West Africa: Indigenous, Islamic, and Christian." *History Compass* 5, no. 5 (2007): 1468-1482.

"Truth and Reconciliation Commission, Faith Community Hearings, 17-19 November 1997." <http://www.justice.gov.za/trc/special/faith/faith_b.htm>. Accessed 15 January 2012.

Turner, H. W. "A Typology for African Religious Movements." *Journal of Religion in Africa* 1, no. 1 (1967): 1-34.

Tutu, Desmond and John Webster. *Crying in the Wilderness: The Struggle for Justice in South Africa*. Grand Rapids, MI: W. B. Eerdmans, 1982.

Umar, Muhammad S. *Islam and Colonialism: Intellectual Responses of Muslims of Northern Nigeria to British Colonial Rule*. Leiden: E. J. Brill, 2006.

Van Wing, J. "Le Kimbanguisme vu par un temoin." *Zaire* 12, no. 6 (1958): 563-618.

Venuti, Lawrence. *The Translator's Invisibility: A History of Translation*. 1995. 2nd ed. London: Routledge, 2008.

Vilakazi, Absolom with Bongani Mthethwa and Mthembeni Mpanza. *Shembe: The Revitalization of African Society*. Johannesburg: Skotaville, 1986.

Waldman, Marilyn Robinson and Robert M. Baum. "Innovation as Renovation: The 'Prophet' as Agent of Change." In *Innovation in Religious Traditions*, edited by Michael A. Williams, et. al., 241-284. Berlin: Mouton de Gruyter, 1992.

Walker, Cherryl. *Women and Resistance in South Africa*. London: Onyx Press, 1982.

Wallis, Jim and Joyce Hollyday. *Crucible of Fire: The Church Confronts Apartheid*. Maryknoll, NY: Orbis Books, 1989.

Walshe, Peter. *Prophetic Christianity and the Liberation Movement in South Africa*. Pietermaritzburg: Cluster Publications, 1995.

Weber, Max. *Max Weber on Charisma and Institution Building*. Edited and with an introduction by S. N. Eisenstadt. Chicago: University of Chicago Press, 1968.

Welbourn, Frederick Burkewood. *East African Rebels: A Study of some Independent Churches*. London: SCM Press, 1961.

Wells, Nattie. *Natal Mercury*, 30 July 1929.

West, Gerald O. "Reading Shembe 'Re-membering' the Bible: Isaiah Shembe's Instructions on Adultery," *Neotestamentica* 40, no. 1 (2006): 157-184.

Wipper, Audrey. *Rural Rebels: A Study of Two Protest Movements in Kenya*. Nairobi: Oxford University Press, 1977.

Index

• N •

Natal, 1, 117, 165, 196 n. 3
   citizens of, 83-95, 104-106
   officials of, 83-95, 96-103
   Supreme Court of, 8
Natal Mercury, 104
Natalia, 4
Native Affairs Department, 21, 70, 83-95,
   102-103, 116
   Secretary of, 83, 89
Native Economic Commission, 23, 81
Natives' Land Act, 102, 116
Nazareth Baptist Church
   academic studies of, 105-106, 163-167,
     171-177
   accusations against, 83-95, 174
   annual festivals of, 96-99, 142
   and baptism, 147-151
   biblical applications of, 23-24, 57-59,
     80, 91, 145-147, 158, 164
   and central leadership disputes, 8-9
   as chosen people, 2-4, 108, 113-115,
     123-124, 157, 161-162, 176-177
   and colonialism, 13-17, 83-95, 96-103,
     104-112, 147
   documentary history of, 21-54
   ethnic composition of, 108-109
   founding of, 7-9, 73
   growth of, 29, 32, 108-109, 117-119
   historical notebooks of members, 23,
     26-27, 44, 59
   and identity, 113-115, 119, 139-140,
     164, 179 n. 4
   and legitimacy, 22, 30, 44-46, 148, 156-
     157
   laws of, 35-37, 118, 122
   liturgies of, 25
   and Lord's Supper, 140-147
   news coverage of, 104-105, 142-143
   parallels with early Christianity, 22, 30,
     37-40, 57-59, 119-121, 155
   priesthood of, 29, 117-118
   sacraments of, 8, 139-162
   and seventh day Sabbatarianism, 8, 125-
     128
   soteriology of, 113-115, 124-133, 151
   split in, 8-9
   standardization of history, 29-32
   temples of, 102-103, 108-109

   and theophanic sites, 115-124, 134
   and *ukusina*, 152-157
   and *umnazaretha*, 157-161
   and Zulu culture, 134-138, 154-156,
     166-167
   worldview of, 3, 13, 81-83, 91-93, 115-
     116, 125, 132-133, 139-140, 161-162,
     164, 165-167, 174-177
   see also prophecy, Shembe, Isaiah
nazirite, 129, 131, 146-147, 203 n. 39
   see also God's chosen people
Ndadano, Setshebe Mbhele ka, 88
Ndelu, Khaya, 149
Ndwedwe, 83-95, 97, 104
Nemithetho, Imilando, 28
NERMIC, 42
New Jerusalem, see Ebuhleni, Ekuphakameni
Ngada, N. H., 169-170
Ngcobo, Eliot, 117, 150
Ngcobo, Montane, 40
Ngubane, Philip, 28
Ngunzists, 168
Nkabinde, Johane Zandile, 160-161
Nkandhla, 86, 87
Ntanda, 145

• O •

Ondeto, Simeo, 75-76
oralture
   church's establishment of, 23-27
   intersection with literature, 23, 26-27,
     44
   as legitimating device, 22, 54, 148
   preservation of, 27-32
   and provenance, 47-49
   see also literature
Oosthuizen, G. C., 33, 41-42, 163-164

• P •

Papini, Robert, 33
Petersen, Robin, 175-176
Pietermaritzburg, 23, 73
pilgrimage, 55, 85, 89, 120-122
   rules of, 122
   and the state, 96-99
police, 81-83, 84-86
Pondo, 108-109, 137
Pondoland, 67, 70, 100

• U •

• V •

• W •

• X •

• Z •